TYPES OF RELIGIOUS EXPERIENCE
CHRISTIAN AND NON-CHRISTIAN

by the same author

★

SOCIOLOGY OF RELIGION

TYPES OF
RELIGIOUS EXPERIENCE
CHRISTIAN AND
NON-CHRISTIAN

BY

JOACHIM WACH

THE UNIVERSITY OF CHICAGO PRESS

International Standard Book Number: 0–226–86709–9 (clothbound)
Library of Congress Catalog Card Number: A51–9885

THE UNIVERSITY OF CHICAGO PRESS, CHICAGO 60637

The University of Chicago Press, Ltd., London

TO MY DEAR COLLEAGUES
OF THE FEDERATED THEOLOGICAL FACULTY
OF THE UNIVERSITY OF CHICAGO

As though there were any kind of science in the world which leadeth man into knowledge without presupposing a number of things already known. No science doth make known the first principles where it buildeth, but they are always either taken as plain and manifest in themselves or as proved and granted, already some former knowledge having made them evident.—Richard Hooker, *Laws of Ecclesiastical Polity*, III, 8.

Only if God is revealed in the rising of the sun in the sky, can He be revealed in the rising of a son of man from the dead; only if he is revealed in the history of Syrians and Philistines can He be revealed in the history of Israel, only if he chooses all men for His own can He choose any at all; only if nothing is profane can anything be sacred.—William Temple, *Nature, Man and God*, p. 306.

But before we compare, we must thoroughly know what we compare.—Max Müller, Letter to Renan, 1883.

ACKNOWLEDGMENTS

THE author wishes to thank the following publishers and editors for the permission to use the material listed: *The Journal of Religion*: 'The Place of the History of Religions in the Study of Theology' (XXVII, 1947), pp. 157–77; 'Spiritual Teaching in Islam' (XXVIII, 1948), pp. 263–80; 'Caspar Schwenckfeld. A Pupil and Teacher in the School of Christ' (XXVI, 1946), pp. 1–29. Seabury-Western Episcopal Seminary, Evanston, Illinois: 'Church, Denomination, Sect' Dwight Johnson—Memorial Inaugural Lecture, 1945. *The Journal of the History of Ideas*: 'The Role of Religion in the Social Philosophy of Alexis de Tocqueville' (VII, 1946), pp. 44–50. All these essays are reprinted without any major changes. Christophers, London: 'Der Begriff des Klassischen in der Religionsgeschichte' from *Quantulacunque, in honour of Kirsopp Lake* (1937), pp. 87–97, which appears here for the first time in an English translation.

CONTENTS

CONTENTS

INTRODUCTION

T HE essays collected in this volume date from different times; they have been written at different places, and they treat of apparently quite different topics. What then can be said for presenting them to the reader in this unified form? The answer is, their author feels, that the studies which he has carried on during the last decade have all been directed toward *one* goal: the deeper understanding of the religious heritage of West and East. Comparison is for him no end in itself but rather a means used in the service of a greater purpose: to help him and others to a more intimate acquaintance with the witness and the witnesses of genuine religious experience at various times and in various places. He admits that he delights in the variety which the expressions of this experience the world over offer—in this he sympathizes with the author of the wellnigh classical *Varieties of Religious Experience*, William James, the greatest modern American religious thinker. But he is also aware that fifty years have passed since James's book made its first appearance and that there has been much opportunity to learn since his day. We are no longer so ready to glory in the vindication of a pluralism of which historism is just an instance, for over twenty-five years ago Ernst Troeltsch voiced his conviction that the great work in which he had summarized the philosophy of this worldview was also to be its epitaph. Not that we should ever wish to neglect or forget the enormous debt which we owe to a generation of scholars and thinkers who have increased a thousandfold our knowledge of civilizations, societies and religions different from our own. None of the modest contributions collected in this volume could have been written without the painstaking work of the generation which preceded ours. Yet, we do not any longer believe that history *as such* can supply us with norms by which to regulate our lives. And with norms we have again become desperately concerned. We realize that habits and mores, customs and institutions vary with each civilization. But does that mean that religion also should be regarded as a 'function' or aspect of culture, as many contemporaries want us to think? There can certainly be no doubt that a good deal of what is called religion belongs to the category of culture and of custom. But it is the conviction of the author of the following essays that we must carefully distinguish between religious *experience* and its *expression*. We need history, we need to study it well; but, beyond that, we need to reflect most assiduously on the foundations upon which our own faith can be built. The traditional argument is that, because it has been the dominant religion in the history of the Western world, Christianity is or ought to be the 'natural' form in which our faith should be cast, just as Hinduism, because it has served India in the past, or Buddhism, because it fits the Eastern temper, are the appropriate religions for those parts of the world. This argument implies a grave misinterpretation of the nature of religious experience. What we wish to know is: what is *true?* To decide for Christ does not mean a blanket endorsement of all that has been thought, said, and done in the name of Christianity, just as recognizing deep spiritual truth in Mohammedan or Buddhist insights need not imply a total appropriation of whatever has at any time been offered or regarded as Islam or Buddhism. We have rather to apply ourselves again, as each generation will have to do, to explore and investigate, as we said above, the religious heritage of the past with the intention of learning from it for the constructive task with which we are faced. This means that we should avoid two extremes: that of taking over notions and practices uncritically for no other reason than that we have inherited them; and that of rejecting, equally uncritically, tradition because it is tradition. To tackle the task of articulating for our contemporaries the content of our faith on a level such as its dignity requires, means to refuse to be satisfied with artificial syntheses or cheap short-cuts of the kind offered as a new World-faith, etc. But the author of the following essays does not promise to propose a programme or system that would fulfil a need which requires the co-operation and sustained effort of a whole generation of dedicated scholars and thinkers. He has concentrated on a preliminary task, that of helping to foster understanding by interpreting the results of spiritual quests at different times and in different cultural and sociological contexts.

The need for *understanding*, understanding people and peoples, their thoughts and affections, their words and deeds, has impressed the author from his youth. He chose the problem of hermeneutics—the theory of interpretation—as the subject of an extensive historical study (1). He has tried to carry out his work both as a scholar and as a teacher, in two continents, with a view to practising and teaching understanding. Two wars brought home to him even more clearly the urgency of helping to create the conditions for understanding among nations. Scholars ought to be interpreters. That is their *raison d'être*. And their interpretation should concern matters of existential significance. That is their *raison d'être* to-day. The nineteenth century, living in outward security, could afford lovingly to investigate the minutest details of phenomena far removed from immediate exigencies; but in the middle of the twentieth century we have to realize that first things must come first. Our decision as to the order of precedence in our work as scholars and teachers will, of course, be dependent upon the scale of values to which we are committed. But an agreement on the necessity of three things seems to be not impossible: a rule of frugality, in the sense of a concentration on essentials; a concern with meanings, rather than with facts for the sake of collecting them; and a striving for the achievement of a unified outlook on life. While there is no discipline within the vast area of scholarly pursuits which would not be called upon to contribute towards this goal, we shall have to expect leadership from two fields: *theology* and *philosophy*. This is not the place to detail reasons for the apprehension with which not a few of us have watched developments in both disciplines here and abroad since the turn of the century. In the case of theology it is the divisiveness of efforts, in the case of philosophy the preoccupation with technical problems, that have caused widespread disappointment and alarm. We are in these pages primarily concerned with the study of *religion* and the problems it faces. As the author of these essays has indicated elsewhere, he is of the conviction that the study of religion has a double task: as

general science of religion, it is concerned with the phenomenological, historical, psychological and sociological examination
of all religions; as theology, it analyses, interprets, and promul-
gates *one* particular faith. While the method of the former
discipline is primarily descriptive, that of the latter is normative.
The problem of the relationship of the two is the subject-
matter of the first of the following essays.

This collection of papers is divided into *three parts*. The first
three contributions which make up the first part are methodological in character. Since there is no equivalent for the
German and French expressions 'Religionswissenschaft' and
'science des religions' in English, 'History of Religions' has been
used *pars pro toto* as the term for the field of descriptive studies.
The *Place of the History of Religions in the Study of Theology* (2) is
discussed in the first paper. The second, which, in many respects,
contains the core of the author's thought, summarizes his concept of the nature of religious experience and a phenomenology
of its forms of expression. It is entitled *Universals in Religion*
because it offers an outline of the structural elements the author
believes to be characteristic of religion wherever and whenever
found. It represents an attempt to go beyond the traditional
exposition of the manifestations of religion (cf. van der Leeuw's
Phenomenology; Lehmann's *Lehre von der Erscheinungswelt*; Eliade's
Morphologie) in the direction of what used to be called 'Natural
Theology,' but with the endeavour to avoid the rationalistic
preoccupation of the earlier (eighteenth-century) conceptions.
This essay has not been published before. The third essay on
The Notion of the Classical in the Study of Religion (3) develops a
construct to be used by the teacher and student of religions to
steer a middle course between a historistic preoccupation with
completeness of data in the history of religions, and arbitrary
selection based upon a traditional or freely chosen viewpoint.
All three papers owe their existence to reflections which have
grown out of the experience of teaching; they, as well as several
of the following contributions, are meant to stimulate thought
on the way in which instruction in our field might be
improved.

The second and third parts consist of a series of seven articles,
three of them not previously published, of which one part deals

with certain aspects of non-Christian religions, the other part
with certain aspects of Christianity. Of the former, one paper
each is devoted to the ancient and to the medieval Near East,
and one to the Far East. The first of these, published in outline
in German some time ago (4), examines the concept of the
Nature of Man in the Religious Thought of Western Asia in a typological fashion. The second, under the title *Spiritual Teachings
in Islam*, is dedicated to an important aspect of Islam, Sufism,
and analyses the teachings of one representative thinker of that
movement who lived in the early Middle Ages. Here the
opportunity offers itself to compare these mystical and spiritual
doctrines with those of other religions. The third essay proposes
to introduce the student of the history of religion to the study of
Mahāyāna Buddhism, after Islam the most important com-
petitor of Christianity, and to summarize some important work
done on this difficult subject which is not too readily available
to the general reader. This paper has not been published before.

The last four papers pertain to the history of Christianity.
The first of them analyses the religious thought of a Protestant
sixteenth-century spiritualist, the much neglected German
theologian, *Caspar Schwenckfeld* (5), who deserves a place in any
history of outstanding Christian witnesses. This small contribution belongs to the increasing number of studies of the so-called
Left-wing Reformation. The second takes note of the *Role of
Religion in the Social Philosophy of Alexis de Tocqueville* (6), a
Catholic historian and statesman whose efforts were concentrated on the demonstration that principles—religious principles—and progressive thought were not mutually exclusive.
This essay, like the third included in this collection, grew out of
the author's interest in the sociology of religion (7). As a
typological study of three great forms of organization within
Christendom, namely of *Church, Denomination, and Sect* (8), it
attempts to satisfy both historical and systematic interest in the
dialectics of religious development as it expresses itself societally.

The fourth and last study seeks to characterize the work
of one of the most outstanding theologians and historians of
religion in the beginning of the twentieth century, a man to
whom the author owes a great deal. It is devoted to *Rudolf Otto
and the Idea of the Holy* (9).

INTRODUCTION

Since these papers were not conceived and written with the intention of including them in a collection such as this, it has been thought best not to alter their original form, but to trust that the reader will bear in mind that they owe their origin—and hence their mode of presentation—to different occasions. Four, the second, fourth, ninth, and tenth, were first delivered as lectures.

[A]
METHODOLOGICAL

CHAPTER ONE

THE PLACE OF THE HISTORY OF RELIGIONS IN THE STUDY OF THEOLOGY

I

INTEREST in religious experience other than one's own can be found in various cultures and religious communities (1). The Greeks, Romans, Hebrews, Babylonians, Egyptians, Moslems, Zoroastrians, Hindus, Mongols, Confucians, and Buddhists were aware of and showed interest in religious attitudes and institutions differing from their own. In most cultures this interest remained pragmatic, while in some it developed into a systematic study of the religious concepts and practices of other peoples and groups, as among the Greeks, the Romans, the Hindus, the Moslems, the Buddhists, and the Confucians. We find such interest arising on three different sociological levels: as the concern of rulers faced with the task of integrating peoples of different religious persuasions into a politically unified realm; as that of the theologian in defending his faith against one or many competing cults and in buttressing the intellectual and moral presuppositions upon which his own faith rests; and, finally, as an interest among the rank and file of the people as a result of local contiguity. However, syncretistic practice and theological concern are two different things, though the former may be conducive to a development of the latter.

The history of the study of alien religious experience in Judaism, Islam, Hinduism, Buddhism, and Confucianism remains to be written. As far as the Western world is concerned, the task has been done (2). We have learned of the development and growth of knowledge of other religions among the Greeks and Romans, in early and medieval Christianity, and, finally,

3

in modern times. However differently we may regard the result or effect of this increase in our knowledge of the varieties of religious experience upon our faith, the fact that our horizon has been constantly widened cannot well be denied. The reaction of the Christian theologian—theological thought, not the layman's reaction, will concern us here—has been defined differently in different periods and in different Christian communities (Orthodox, Roman, and various Protestant groups), and it has differed from individual to individual.

Three main types of reaction can be distinguished: (i) unintentional or intentional disregard of the growing material in the field of non-Christian religions; (ii) negative reaction, that is, wholesale denial that any value or importance is to be attributed to these forms of expression of experience when contrasted with the Christian; and (iii) positive reaction, which has taken different forms: (a) acknowledgment of the existence of some grain of truth in or hidden under these expressions, coupled with insistence upon the superiority of the Christian claim; (b) the conclusion that the several expressions of religious experience are equally valid, and hence that Christianity should be regarded as one among many faiths, possibly the one especially adapted to the religious quest of those reared in its tradition or in the environment which produced it; (c) a sceptical attitude, which draws from the study of religions the conclusion that the truth is not to be found in any of them.

The first position, though still widely held to-day, will not interest us here, since no constructive contribution can be expected from the ostrich hiding its head in the sand. History shows that vital developments are not arrested by those who attempt to ignore them. The second conclusion has had its defenders through all the ages of Christian history. It has been reached in abrupt and dogmatic fashion, or again in and through subtle and protracted processes of reasoning and argumentation. According to this view, we cannot expect any major contribution from non-Christian sources to the formation of Christian thought because, in the first place, such addition is not needed, owing to the fact that the fullness of truth is contained in the original Christian experience and safeguarded by its theological tradition, and, secondly, because there are no valid insights discoverable in the non-Christian religious expressions. It may be conceded, however, that certain non-Christian faiths do contain some such insights, the validity of which is judged to be impaired by the form in which they appear or the context in which they are found. In a theology identified with these assumptions there is no place for the study of non-Christian religion other than as a catalogue of errors and falsehoods. It is interesting to observe that, contrary to popular opinion, this position (discontinuity) is more strongly maintained by Protestant theologians; Catholics may uphold it in practice, but the doctrine of the church, though not uniform on this point, provides by its concept of natural theology for an emphasis upon continuity.

It cannot be denied that positive appreciation of non-Christian religious expression has in the past frequently been achieved at the cost of a weakening of basic Christian convictions. The period of the Enlightenment (3) is marked both by an increased interest in non-Christian beliefs and by great progress in the study of these beliefs, their rites and lore, and by a diminution of the substance of the Christian faith. A casual relation between these two facts has frequently been pointed out and commented upon by those who felt that the gain was outweighed by the loss which Christianity and Christian theology suffered. That such a causal relation exists cannot be denied. Yet the trend of the new development could not easily be arrested before it had run its full course.

During the nineteenth century a tremendous expansion of the frontiers of our knowledge of foreign religions took place (4). Archaeological, historical, philological, and anthropological research, which had yielded such astonishing results in other fields, was applied by theologians and non-theologians to the Christian religion, with the result that for many expressions, regarding which the contention of uniqueness had been asserted, doublets and parallels in other religions could be exhibited. A new discipline emerged, to which the ungainly name 'comparative religion' was given (5). Moreover, voices were heard calling for the substitution of a science (history of religion) for Christian theology (6). It was felt that, if one could not be a theologian with a good conscience, it might be better to cease

5

being a theologian altogether (7). The theory of isosthenia (equal validity) of Christian and non-Christian religious values became common ground to students of religion and educated laymen alike. The problem was recognized and stated perhaps most convincingly and comprehensively by Ernst Troeltsch (8). While the number of sceptics increased, strengthened in their conviction with regard to religion by the growing impact of the philosophies of materialism, evolutionism, and pragmatism, an 'enlightened' but non-committal attitude, which was understood as tolerance, tended to exclude all value judgments from the discussion of the problem of religious truth, if it did not eliminate that problem altogether. With the more conservative this tendency expressed itself in claiming superiority for Christianity, especially on moral grounds, and in view of the fact that it appears better suited than the more 'exotic' cults to our own culture, to which it has so heavily contributed.

Now it is significant that in our own day a twofold movement of thought similar to that which we discovered in the age of the Enlightenment can be recognized, though it is of a different if not opposite character. This consists of a trend in theology and a corresponding development in the study of religion. Since the predominance of the historical quest in theology towards the end of the nineteenth century and at the beginning of the twentieth, a new interest in 'systematic' or constructive thought has become apparent; and in the field of the history of religions a preoccupation with the amassing of data and indiscriminate 'comparing' has given way to the attempt to view these data structurally and functionally and to understand their religious meaning. I consider this tendency to have been in the ascendant since the publication of Rudolf Otto's important and influential *Idea of the Holy* (9). With this reorientation in both theology and the study of non-Christian religions, the situation seems to warrant a renewed examination of the place of the history of religions in the study of theology.

II

Part of the contemporary confusion as to the nature and function of the study of non-Christian religion is due to the failure of so many, scholars and laymen alike, to distinguish between statements of fact and value judgments. That Mohammed was the founder of Islam, with all that this simple assertion implies, is a fact which can be ascertained with reasonable certainty. How to react to his claim to be the 'seal of the prophets' is a question not of fact-finding but of evaluation (10). It was an error of earlier times that no clear distinction was made between these two functions in the study of religions. It was the mistake of the school of 'comparative religion' at the turn of the century to advocate the elimination of value judgments in favour of a completely 'objective' approach. The result was an unsatisfactory relativism incapable of contributing to the eternal quest for 'truth,' that quest which is actually the prime motive in all our desire for knowledge.

We have now learned that the task of interpretation of all expressions of religious experience is twofold: first, to discover the facts, a procedure exclusively committed to the idea of objectivity, and, second, under the guidance of the motto, 'Tua res agitur,' to formulate and define our reaction to these facts, that is, the question of their evaluation. Hence the most important methodological requirement is a clear distinction between these two tasks that will be sufficiently articulate as we pursue the task of interpretation and convey our findings to others. Before we try to answer the important questions where and how the task of evaluation shall be performed, we shall attempt to describe further the implications of the two tasks formulated above.

Careful analysis of the procedure of fact-finding, as actually practised in the natural and historical sciences, has revealed it to be a complex process. Consider the *modus procedendi* of the historian (11). We call the study of the material available (relics, sources, monuments) *heuristics*. This material has to be examined with the utmost care and by use of the method of combination. Next, the critical task has to be performed; that is, we must attempt to correlate the material with the thoughts and intentions to which it bears witness. The question of the genuineness of the material has to be answered with reference to its possibility or impossibility as judged by our knowledge of human experience and the circumstances. Thus the material is made ready to yield its testimony. To ascertain it the fine art of interpretation is employed. By means of hypotheses the actual course of events is reconstructed and then checked by what we know of the laws of motivation and of cause and effect. Conditions such as time, place, technological level, and the prevailing moods and thoughts of the period and place are taken into consideration. The psychological pattern of the actors in the historical drama is studied generally according to known, psychological rules. Further, the ethical horizon (*Droysen*) is investigated to determine what moral ideas and forces conditioned the actions of the individuals and groups at the given epoch. Thus the elementary tasks of analysis of sources and criticism culminate in a pragmatic, technological, psychological, and ideational interpretation, and thus an integral understanding of the historic phenomenon is ensured (12).

All these methodological considerations apply to the work of the historian of religion, who shares with the general historian and with the student of the history of law, economics, politics, art, or philosophy a subject matter of historical character. His method, as far as this side of his task is concerned, does not differ from that of the historian of Christianity in the disciplines known as church history and the history of Christian thought and experience, or from that of the student of the Old and New Testament. The latter will have to proceed from the task of textual criticism to that of exegesis; he will find himself concerned with the business of relating individual phenomena to the system of concepts, practices, and institutions which emerges from the concentrated efforts of biblical studies, and is known as Old and New Testament theology respectively (13).

The parallel to the work of the historian of religion is obvious: he, too, cannot be satisfied with the isolated data gleaned from a thorough use of the sources, but will have to attempt to ascertain their meaning and significance by interpreting them in the contexts indicated above. One example will suffice to illustrate this parallelism. The historian of religion desiring to understand

Mohammed's eschatological teachings will analyse the material available in the pertinent passages of the Koran, taking into account the results of textual criticism with reference to the nature and sequence of composition of the suras in question. He will then proceed to interpret the meaning of the emergent concepts and ideas within the context which the study of Koranic and Islamic theology in general has provided, testing and probing the validity of his assumptions by the results and vice versa. Now, recent discussions of the nature of biblical theology have revealed a divergence in the concept of its purpose (14). One school is inclined to limit the task of Old and New Testament theology to the exposition of basic ideas as indicated above. Typical of this are presentations such as Robinson's *Ideas of the Old Testament* or Eichrodt's *Theologie des Alten Testaments* (15). Others, however, feel that it is the task of biblical theology to concentrate upon the normative aspect. This brings into the picture a new element. The question immediately arises: 'From whence are we to derive the norms which shall be rendered discernible in and through the study of the Bible?' Different answers have been given to this question. The documents themselves are, according to one view, supposed to contain these norms. Again two different views can be discerned among those who hold to this principle: (a) that the documents are the exclusive source, and (b) that their testimony is to be supplemented by other additional sources, such as the tradition of the early and later community as codified in the body of doctrine or dogma or as existing in the consciousness of its believing members, that is, the collective or individual experience ('das fromme Selbstbewusstsein' (16) . . . 'der Kirche' (17) oder 'des einzelnen Christen'). The first position is represented by Protestant theologians of the biblicist type, the second by Catholic theologians and by Protestants of the classical and liberal schools. The introduction of the normative viewpoint into the task of interpretation is repudiated by those students of the Bible who desire to limit the task of the exegete to the exposition of the texts, while others feel that, in order to find the full meaning, recourse to the before-mentioned norms has to be made (18). Whereas the former group is inclined to regard this procedure as an intrusion of systematic theology (dogmatics) into the field of interpretation, the latter welcomes it as conducive to the integration of the theological disciplines and their work.

The historian of religion will have to leave the resolution of this controversy to the biblical scholars. As indicated above, he also is faced with the task of interpreting religious documents. Philological or historical exegesis alone cannot suffice him. He strives to understand his material in the context of systematic concepts elaborated in and through the various methods of interpretation. However, his interest is somewhat different from that of the student of the Bible. The Koran, the Tripitaka, or the Lun Yü are not normative writings for him, nor can he pretend to speak with the authority which membership in the religious tradition and community provides. So it seems that the ways of the Christian theologian and of the student of non-Christian religions definitely part. Can the work of the latter, if he does not share in the basic presuppositions of the theological quest, have any place in a programme of theological studies?

III

The last twenty-five years have witnessed a widespread renewal of interest in systematic or constructive theology succeeding the sovereign rule of the historical quest in Protestantism at the beginning of the century. After World War I it became apparent in Europe that the best minds among the younger theologians were no longer exclusively attracted by the appeal of historical studies. The crisis of historicism became apparent in theology, though this was by no means the only field affected by it. The rise of comparative studies and of the history of religions in general had occurred in times which found Protestant systematic theology in retreat and on the defensive— as was the case in the eighteenth and nineteenth centuries. Now they faced the need to redefine their aim, their method, and their position within the context of theological studies with a view to the renascence of constructive theology.

Theology wherever it occurs—the historian of religion is aware of its rise and development in different cultures and religions—has a double function: to defend its own position against other claims and to deepen and widen the understanding of the insights, experiences, and norms upon which it is itself based. These two tasks appear inextricably intertwined in the early stages of Christian theology and continue to be most closely allied in the patristic and scholastic ages. Hence the apologist, in formulating the arguments he would submit, has been obliged to recognize the demand upon him for a modicum of knowledge and understanding of the expressions of other forms of religious experience. As a consequence of the recognition of this demand by the Fathers and Doctors of the Middle Ages, a considerable amount of most valuable knowledge was accumulated. Inasmuch as this information concerning other faiths was acquired and organized with a pragmatic interest, that of buttressing and reaffirming one's own religious convictions and theological principles, criteria had to be developed for the evaluation and explanation of the variety of expressions of religious experience. Such concepts as 'demonic interference,' 'plagiarism,' and 'condescendence' served the Fathers and the medieval theologians in formulating doctrines concerning the origin and nature, and hence the subsequent evaluation, of other religions. This procedure assumed the implicit and frequently explicit admission of some positive values discernible in these alien insights.

The heritage of Greek philosophical thought, in itself an element alien to the gospel, though very early seized upon for its elucidation by the followers of Jesus Christ, fostered a qualified incorporation of the insights of non-Christian experience into Christian theology. It was, more especially, the Stoic doctrine of the *logos spermatikos*, the scattered germ of truth, which played, since the Alexandrian Fathers made use of it, an important role in the arguments of Christian theologians (19). This, however, like other borrowings from ancient or generally 'pagan' sources, was staunchly opposed by a chain of Christian thinkers which stretches from Tertullian down through the ages, marking the endeavours of a group of theologians to disavow any attempt to find any value whatsoever outside the Christian tradition. The great teachers and scholars of the medieval period, whose views were to be regarded as authoritative by the post-Tridentine Catholic church, however, elaborated upon the basis of the before-mentioned ideas the concept of natural insights which could be possessed and developed by those as yet outside the reach of the Christian message. This concept permitted them to regard the illumination which divine grace confers as the perfection rather than the complete abrogation of natural insight (20).

The theology of the Reformers, developed under direct appeal to the scriptures and with a critical appraisal of the patristic tradition, did not concern itself extensively with the question of truth in regard to non-Christian religions. It implied, however, a sharp distinction which left little room for the development of concepts similar to that of the *logos spermatikos*. Classical orthodoxy, in reintroducing at least *de facto* an appeal to Protestant tradition (Lutheran and Calvinist) and the exigencies of the church, as auxiliary norms, in defining the basic Christian teachings, defined the doctrine of revelation in a manner which left no ground upon which to construct a 'natural theology' (21). Essentially this position has been maintained by conservative Lutheran and Calvinist theologians ever since the seventeenth century, and it has lately become the refuge for certain modern Protestant thinkers who have become dissatisfied with the theology of liberalism (22).

Meanwhile the philosophical movement known as the Enlightenment, resulting from (*a*) a recoil of outstanding thinkers of various European nationalities from dogmatic controversies and (*b*) a growing acquaintance with and interest in different forms of religious expression the world over, endeavoured to develop just such a natural theology (23). The attempt, in itself praiseworthy, was abortive, for two reasons. In the first place, the implicit trust in human reason which characterized the thinkers of this movement prevented them from doing justice to the true nature of religious experience, and, more significantly, it rendered their attainment of an understanding of its (historical) forms of expression impossible. Kant's judgment of religious observances and institutions illustrates this point. Secondly, their insight into the nature of Christian experience was insufficient, partly because of the above-mentioned intellectualism and moralism. The alternative to the absolutism of classical Protestantism thus appeared to be a latitudinarian indifference to the individual, peculiar, and characteristic trends not only of Christianity but of other religions as well.

It has been rightly seen by Troeltsch that the development in the Anglo-Saxon countries and in Germany since the Enlightenment has been along different lines (24). While the former preserved in their thinking the orientation which the 'natural system' had evolved, the latter, under the impact of the Romantic movement, was swayed by what is known as historicism (25). Schleiermacher, deeply influenced by Herder, is the first great exponent of this trend in theology (26). The implications of this school tended to emphasize the studies of the origins of historical phenomena—everything had to be viewed under this aspect—and to reduce norms to expression explicable only in terms of historical conditions. The danger of historicism (i.e., historic relativism), keenly sensed by the opponents of the movement from the beginning, actually became manifest in the relativism at the turn of the nineteenth century. The metaphysics of the transcendental school of philosophical and theological idealism of the early nineteenth century tried in vain to counteract this danger (antagonism between the 'Historische Schule' and Hegel (27)).

Following on the collapse of the Hegelian system, in which a gigantic attempt was made to incorporate individuality and individual historical variety into a unified comprehensive view of the development of the mind, the quest for the establishment of norms seemed definitely frustrated in the face of historical and, in due course, of psychological and sociological relativism. Inasmuch as the main contributions to Protestant theological thinking and writing during the nineteenth century were made by Germans, the impact of this orientation was very great indeed. While historicism has turned out to be the peculiar danger of German scholarship, rationalism has been the great temptation of Anglo-Saxon thought. Here not history but philosophy (28) (and its tributaries, e.g., psychology) tended to monopolize the inquiry into the nature of religion and the forms of its expression. Philosophy of religion as a specific discipline emerged (29). Since it was concerned from its inception with the width and breadth of the religious experience of man (Herbert of Cherbury, Hume), it concentrated either upon the analysis of the nature of this experience philosophically, epistemologically, and psychologically, or upon the problems of religious values and of truth and their apprehension. Three typologically different attitudes towards the religious quest can be observed: the critical, the idealistic, and the naturalistic. In all three cases reason precedes or supersedes revelation. 'Philosophy of religion is an attempt to discover, by rational interpretation of religion and its relation to other types of experience, the truth of religious beliefs and the values of religious attitudes and practices' (30). How to define the relation between systematic theology and philosophy of religion is one of the most difficult questions confronting us to-day (31). There is less friction between the history of religion and the philosophy of religion. While the former investigates the individual, the specific, and the historical, the latter is interested in general and universal validity.

The tremendous amount of material concerning non-Christian religions which we owe to the combined efforts of scholars of a variety of European nations, archaeologists, philologists, anthropologists, historians of religion, and theologians during the nineteenth century, confronted the German, English, French, Dutch, Scandinavian, and American theologians who were acquainted with it with a difficult task, that is, to combine the understanding and appreciation of religious insights and values outside our own tradition, as we glean them in our study and interpretation of non-Christian religions, with the endeavour to reinterpret the Christian truths to our own generation (32). This task, as such, is not new, but the difficulty is greatly aggravated by the quantitative and qualitative increase in knowledge. Three types of reaction can be noticed: (a) a yielding to historicism and relativism; (b) a reversion to 'classical' standards (33); (c) new attempts at a constructive solution. Let us look at some of the latter.

IV

The first theological solution to the problem which we will briefly examine here is that presented by Nathan Söderblom in his two treatises *The Nature of Revelation* (1903; 2nd ed.,

THE HISTORY OF RELIGIONS

1930) and *Natürliche Theologie und Religionsgeschichte* (1913) (34). Söderblom traces the historical development of the concept of natural religion through four stages: a preparatory stage, a stage of formulation, a stage of universal application, and a stage of rejection, the last dating from Schleiermacher. He discards rightly the idea of a universal religion to be abstracted from the positive faiths, usually with 'reason' as a criterion. 'No general theory,' according to him, 'is able to comprehend without doing violence to it the wealth of the extra-biblical history of religion' (35). No simple scheme of true-false or of unilinear development is sufficient. The variety of historical religious expression has to be faced. All religion, according to Söderblom, is positive, that is 'a concrete whole of rites, customs and traditions,' not a 'conclusion of reason' (36).

One of the most important achievements of modern scholarship is the discovery of a 'new inner unity of all genuine religion' (37). Each positive religion, inasmuch as it is real, stands under an unconditioned obligation ('unbedingte Verpflichtung'). The characters of holiness and obligation ('Verbindlichkeit') are the surest criteria of genuine religion. It is well known that the Swedish scholar anticipates with this insight Rudolf Otto's central concept of the experience of the holy (38). Within this unity of all religion belongs, as Söderblom insists, the biblical also. Whatever religious truth is to be found in the non-Christian world thus is to be regarded as of divine origin (39). The subject matter of theology, he feels, ought not to be defined more narrowly than that of religion (40). Newman's conclusion that natural religion is also revealed is approvingly quoted by Söderblom (41). Theology, therefore, is concerned with 'the whole field of religion.' Now the concept of revelation, and revelation is defined as 'knowledge of or insight into the essential nature of reality,' is constitutive for theology, inasmuch as all organized knowledge (*Wissenschaft*) has thus proceeded from the assumption of the reality of its object. 'A revelation of God is present wherever a real religion is found' (42). This understanding, current among the earlier Christian theologians, was later abandoned, partly because of the exclusively theological point of view in the past century and partly because of a lack of acquaintance with the spiritual treasures of

15

the ancient world (43). It is high time, according to Söderblom, for the church, emulating the example of an Origen,
to acquaint itself with the thought of the general revelation of
God. Inasmuch as this revelation is always given within a
cultural context, the two viewpoints, the religious and the
cultural, belong together. We should not think in terms of a
parallelism in the sense of a unilinear development, because
there is also disparity and unevenness (44). God and man,
nature and revelation, commingle from the crudest to the highest
forms of religion (45). Christianity appears from this perspective
not as the end of the journey of religion aided by culture but
as the full completion of a special revelation of God (46). It is
felt to have something of its own, and this particularism has
proved the strongest religious power in all the world. It is its
concept of God, his unity and personality, active and thus
revealed in history, which, according to the Scandinavian
theologian, makes this religion not only superior in degree but
essentially different in quality. Söderblom claims to arrive at
this judgment not as a dogmatician but *qua* historian (47).

In the two types of revealed (or prophetic) religion and the
religion of mysticism (infinity) Söderblom finds two basically
different yet legitimate types of the communion of man with
God (48). Biblical religion is of the first type. Though the
Swedish scholar agrees with Frank and Ihmels, two theologians
of the Erlangen school (49), in defining the task of Christian
theology, and more especially of dogmatics, as the scientific
interpretation of the self-consciousness of the church (anticipat-
ing the results of full historical and psychological investigation),
he stresses the necessity of 'including the entire historical reality
of religion on our earth' (50). Thus it will become manifest
that the certainty of revelation which the church possesses is not
reduced to that certainty which every other religion claims for
its object (51). For Christian theology the history of religion is,
according to Söderblom, 'a divine self-disclosure' (52). While
the student of religion leaves the question of revelation open,
'with the readiness of the scientific spirit to bow before the
actual fact' (53), biblical faith is animated by the conviction that
one part of the history of religion constitutes revelation in a more
real and a richer sense than in the history of religion in general.

He suggests that perhaps there ought to be found revealers as re-markable as Christ. Yet he adds significantly, 'but in fact there are none' (54).

This doctrine of a special revelation must, however, be tested in the light of that historical reality which is disclosed in general revelation. Confidently the Scandinavian historian answers 'Yes' to the question: 'Does revelation continue?' (55). It continues in the three areas of nature, history, and moral life (56). This point is of great importance for the understanding of the relation of the general and special study of religion. As in the study of history, language, and law, the Western scholar is justified in concentrating on the history, language, and law of his own culture—of course, not exclusively; so the study of Christianity must receive the lion's share in the efforts of the study of religion organized in the Christian universities and faculties (57). But a more important reason calls, according to Söderblom, for this emphasis: the breadth and length and depth of the Christian experience. The remarks which the great historian of religion devotes to proving this point are highly deserving of attention (58). But we cannot dwell on them here.

Nearly half a century has passed since the Swedish theologian began his work. The problem that confronted him has been taken up and somewhat differently resolved in our day by an American philosopher, W. E. Hocking. The two treatises which will concern us here are *Living Religions and a World Faith* (1940) and an article by the same title in the *Asian Legacy and American Life* (1942) (59). Though not the work of a theologian, Hocking's analysis, focusing clearly the dilemma of universality and particularity in religion, is of considerable importance because it is undertaken with a wide knowledge of and insight into the nature and variety of non-Christian faiths, and because it introduces a new normative element not present in the approach which we have just examined (60).

While Nathan Söderblom's work reflects the immediate response to the new situation which a vastly extended study of the religions of the non-Christian world had created at the close of the last century, William Ernest Hocking's thought repre-sents a sophisticated digest of the problems arising from the actual contacts among the world faiths of our own day. Like

Söderblom, Hocking stresses the dual nature of positive religion. It reaches out for the eternal and it is bound by and to historical situations. As a result, we notice 'a conflict between the sober rationality of the universal and the element of the irrational which enters with the particular' (61). Without discussing the adequacy of this characterization of the universal, we identify ourselves with the philosopher's insistence that simple abstraction from the particular will not and cannot solve the dilemma. An abstraction has no life, 'the price of existence is to be paid' (62). The philosopher is aware of the error of those who look upon the local or particular in religion as just a historical accident (the mistake of most thinkers of the age of the Enlightenment) and rightly claims that it is of the nature of religion, defined by him as 'a passion for righteousness' (63), to contain, as the 'farthest reach of universality of which the race is capable' (64), 'release from all localism', and yet, because it has to be communicated, to be identified with the destiny of one particular group and hence to be 'immersed in regional character and history' (65).

With a view to the particularization of the historical faiths, it becomes imperative to look for criteria which would help us to organize in our thought the multiplicity of phenomena with which the historians of religion have presented us. A unilinear development, such as was constructed by leading thinkers and scholars of the end of the nineteenth century under the influence of both the German transcendental and the French-English positivistic philosophy, can no longer be envisaged because of the trenchant criticism to which Rudolf Otto has subjected the theory of Wilhelm Wundt (66). The typological approach (67) essayed already in the work of C. P. Tiele and brilliantly carried through, theoretically and practically, in the work of his countryman, Gerardus van der Leeuw (68), has won the day.

Hocking, equally dissatisfied with relativistic historicism and unilinear evolutionism, not only suggests a classification of religions (69) on a typological basis but also isolates, with the use of this method, some important characteristics of Eastern religions (plural belonging, relative formlessness, variety of personnel, place of thought and doctrine, immunity to proof, adaptability to change) (70). It is not with the latter attempt, significant and worthy of consideration though it is, that we are here concerned, but with the philosopher's criticism of the typological principle which we found looming so large in Soederblom's theological interpretation of the variety of religious experience: the concept of revelation as the criterion of truth. With the Scandinavian, Hocking distinguishes revealed and non-revealed religions, the former comprising, according to him, the 'Semitic' religions of the book, and the latter the religions of eastern Asia, especially Hinduism and Buddhism (71). He disagrees with the propounders of the idea that—inasmuch as Judaism has been absorbed by Christianity, and Islam is a 'poorly edited adaptation of the two other faiths to the desert environment,' hence a 'very impeded' revelation or per- haps 'no revelation at all'—only Christianity is left as 'the one legitimate vessel of the world faith' (72). The philosopher is right in protesting against such manipulation, but how is he going to escape radically relativistic consequences?

Hocking is thoroughly opposed to any concept of revelation which limits to a single source the channels through which truth becomes available, and he insists that revelation should not be thought of as opposed to insight or reason (73). He protests that the question of truth must be taken seriously. It will not do to say: 'I believe because I decide to believe.' Such procedure would leave us with a 'confusion of decisions without means of rational conversation.' Hocking, however, does not side with rationalism. He holds that we know in a way other than by pure reason and by experience. Revelation in the general sense is understood by him as the 'empirical element in religious knowledge which does not exclude but lies beyond thought' ('God becomes perceptible through the medium of experience in time') (74); in the special sense it refers to the knowledge of the will of God, inasmuch as he acts and reveals himself in events. Hence it can be said that 'to each individual self, his world of experience is a direct address of God to man' (75). In addition to such general divine self-communication, some events will convey in a more particular sense a notion of the quality of God's being. For each individual person, Hocking states, his revelation is *his* 'Burning Bush,' his response being *his* response to objective historical fact. But what is responded to cannot be the 'arbitrary or unintelligible' which rebuffs man's apprehension and demands 'blind obedience.' That would mean to 'revel in the abasement of the human,' contrary, the philosoper feels, to the meaning of Jesus' words and spirit (76).

Hocking discusses in detail the rival claims of the religions of revelation—an important task, one of the most important perhaps, for a comparative study. His interest is not, like that of Söderblom, centred upon the question of the truth of Christianity as such but, as indicated above, on an inquiry into the feasibility and the nature of a world faith. Here we find it more difficult to follow him. He feels that the need for a world religion is urgent and, further, that something like a world faith is actually emerging. In this diagnosis he is in accord with scholars like Charles Morris and Filmer S. C. Northrop. Yet Hocking does not believe in achieving such a world religion simply by *laissez-faire*.

Of the three ways in which, according to Hocking, the goal of a world religion can be reached, the first—that of radical displacement of the existing non-Christian religions ('be done with the old allegiance and take on the new one')—must be abandoned. Its presuppositions and methods are discredited. 'Discontinuity means isolation.' Yet, he believes, opportunity must be provided for individual conversion in the form of a radical break. Those who feel strongly ('fanatically') about their religious ideals, he says, should be allowed to be individual missionaries. The second way, that of synthesis, is, inasmuch as there is something unavoidable about it, legitimate. But it does not really lead to the planned result—the solution of the great issues. It happens anyway that contacts lead to mutual influencing and convergence, yet this event is 'but the assembling stage, preliminary to a further process of thought' (77). Hocking himself prefers the third way, that of reconception. It differs from the second method, that of broadening, in that it involves the deepening of our own and of the alien religious experience. 'The great effort now required is the effort to discern the substance of the matter underlying all this profession of religious expression, to apprehend the general principle of religious life and of each particular form of it' (78).

Inasmuch as the formulation of this task does not funda-
mentally differ from the ideal which has motivated the leading
lights of the eras of the Enlightenment and of classical idealism, a
great deal depends upon the method which its advocate suggests
for its achievement. How is this essence to be found? Hocking
answers, not primarily by comparison or analysis but by induc-
tion or, more precisely, by 'a perception of the reason why a
given group of facts or experiences belong together' (79). This
definition is very illuminating, because it stresses the functional
nature of the forms of expression of religious experience which
has so often been overlooked or ignored by recent students of
the history of religions. Its author is aware of the danger which
earlier seekers after essences have not avoided: 'reduction of
religion to bare bones' (80). 'Something is final in what I have;
but not all that I have is final.' He knows that the search for
'essence' cannot stop; that it is progressive (81). Our finite
apprehension of that which is not final cannot be thought to be
beyond improvement. The philosopher objects equally to a provincialism which posits one's own position as absolute and a
flabby relativism which gives up the 'central citadel of finality'
(82). Our judgment contains elements both of certainty and of
uncertainty, and develops in a dialectical manner. All this,
Hocking holds, is true of all religious statements, Christian as
well as non-Christian. Thus he can say that 'in proportion as
any religion grows in self-understanding through grasping its
own essence, it grasps the essence of all religion and gains in
power to interpret its various forms' (83).

Such attempts at a deepened self-understanding are made in
all contemporary great religions, and this fact is regarded as a
source of encouragement (84). Hocking seems to imply that
truth is one (85). He feels that that faith, that concrete faith,
which shall prove its genuineness by its fruits, redeeming contemporary man from his deep sense of frustration and from the
vices that plague him, that which is most fertile in stimulating
his creative capacities and yet is capable of legitimately asserting
its authority, will win and create the body it needs to live (86).

There is no need here to dwell on Hocking's discussion of
certain contemporary trends which seem to him to point in the
direction of a growing world faith, and which he does not hesi-

tate to call an 'incipient natural religion': a belief in obligation and in a source which is good; the longing for some participation in permanence in view of transience; the sobered recovery of supernature (87) and the dissatisfaction with the excess of humanism. However, we are vitally interested in what he has to say about the role he envisages for Christianity (88). The role of any religion will be, according to him, very largely determined by 'the disjecta membra of a possible world faith' (89).

As the great assets of Christianity, Hocking regards the facts that in its potential or ideal self it 'anticipates the essence of all religion,' especially in the Sermon on the Mount and in the concept of universal incarnation, and so contains 'potentially all any religion has' (90). Christianity means, moreover, 'faith in the significance of the particular event and of the individual person,' a need especially great with the 'deepening lostness of the soul in an expanding world' (91). Furthermore, it has a superior power of self-expression, demonstrated in its history and increased by it. It is not committed to a fixed social institution, and it possesses an essentially democratic character. But it also suffers a great disadvantage in that it has become a Western religion. Though it has been a spiritual motor in the development of Western culture, it has need to dissociate itself from a fatal entanglement (92). Moreover, two facts indicate that, in Hocking's judgment, Christianity is not yet ready to serve as a world religion: first, it is not brought to bear upon the social life in our own society and is liable to corruption by institutionalism; and, second, there are still important values outside Christianity (93). As such Hocking regards, for example, the Moslem emphasis upon the majesty of God and the solidarity of the brotherhood of Islam; the reflectiveness, spirituality, and serenity of spirit of the Indian faiths; the enjoyment of the impersonal element of ultimate truth in Buddhism; and the intense humanity, naturalness, and gaiety of the Chinese religions (94). Though conscious of the subjectivity of this appraisal, the philosopher holds that the challenge of such an enquiry should be taken seriously by the Christian theologian.

It is just this problem, that of religious values outside Christianity, which very recently has been fruitfully and suggestively discussed by a Christian theologian with a deep insight into a non-Christian religion, in this case Hinduism. In *Studies in History and Religion*, Professor Wenger of Serampore College, Bengal, has contributed a paper on 'The Problem of Truth in Religion' (95). His thesis is that Christian theology, as it has developed in the West, has a great deal to gain from non-Christian Eastern sources. New forms of thought may emerge to give a 'more adequate interpretation and expression to religious experience' (96). The author, however, in contrast to Söderblom's procedure which we outlined above, does not set out from a general concept of religious experience. He desires, as indeed as a Christian he must, to start with what, he is confident, is 'the truth.' But he is—and this statement is of great importance for the understanding of his position—convinced of the inadequacy of his apprehension of the Christian revelation. A criterion has to be found to distinguish between the more and the less essential therein. Appeal to the working of the Holy Spirit or to the scriptures will, according to Wenger, not serve the purpose; the variety of interpretations given to the manifestations of the former and the teachings of the latter shows that the problem is thus only pushed back, not solved. And even if a 'correct' or adequate exegesis would ascertain the meaning of a particular manifestation of the Divine Will and Word, the latter is conveyed to us by prophets or saints who deliver the divine message on the basis of their human apprehension. Thus the 'personal equation' enters in. The author therefore sees a 'need for an epistemological investigation to test the instruments by which we claim to know' (97). He criticizes dialectical theology for its insistence that whatever can be shown to have the form of the Word of God has to be obeyed unquestioningly (herein agreeing with Hocking) and for its rejection of all discussion and evaluation of the contents. How do we know, he asks, which is the voice of God except by examination of these contents? The criterion cannot be sought in the realm of subjective psychological evidence.

There is still another point which causes Wenger to take exception to the position of the dialectical theologians: their unqualified identification of revelation with divine activity without regard to human receptivity (98). Their limitation of the meaning of the term 'revelation' in the interest of safeguarding

23

the uniqueness of the incarnation of God in Jesus Christ involves them in difficulties, inasmuch as they cannot do justice to 'other occasions where God's activity is manifested' (99). The interpretation which Wenger gives to the term 'revelation' implies three things. First, revelation does not mean the conveying of facts about God but is actually the establishment of a communion between man and God in various forms and categories, and this communion, though initiated by divine activity, presupposes a measure of human receptivity (100). The conclusion to be drawn from this understanding is that 'God's revelation of Himself to men is not the same for every man but varies according to their powers and natures.' This notion concurs with the Buddhist doctrine of the *upayakauśalya* (skilfulness in the use of means) employed by the Buddha. Second, it becomes apparent that man hears God according to his powers of reception; man is passive, and the moment of hearing 'may be the product of his own past activities.' Finally, the experience sustained in receiving revelation must be communicated and can be communicated only in human terms.

The author is in agreement not only with Söderblom and Hocking but also with Luther and in opposition to Barth and Krämer in suggesting that God does not necessarily reveal all of himself all the time (101). Though the term 'progressive revelation' has been misinterpreted as meaning merely man's progressive apprehension, it is appropriate if used with the understanding that it actually denotes God's progressive self-revealing activity. Wenger is, in accord with biblical teaching, inclined to believe that this activity has been universal, that God is 'everywhere personally active.'

This understanding of revelation suggests three questions, according to our author. Is the truth, so far received, the maximum God can give? Has it been adequately apprehended? Is it adequately expressed? (102). While he replies to the first question in the affirmative, the other two questions cannot be so answered. Even the earliest apostle's interpretation of God's revelation in Christ was not sufficient. The thought-forms in which the West has expressed its understanding of divine revelation have, says Wenger, been strongly influenced by concepts developed elsewhere in pre-Christian times (Greek,

Latin, Nordic, *et al.*). The fact that the home-made theologies of these sections of the originally non-Christian world have been incorporated justifies the expectation that there will be a new expression of the gospel in India, where God has revealed himself through the ages (103). What Wenger has in mind is, according to his own words, not a 'mere translation of Christian doctrine into the idiom of Hinduism but a constructive working out of the meaning of God in Christ as led up to by the early preparatory revelation by God in India.'

An interesting instance of such implementation of our apprehension of divine truth is the methodological problem of its evidence. While perception and inference are the generally recognized sources of knowledge in the West, 'authority,' claimed by Christian theology, is not. Indian epistemology, highly differentiated as it is, makes provision for *śābda* (authority) as a legitimate *pramāna* (method of knowledge). All normative disciplines have to face the question of what to do if authorities differ (104). A conflict as such does not necessarily invalidate all claims of authority. Wenger reminds us of Robinson's suggestion to regard the saint as the 'expert' in religion who should be heard when the religious truth is discussed, but he warns of the one-sidedness of the insight of all who detach religion from its broad context in life. Because the saint is, as a rule, no critical thinker, the theologian and the philosopher hold the responsibility of testing the authoritarian utterances of the saint; to them must fall the explicit working-out of the message of the saints to test it 'in the totality of life' (105).

V

It behoves us to state to what extent we are inclined to identify ourselves with the views of the three scholars which we have tried to summarize in the foregoing paragraphs. Their common argument for an inclusive concept of revelation according to which the whole history of religion should be viewed as divine self-disclosure seems to us irrefutable. The theologian cannot afford to neglect the contribution to his work that will be gained from a thorough acquaintance with non-Christian religions. However, we feel that the relationship of Christianity to these religions has not been satisfactorily determined by Söderblom, owing to the fact that he fails to distinguish clearly, as do the two others, between truth and the apprehension of truth. While Söderblom is aware of the 'particularization' of religion, owing to the environmental context in which it develops, he does not apply this insight to the work of the Christian theologian. Moreover, Söderblom does not indicate how the Christian theologian should proceed if he would utilize non-Christian insights and forms of expression. Both Hocking and Wenger have profited from the result of the process of self-examination in Christianity which began after World War I. Hence they distinguish between truth and its apprehension and expression in *all* religions.

While all three authors reject the notion of a radical replacement of Christianity by another faith, old or new, and are averse to any artificial 'synthesis,' only one, Hocking, wants to go beyond Christianity in favour of a new world faith. We indicated above that we cannot follow him here. His analysis of the assets and shortcomings of Christianity has led him, we feel, to a surrender which his own concept of reconception actually makes unnecessary because the shortcomings he mentions are due to inadequate apprehension of the Christian truth. Here we side with Wenger, who rightly sees that a decision is necessary but also rightly avoids an identification of this decision with the 'blind obedience' to which Hocking objects. His definition of revelation as communion between God and man (106) excludes such misunderstanding. We concur in his negation of a purely passive notion of human receptivity. The rational element, on which Hocking insists as constitutive for the religious act, lest there be a 'confusion of decisions without means of rational conversation,' is thus safeguarded without being elevated to the dignity of sole arbiter as in the theology of the Enlightenment.

It is again Wenger who poses, with precision, the essential question of the criteria of evidence for what is claimed as revelation. Neither he nor Hocking would follow Söderblom's stress upon the scriptures. Both are keenly aware of the ambiguities to which their interpretation is exposed. Wenger's reference to the saints as the experts in religion seems to us an indication of his realization of the value of the tradition of the religious community, a factor so universally neglected by modern Protestant theologians. In view of this realization it is difficult to see why he dismisses so summarily the chance to avail himself of the possibilities which the concept of the Holy Spirit in Christian theology offers for an epistemological analysis of the apprehension of truth (107).

Because the spirit of God illumines his saints as spokesmen, they are enabled to apprehend, express, and communicate as much of his truth as they are open to. By the same token, we who are hearers understand, on the basis of an affinity of spirit, the message which they convey to us in oral or written form. Where this 'congeniality' is lacking, all ingenuity of interpretation is of no avail (108). But it takes all this ingenuity (cf. above, Sect. II) to do justice to a document of religious experience. That is why students of the disciplines among which the study of religion is parcelled out must work together. The work of the theologian who is conscious of this necessity will gain in width and depth. The provincialism which is, at least in part, responsible for the suspicion and lack of response which so often meet theological efforts in the contemporary world will thus be overcome. The historian of religion who is aware of the same necessity will cease to be an antiquarian. He will find meaning in the manifestations and phenomena he studies, and, to the extent to which he does justice to this meaning, he will contribute his mite to the search for the truth.

As in other fields of knowledge, in the sciences and in the humanities there are also axioms or basic principles in theology, the existence of which, instead of being regarded as *partie honteuse*, to be concealed or altogether denied, should be acknowledged and clearly formulated in methodological prolegomena. Here is an attempt at such a statement. The place of the history of religions in theological studies should be determined on the basis of the following considerations.

1. The primary concern of the Christian theologian is the hearing, understanding, and promulgating of the gospel of God's redemption of man the culmination of which he understands to be the work of Christ Jesus. His sources are God's continuous disclosure in nature, in history, in his world, and in the

community of those he has drawn to himself. All that proves helpful towards the consummation of this task of interpretation and communication can be judged to belong within the sphere of theology.

2. The theologian cannot but be aware that, in his infinite love and mercy, God has at no time left himself without witness. It is not in the theologian's competence to delimit for past, present, or future the self-revealing activity of God. He is deeply aware of the inadequacy and the provisional character of all apprehension of divine revelation, including his own.

3. To the divine self-disclosure and call through the ages corresponds the seeking and thirsting of man's heart and mind after God and his righteousness, part of which is recorded in the history of the religion of mankind.

4. The theologian, though conscious of his special task to illuminate the content of the divine message in the sense indicated above (under 1), cannot but utilize for this purpose, drawing from the sum total of man's religious experience, the insights 'revealed' to men of God everywhere.

5. While the theologian is at pains to interpret the above-mentioned sources (under 1), thus continuously formulating and revising the Christian apprehension of divine truth, the historian of religion provides a comprehensive but articulated inventory of the varieties of expression of this experience.

6. This material cannot be regarded as an extra of which the theologian may or may not avail himself, but is indispensable for that approximation to the understanding of God's self-disclosure which he must set himself as goal. If constructive theology of necessity be in some measure apologetical, it must be remembered that genuine apologetics is inconceivable except as a serious discussion of the claims of all non-Christian religion.

7. Discussion of the claims of non-Christian religion does not fall within the competence of the historian of religion as such. Inasmuch, however, as the facts provided by him remain without meaning for us if not evaluated in a normative context, such evaluation has to be essayed.

8. Interpretation of expressions of religious experience means an integral understanding, that is, full linguistic, historical,

psychological, technological, and sociological enquiry, in which full justice is done to the intention of the expression and to the context in which it occurs, and in which this expression is related to the experience of which it testifies. Comparison, an important means of ascertaining analogies and differences between various forms of expression of religious experiences and between experiences themselves, is not an end in itself. Neither is the construction of types of religions such an end, valuable as they will be.

9. Objective study, comparison, and typology are the indispensable preparation for evaluation. Evaluation presupposes standards. Such standards, ascertained and formulated in the course of the history of Christian experience and theological thought, have been indicated above (under 1). The result may be 'a comprehension of the various religions deeper and more adequate than their own understanding of themselves' (109).

10. It is the task of the theologian to determine the depth of insight into divine truth manifested in non-Christian religious expression, from his awareness of the love and grace of God, revealed in Christ and in the manifestations of his will in nature, in history, in the community, and in the soul of man, while remaining conscious of the limitations of this apprehension (cf. under 2).

11. It is precisely the concept of the Holy Spirit of God, unduly neglected by modern theologians, which should be the guide in all attempts at the determination of the 'germs of truth,' inasmuch as it represents the only legitimate criterion by which to judge where God speaks and is present.

12. It seems difficult, if not impossible, to outline the main features of the 'world faith' which some believe is emerging from the conflicting claims of competing world religions. Who will say that we have, as yet, fully appropriated to ourselves the incomparable spiritual heritage which is ours?

CHAPTER TWO

UNIVERSALS IN RELIGION

I

THE careful research of many a generation of scholars, the travel reports, not only of adventurers, missionaries and explorers, but of many a person you and I count among our personal acquaintances, have brought home to well-nigh all of us a realization of the variety of religious ideas and practices that exist in the world. The result of this realization has been bewilderment and confusion in many hearts and minds. Roughly three different types of reaction to the situation can be discerned: (i) scepticism, that is, the refusal to see in all these religious ideas and usages more than the expression of ignorance and folly, in other words a cultural and/or religious 'lag'; (ii) relativism, that is, a disposition to dispense with the problem of truth in favour of a non-committal registration of all there is and has been, an attitude which has found much favour in the latter-day circles of scholars and intellectuals; and finally (iii) the desire to investigate the variety of what goes under the names of religion and religions in order to determine by comparison and phenomenological analysis if anything like a structure can be discovered in all these forms of expression, to what kind of experiences this variegated expression can be traced, and finally, what kind of reality or realities may correspond to the experiences in question. It is the last of the three types of reaction to the predicament characterized above which seems to us the only promising and fruitful one, and we propose to follow it in what we have to say here.

The first difficulty we encounter in trying to bring some order into the bewildering mass of material that geography, anthropology, sociology, archaeology, philology, history, and the history of religions have placed at our disposal, is the need for criteria which would enable us to distinguish between what is religious and what is not. Now you will not expect me to discuss the well-nigh endless series of definitions of religion which have been proposed by the great and the not-so-great during recent decades. We shall also find it impossible to use as our yardstick one of the classical historical formulations evolved in one of the great religious communities itself, say in the Christian. For we should soon discover that it is not possible to identify religion with what we have come to know as Christian or Jewish or Hindu, even if we forget for the moment that it would be far from easy to agree on which of the available formulations we want to use. Some of us might feel, at first thought, that it is after all not so difficult to determine what may be called religious and what is not religious; they would point to the neat divisions which we are accustomed to find in our text-books, dealing with the lives of individuals, societies and cultures, past and present, in which separate chapters deal with man's political views and activities, his economic situation, his interest in the arts, and his religious orientation, or with the social organization, the economics, the legal institutions, the arts and sciences, the moral life, and the religion of a given tribe, people or nation. But, on second thoughts, the unsatisfactory character of such parcelling becomes evident; and that not only in the repetitions and omissions which this procedure entails. No wonder then that some investigators—and we find among them distinguished anthropologists, philosophers, and theologians—have come to the conclusion that religion is not anything distinct and *sui generis*, but is a name given to the sum of man's aspirations, to the whole of the civilization of a people. If we reject this view, it is not because we want to separate sharply between religion on the one hand and on the other all that makes up an individual's or a society's other experiences and activities. But we are of the opinion that, in order to be able to assess the interrelation and interpenetration of the various interests, attitudes, and activities of man, we have to examine very carefully the nature of his propensities, drives, impulses, actions, and reactions. William James has rightly said: 'The essence of religious experiences, the thing by which we must finally judge them, must be that element or quality in them

31

which we can meet nowhere else. (1) We disagree with those who are prone to identify religion with just one segment of man's inner existence: feeling, willing, or cogitating. In order to lay down our criteria, we cannot be satisfied to examine only the conceptually articulated perceptions or only the emotions and affections and the respective expressions in which they have become manifest. We propose rather the following *four formal criteria* for a definition of what might be called religious experience:

1. Religious experience is a response to what is experienced as ultimate reality; that is, in religious experiences we react not to any single or finite phenomenon, material or otherwise, but to what we realize as undergirding and conditioning all that constitutes our world of experiences. We agree with Paul Tillich when he says that 'the presence of the demand of "ultimacy" in the structure of our existence is the basis of religious experience' (2). Before him William James said in his book on the *Varieties of Religious Experience* (3)—a passage quoted in Paul Johnson's *Psychology of Religion* (4): 'It is as if there were in the human consciousness a sense of reality, a feeling of objective presence, a perception of what we may call "something there," more deep and more general than any of the special and particular "senses" by which the current psychology supposes existent realities to be originally revealed' (5). Or as the author of a recent text-book on Psychology of Religion formulates it (6): 'Religious experience is response to stimuli that represent an active reality viewed as divine, or as creative of values.'

This response has the tendency to persist, once communion with the source of life and values is established, and man is restless to reassure himself of its continuance.

2. Religious experience is a total response of the total being to what is apprehended as ultimate reality. That is, we are involved not exclusively with our mind, our affections, or our will, but as integral persons (7).

3. Religious experience is the most intense experience of which man is capable. That is not to say that all expression of religious experience testifies to this intensity but that, potentially, genuine religious experience is of this nature, as is

instanced in conflicts between different basic drives or motivations. Religious loyalty, if it is religious loyalty, wins over all other loyalties. The modern term 'existential' designates the profound concern and the utter seriousness of this experience.

4. Religious experience is practical, that is to say it involves an imperative, a commitment which impels man to act. This activistic note distinguishes it from aesthetic experience, of which it shares the intensity, and joins it with moral experience. Moral judgment, however, does not necessarily represent a reaction to ultimate reality.

It should be borne in mind that one, two, or three of these criteria would not suffice to reassure us that we are dealing with genuine religious experience. All four would have to be present. If they are, we should have no difficulty in distinguishing between religious and non-religious experiences. However, there are *pseudo-religious* and *semi-religious* experiences. The former are non-religious and known to be such to the person or persons who pretend to them by using forms of expression peculiar to religion. The latter may show the presence of the second, third and fourth characteristics, but refer not to ultimate but to some aspect of 'finite' reality. The intense and possibly sacrificial devotion with which somebody may 'worship' a loved person, his race, his social group, or his state are instances of semi-religious loyalties. Because they are directed toward finite values, they are idolatrous rather than religious.

Now it is our contention, and this is the first proposition in regard to our topic, that religious experience, as we have just attempted to define it by means of these four criteria, is *universal*. The empirical proof of this statement can be found in the testimonies of explorers and investigators. 'There are no peoples, however primitive, without religion and magic,' is the opening sentence of one of Malinowski's well-known essays (8). In practically all cases where a rash negative conclusion has been reached, more careful research has corrected the initial error.

A *second* proposition is this: religious experience tends towards *expression*. This tendency is universal. Only in and through its expression does any of our experiences exist for others, does any religious experience exist for us, the students of the history of religion. The religious experience of another person can never become the object of direct observation. Some important hermeneutical consequences result from the recognition of this fact.

Now for the *third* step in our search for universals in religion. A comparative study of the *forms* of the expression of religious experience, the world over, shows an amazing similarity in structure. We should like to summarize the result of such comparative studies by the statement: all expression of religious experience falls under the three headings of *theoretical expression, practical expression,* and *sociological expression* (9). Everywhere and at all times man has felt the need to articulate his religious experience in three ways: conceptually; by action, or practically; and in covenanting, or sociologically. There is no religion deserving of the name in which any one of these three elements is totally lacking, though the degree and, of course, the tempo of this development may vary. Notwithstanding numerous attempts at establishing priority for one of these three modes of expression, we feel that it would be futile to argue that myth precedes cult or that both precede fellowship: history teaches us that the dynamics of religious life is made up of the interpenetration of these three aspects.

Before we can discuss in any greater detail the structure of these fields of expression of religious experience and the common elements to be found within an apparently endless variety of forms, we have to consider briefly some general factors which help to determine their development. Man finds himself always situationally conditioned: whatever he experiences, he experiences in *time* and *space*. Even if, in his religious experience, he seems to transcend these limitations—a feeling to which the mystics of all religions have given vivid and often paradoxical articulation (Eckhart: 'Time is what keeps the light from reaching us. There is no greater obstacle to God than Time' (10))—he cannot but give expression to what he has seen, felt, etc., *per analogiam entis,* by means of *analogy* from what is known and familiar to him (11). The way of negation, of analogy and of eminence is used in all religious language. That we have to remember when we review the concepts of sacred time and of sacred space which are the framework within which religious thought and religious acts enfold themselves. Holy times and holy places are universal notions; no myth or doctrine, no cult or religious association is found without them (12). Closely related to these categories within which religious apprehension expresses itself is the notion of a *cosmic* (that is natural, ritual and social) *order* upon which life, individual and collective, depends. The well-known Chinese concept of *Tao*, the Hindu *ṛta*, the Iranian *asha*, the Greek *dike*, designate the order upon which man and society depend for their existence (13). In the religions of the American Indians, the Africans and Oceanians the directions, the seasons, the celestial bodies, colours, social organization, all follow this orientation, the cosmic law which the physical, mental and spiritual life of all beings has to obey (14). Nature and its rhythm, culture and its activities, and polity and its structure are but aspects of this order. It is the foundation for all 'ethics.'

Religious experience, we saw, may be characterized as the total response of man's total being to what he experiences as ultimate reality. In it he confronts a *power* greater than any power which he controls by his own wit or strength. I should like to stress *two* points here. This encounter is not a question of intellectual inference or speculative reasoning, of which there are few traces in many of the lower so-called primitive religions (15). That is to say, religion is emphatically not a kind of underdeveloped 'science' or 'philosophy.' This misinterpretation, still widely current, is an unfortunate legacy from the rationalistically-minded era of the Enlightenment. The experience which we call religion is rather an awareness of apprehension, not lacking a cognitive aspect but not defined by it, a reaction to something that is sensed or apprehended as powerful. Rudolf Otto has spoken of a *sensus numinis* (sense of awe) (16), and this term seems to me a very apt designation. We must reject all theories of religion which conceive of it as the fulfilment which imaginative or crafty individuals have supplied for a subjective, that is illusory, need. True, many a testimony to religious experience lets the latter appear as the result of a search, a struggle, but more often this experience has come as a bolt from the blue, with a spontaneity which contradicts the theory of need. Hence we prefer to say that there is a propensity, a *nisus* or *sensus numinis* which is activated in the religious experience proper (17). The aspect of power which the comparative study of religion has recently vindicated as a central notion in the religions of widely different peoples and societies, indicates the 'point of contact' between the reality which is confronted in religious experience and life in the everyday world: the 'immanence of the transcendent.' Religions differ in their notions as to the how, where, and when of the manifestations of power in the phenomenal world. But the acknowledgment that this power manifests itself in experienceable form is universal. To the degree that it appears diffused, we speak of *power-centres* such as are known in all primitive, higher and fully developed cults (18). The Swedish historian of religion, Martin Nilsson, has recently (19) stressed the adjective character of terms for power such as *mana, orenda,* etc. Not the phenomenon, object or person in which this power manifests itself, but a power that *transcends* it, is the object of man's awe. It is of great importance to understand that this power is apprehended as an elementary force which transcends moral or aesthetic qualifications. As such it is 'mysterious.' It was one of the great insights of the author of the *Idea of the Holy,* Rudolf Otto, that he caught the double notion of the *mysterium magnum* in the twin ideas of its terrifying and its alluring aspect. These *two aspects* are known to the theologians of all religions as Divine Wrath and Divine Love or Grace. Though their natural roles and relationships are differently conceived in different faiths, these two aspects of power are universally recognized. But we can still go one step further in our analysis of universal features in religious experience. It is possible to discern a double consequence of man's apprehension of numinous power at all times and everywhere: he either bows to it in submission, or he reaches out in an attempt to manipulate and control the mysterious forces of which he has become aware. The first, the *religious* way, leads up to the highest religious act, that of adoration; the second, the way of *magic,* sets him on the road to conquer and to appropriate as much of the power as will yield to his command. These two developments are not to be thought of in terms of a chronological and evolutionary sequence: on the one hand the magical is always with us, and on the other the presence of genuinely religious response to the numinous even in the primitive cults cannot be denied. Hence both are universal. It is only the *intention* inherent in it which distinguishes the religious from the magical act. The very complicated question of the origins, the nature of the development of 'science' (in the broader as well as the narrower sense of the natural sciences), and of its relation to both magic and religion, can be answered when we are more fully conversant with the nature of knowledge (20), with the psychological motivations for wanting to know (21).

Perhaps the sociology of knowledge will help us at some time in the future. On the cognitive factor in the experience which we call religious we shall have a word to say presently.

II

After these brief remarks, which were meant to put in relief some universally valid features of religious *experience*, we will now turn to the examination of universals in the forms of *expression* of this experience (22). We have said that the very fact that this experience tends to expression constitutes in itself a universal. We shall enlarge this statement now by asking: What *motivates* expression? There is first what I should like to call the demonstrative type of expression with which we are familiar from all kinds of experiences other than religious. The shout of joy or pain, witnessing to a profound emotion, is paralleled by the ejaculatory expression of awe or devotion. Then there is the communicative motif: we like to share our experiences with others, and we can do so only by means of sounds, words or acts. Finally the missionary purpose has to be considered. We want to attract others, a purpose not alien to other types of experience, but constitutive of the religious. Finding these motives making for expression universally valid, we may ask further: What of the *modes* in which the expression of religious experience is cast?

Here we face the difficult question of the interrelationship of what we have called the intellectual, the practical and the sociological expressions of religious experience (23). Bevan, Cassirer, Urban, Susanne Langer and others have studied the problem of symbolism and analysed the structure of logical, aesthetic, and religious symbols (24). The *symbol* is the primary means of expressing the content of any experience which we call religious. The use of symbolic expression is universal. By symbols a meaning is conveyed the nature of which may be conceptually explained, which may be acted upon, and which may serve as an integrating factor in creating religious fellowship. An example of a simple symbol is the *churinga* of the Australians (the bull-roarer, standing for the presence of totemic ancestors), on a higher level the *shintai* (sword, mirror, stone) of the Japanese, or finally, in the great world religions, the Buddhist wheel and the Christian cross. In each case theoretical explanations, cultual use and sociological effect contribute to unfold and explain the meaning of the symbol (25). Stages in the development of these modes of expression can be traced: the African Bushmen, awed by the presence of the numinous at a given place, utter a numinous sound in which they express the vivid emotion that grips them, while throwing a few grains into a hole in the hallowed ground, an act which at the same time expresses and reinforces the communion which exists between fellow-worshippers. A second example: in the Egypt of the ancient kingdom the worshippers of a deity are gathered in a hut before the crude therio- or anthropomorphic images which stand as a symbol of the numinous presence. The myth in which the nature and the significance of this manifestation of the divine is illustrated imaginatively, is alive in the minds of those present. A third example: the original intuition or basic religious experience of the founder of Islam is enfolded in the systematic doctrine of Islam, acted out in acts of devotion and charity, and is the foundation upon which the *umma* or congregation of the faithful rests. All this goes to show the universal presence of the three modes of expression of religious experience and their intimate interrelationship.

We now have to discuss the *means* by which religious ex-experience is theoretically, practically and sociologically expressed. Here too our expectation is to find elements present everywhere (26). We begin with the *intellectual* expression. Religious experience, as confrontation of ultimate reality, entails a cognitive element. When Mohammed received his initial revelation, when the Buddha awoke to the realization of the impermanence of the phenomenal world, when Laotse became aware of the nature of the unalterable Tao, this original intuition ('*Ur-intuition*') in each case implied an apprehension of ultimate reality, of the relation of the visible to the invisible, of the nature of the universe and of man's nature and destiny which invited further conceptual articulation. We do not know to which intuitions the primitive cults owe their existence, but we can infer that generations of seers and priests helped to evolve the mythical concepts in which the numinous experiences of these peoples have come to expression. For *myth* is the *first form* of intellectual explanation of religious apprehensions. 'It is,' says S. Langer (27), 'in the great realm of myth that human conceptions of reality become articulated.' 'These stories,' says Malinowski (28), 'live not by idle interest, not as fictions or even as true narratives; but are to the natives a statement of a primeval, greater, and more relevant reality by which the present life, fate and activities of man are determined. Here the imaginative element prevails over the abstract' (29). Contrary to the assumption of the Positivist school—Comte's theory of the stages—this form of expression is universal; it is not bound to any one stage of development, as the use of mythical language in all the great religions indicates. Myth asks the perennial question Why? Why are we here? Where do we come from? Why do we act in the way we do? Why do we die?—questions which the awakened intellectual curiosity of man is apt to ask and to answer in imaginative, that is symbolic, language. The reason for the persistence of this form of expression of religious experience is to be found in the nature of this experience itself (30). It ultimately transcends rationalization, as the religious thinkers of all times and places well know (31). The *second form* of the intellectual explanation of religious apprehension we call *doctrine*. It grows out of the attempt to unify and systematize variant concepts. Doctrine also is a ubiquitous, that is a universal element. We meet with considerable development or systematization of myth in the priestly schools of Polynesia, in Western Africa, in the Maya and Aztec centres of learning, and we find this process continued in ancient Egypt, in Sumeria, in Israel, in Asia Minor, in

India, in ancient Greece and Rome, among the Celts and the Teutonic tribes. In all the major world religions a doctrinal development which includes reactions and protests can be traced. More often than not we meet with short confessions of faith, some of which have developed into creeds (32).

From the examination of the formal side of the intellectual expression of religious experience, we turn to an analysis of its *content*. The great recurrent themes, treated in the myths as well as in the doctrines of all faiths, are (*a*) the nature and character of supreme reality: the deity of God; evil; the origin, nature and destiny of (*b*) the world and (*c*) of man (personality; sin; hope). In articulated theological doctrine these topics are treated in the disciplines known as theology, cosmology, and anthropology and eschatology. 'The questions,' says P. Tillich (33), 'implied in human existence, determine the meaning and the theological interpretation of the answers as they appear in the classical religious concepts.' In several of the great civilizations in the history of the world, in Greece, in Persia, in India, in China, theological speculation has developed into philosophy of religion and philosophical thought as such, especially metaphysics. Yet not only philosophy but science in practically all its major branches stems from this source. However important the thinking out of the implications of religious apprehension may be, it should never be identified with the total expression of religious experience. We agree here with Wiemann when he says: 'Events rich in value and events transformative of human existence run deeper than ideas and doctrines and are mightier' (34). The history of religious *thought* is only *one* though an essential and ubiquitous part of the history of religions. There are actually other than purely intellectual yet equally universally present means of expression of religious experience. 'Man incited by God,' says the author of the best book on worship (E. Underhill) (35), 'dimly or sharply conscious of the obscure presence of God, responds to him best not by a single movement of the mind, but by a rich and complex action in which his whole nature is concerned, and which has at its full development the character of a work of art.' 'Ritual like art is,' according to S. Langer, 'essentially the active termination of a symbolic transformation of experience.'

The phenomenology of the religious *act* shows a great variety of ways of acting which we shall, for our purpose, arrange typologically. It has been claimed that all life, as it is lived and acted, could be regarded as expressing that relationship that is experienced in the awareness of the numen. The great anthropologist R. R. Marett put it in this way: 'Being inwardly assured of its primacy as the ultimate source of vital and psychic energy, spirit has no need to fear the close intimacy with the natural functions that go with life as pursued on the material plane' (36). Acts which in our view are remote from the religious sphere, such as eating, playing, mating (37), are cultual acts in many primitive and higher religions. In distinction from the general, there are specific cultual acts which we shall call *rites*. They have a special dedicatory character. In and through them the presence of the numen is acknowledged (38). The contact with creative sources of life innervates and stimulates man to action. 'Ritual,' says S. Langer (39), 'is a transformation of the experiences that no other medium can adequately express. It is not prescribed for a practical purpose, even not social solidarity.' The range of *media* employed in the cultual act is very wide: it runs the whole gamut from simple and spontaneous utterances and sounds, tones, words, gestures, and movements to highly standardized practices such as liturgy, sacrifice, sacred dance, divination, procession, pilgrimage. However, in order to determine if an act is genuinely religious or not, we have to examine the *intention* with which it is performed. A bow many be a token of respect, a conventional way of saluting one's acquaintances, and yet it may be, if it is executed in the presence of the numen, an expression of religious awe. The kiss, another general sign, is a token of affection or just of greeting; yet it may become the shibboleth of a spiritual brotherhood and part of a ritual pattern. Prayer, on the other hand, is an exclusive act of recollection by which man establishes and cultivates his communion with the source of power. It is a universal form of worship, as the rich phenomenology of prayer which Heiler has presented convincingly demonstrates. The Australian and the Bantu Negro, the Plains Indian and the Ainu, the Chinese and the Hindu, the Jew and the Christian pray. Universal also are the various types of prayer: silent and

METHODOLOGICAL

vocal, private and collective, spontaneous and standardized.

Life in the universe, in the social unit and in the individual, cannot go on, so it is felt by the religious, if it is not nourished, encouraged, and stimulated by rites which keep it attuned to cosmic or divine powers. *Rites of Passage* (van Gennep) are practised universally. They consecrate the crises and marginal situations in individual and collective life. Prenatal preparations, ceremonies surrounding birth, name-giving, initiation at puberty, marriage, sickness, and burial rites are performed the world over to ward off the dangers lurking in the passage from one stage of life to another and to secure the indispensable contact with the divine source of life. 'Ceremonial life,' says R. R. Marett, 'is the outstanding feature of all primitive cultures' (40). It characterizes, with one great exception— namely, modern Western civilization—all cultures. Not only the extraordinary or crucial events in life but also the regular activities of work and play cannot and must not be carried on unless the accompanying rites render them adequate and effective (41). The making of tools, the building of houses, the construction of boats, the tilling of the soil, hunting and fishing, the making of war, in primitive and higher civilization call for incantation, divination, and dedication. Malinowski has discussed Melanesian garden-ceremonies, Herskovits Dahomean co-operative construction rites, Parsons described the agricultural ritual in the Pueblo settlements. Aztecs and Chinese, Greeks and Romans, Sumerians and Hindus observed the requirements of cosmic orientation in planning their settlements as carefully as the African Yoruba or the nomad North American Omaha. A devout Moslem will not start on any important or even trivial enterprise without placing it, through an '*inshallah*,' in a deeper context. It is the great vision of all *homines religiosi* everywhere that all life is the expression of worship, that every act and deed witnesses to the continuous communion of man with God. The prophets, saints and mystics of the highest religions join in this vision with the humble folks whom we honour with the name of 'Primitive' societies. Perhaps it would not be wrong to say that at no time and nowhere has this vision become actuality. Even if we do not quite agree with P. Radin, who suggests in his book on Primitive Religion (42) that the only men who really can be said to 'have religion' and to practise it have been what he calls the 'religious formulators,' yet we realize that the natural frailty of human nature—man's sinful nature as the Christian would say—prevents him as a rule from enjoying the realization of the Divine presence continually and from expressing it, as it were, uninterruptedly by his deeds and acts. Even in the lives of saints and prophets, their great efforts to sustain this highest level of man's calling have not always been successful. Sluggishness, dullness, disobedience, temptation always work together to cause man to lapse. As he emancipates himself from the power that sustains him, his activities become centrifugal; they become, as we call it, 'secularized.' Yes, the very acts which were designed to witness to the highest communion lose their meaning, become, if they are still performed, empty, fossilized. It is the function of the prophet to revitalize the old forms or to devise new ways by which man can express in acts and deeds his religious experience. Reformation is a universal phenomenon required by the dialectics of religious life (43).

The world over we find that in different religions certain acts are regarded and recommended as especially efficacious in establishing and strengthening the communion between man and the numen which is the goal of all worship. Such are acts of self-discipline or self-denial or the performance of special duties; acts of *devotion* and acts of *charity*. Some may be expected of everyone, and some be defined as *opera supererogationis*. I should be inclined to think that acts of devotion and service to one's fellow-men are universally valid practical expressions of religious experience. It is the exception rather than the rule that in our modern Western civilization worship of one's God and care for one's brother could become separated and one played against the other. If we can be proud at having left behind the cruder practices of an extreme asceticism, there is less reason for rejoicing that so many of us moderns have at the same time, because we see no motivation for it, abandoned all and every act of self-denial.

With the notion that in certain acts of devotion the religious life may culminate or appear epitomized, the concept of the *sacramental* act developed. This has its roots in primitive religion and has come to fruition in the Hellenistic mystery cults, in Zoroastrianism, in Hinduism and Mahāyāna Buddhism, in Gnosticism and Manichaeism, and above all in Christianity. Aptly has E. Underhill defined a sacrament as 'the use of visible things and deeds not merely to signify but to convey invisible realities' (44). Originally (45) the sacramental acts were only special instances of the wider notion (46) according to which the effective and transforming grace of the numinous presence flows into souls (47), especially prepared by acts of dedication; but in the history of our own religion these sacramental foci have become isolated (48) and cut out from the context of the life which they are meant to consecrate.

It behoves us finally to mention one more universal feature of the practical expression of religious experience. All human action will be *conditioned* by the physical *material* in which and with which alone it can work. The word needs no vehicle, the tone may be enforced by the use of instruments, the performance of service hallowed by wearing a special vestment. There are the simple and the complex instruments used for the purpose of creating a numinous atmosphere, the emblems and 'images' which stand for the presence of the unseen, be it the Pueblo feather-sticks, the Plains medicine bundle, the Japanese *shintai*, the Hindu *pratika*, the Hebrew ark, the Greek *agalma*, or the Orthodox ikon. Tone, word, colour, stone, wood and metal are universal media by means of which man has tried to give expression to the profoundest experience of which he is capable. He has become a *secondary creator*. The dangers which must accompany this development have given rise to protests of which the Hebrew prophets, the founder of Islam, and the Christian, Hindu and Buddhist reformers are impressive examples. Some of these protests are directed against the perfunctory or mechanical way in which such acts are all too often performed —cf. the Old Testament prophets and Jesus—others, of a more radical nature, reject all outward forms of expression, as do the spiritualists (49) and some, though not all, mystics. They feel that in spirit and in truth alone can true worship exist, whereas the motto of others is St. Augustine's 'Per visibilia ad invisibilia.' For both extremes—idolatry and evaporation of the *sensus numinis*—the history of religions affords many an example, but, as W. Temple has rightly said (50): 'The goal is to fuse action and worship into the continuous life of worshipful service; in the holy city which came down from God out of heaven the seer beheld no place of worship because the divine presence pervaded all his life (Rev. xxi, 22).'

There is finally, besides the intellectual and the practical, a *third* way in which religious experience expresses itself: the sociological. Here too we meet with a universal trait. We discussed previously the various motives which make for the expression of any kind of experience. True, there is in the confrontation of man with ultimate reality something solitary—the 'flight of the Alone to the Alone.' The solitary visionary is encountered at all stages of religious development from the lonely American Indian in quest of a Guardian Spirit to Søren Kierkegaard and William James (51), but the desire to communicate, to share, is a powerful motif in association and communication between men (52). Here the problem of communication of religious experience poses itself. We moderns are all too prone to look on it as a technical question to which improved techniques of manipulation will supply the answer (53). The history of religion teaches us otherwise. Wherever a true call is felt, a genuine religious experience is had, the means of communicating it miraculously seem to be at hand. Only in a secondary sense did the prophets and teachers feel that the establishment of contact and of fellowship was in their power. Where men were living in a communion with the great reality, they understood each other.

It would be rash to add religious fellowship to other existing forms of association without qualifications. A religious group is not another type of club. If in religious experience man confronts ultimate reality, it is towards this reality that all communion that is to be called religious must be oriented. 'No personal impression,' says R. Otto in his book, *The Kingdom of God and the Son of Man* (54), 'is as strong as the impression of the numinous or so well fitted to bind together a circle of those who receive the impression.' The *first* characteristic which distinguishes the cult-group from all other associations is that it is orientated primarily towards that reality which is apprehended in religious experience. *Secondarily*, it is constituted by the relations existing among its members. These two principles (55), which should guide the work of the sociologist of religion, denote two universal features characteristic of the sociological expression of religious experience. We can test their validity by examining any cult group in primitive, higher, or the highest civilization. What determines the attitude of the members of a secret or mystery society in Polynesia, Africa, or of American Indians but the awareness of power and power centres? What makes the fraternal spirit prevailing in mystery societies, of which we find so many examples in the history of ancient Greece, Rome, and the Near East? The numinous experience reflected in the concept of salvation and acted in the sacred drama! If the atmosphere of the Christian brotherhood is *agape*, can this attitude be meaningful unless it be buttressed by apprehension of the love of God as it is revealed in the life and death of Jesus Christ? All religious communities, furthermore, have specific *notae*, marks by which they desire to be identified (56) (certain visionary experiences, faith, beliefs, a certain esoteric knowledge, an attitude or behaviour).

Universally valid also are the *means* by which the religious community is integrated, namely, a common faith, a common cult, and a common order. Symbols, myths, doctrines, professions of faith, rites and practices, constitute and preserve the identity and integrity of the fellowship. Moreover, every cult-group possesses a structure. Though we find great variety with regard to the degree of differentiation, some differences according to the natural criteria of sex and age, of charismata and skills, knowledge, healing power, etc., make for a diversity of functions. Even in the most egalitarian group reverence is paid to age and experience, to the gift of prophecy or teaching.

We agree with W. Temple (57) that the apparent conflict between *experience* and *authority*, of which we hear so much from our contemporaries, is actually a tension of two indispensable, ubiquitous elements. For the *individual*, Temple says rightly, authority (be it in tribal custom or revelation), is first. He grows and develops within a world in which he finds tradition surrounding him on every side; in the *race*, experience is prior to authority, as can be easily proved. The structure of every religious group implies an *order*. Within this order there is room for freedom and spontaneity as well as for discipline. The history of religions is replete with examples of what happened to religious communities in which one of these two notions was sacrificed for the other.

Leadership is universal, though the sources of its authority and its functions are differently conceived in different cult-groups. Max Weber has convincingly shown that it may be exerted on personal or institutional authority (charisma) (58), the prophet and the priest illustrating these two types of religious leadership.

Here, then, are some universals in religion: man relating himself in the experience which we call religious to ultimate reality. This experience, which is had within the limitations of time and space, tends to be expressed theoretically, practically and sociologically. The forms of this expression, though conditioned by the environment within which it originated, show similarities in structure; there are universal themes in religious thought, the universal is always embedded in the particular. Though the differences and conflicts arise from particular loyalties, these cannot simply be left out (as the Enlightenment would have it). They are the arteries through which the life-blood of religious experience flows. But they have constantly to be checked and purified.

That the particular has not come into its own in this lecture is undeniable, but our topic for to-day was universals in religion. True, we have had to concentrate here on the formal elements which characterize religious experience and its articulation, but this might be also a way of contributing to the important problem of general and special revelation which is vividly discussed in contemporary theology (cf. the controversy between Barth and Brunner). Though we have not indicated here how we conceive of the *relation between* the universal and the particular way in which God has made himself known to man, we have, we feel, demonstrated that there is a ground upon which we can stand in believing that God has at no time and nowhere left himself without witness. We believe, with Temple, that 'natural religion ends in a hunger for what would transform it into something other than itself: a specific revelation' (59).

CHAPTER THREE

THE CONCEPT OF THE 'CLASSICAL'
IN THE STUDY OF RELIGIONS

THE wider the orbit of phenomena which is of interest to the historian of religions becomes, the more necessary it will be to find principles of order, articulation and appreciation which allow for an organization of the wellnigh infinite amount of material unearthed by comparative studies during the ninteenth and twentieth centuries. It goes without saying that there can be, for the scholar, nothing that is actually unworthy of investigation; hence the history of religions has to include in its range of interest and to investigate all that can be called religious. Neither antipathy to nor indifference towards individual expressions, or towards certain temporal or regional forms, should prevent the investigator from letting his sun shine on the just and the unjust. This condition is much more difficult to fufil to-day than it used to be in former times. Then the theologian, who had to see in his own religion the point of reference and the standard for his work, could be satisfied with adducing for purposes of comparison and elucidation the religions which were related in time and space to the world of the Old and the New Testaments. He could do so with a good conscience until, towards the close of the nineteenth and even more since the beginning of the twentieth century, the rapidly progressing studies of the civilizations of the so-called primitive, and of those of many remote middle and higher, peoples began to confront him with an impossible task. Some of the theologians of the *religionsgeschichtliche Schule* reacted to this situation by picking 'parallels' arbitrarily from all available primitive or higher cults, thus turning their commentaries on the books of the Old and New Testaments into something like counterparts of the well-stocked but not equally well-organized ethnological museums. The student of religions, however, who was not orientated by specifically theological concerns, could not but search for systematic principles which would permit him to bring some order into the wealth of new material. For a while the philosophical thought of classical German idealism (Schelling, Hegel) served the purpose. Schemes of development were constructed which followed this pattern, though eventually in a rather epigonal fashion. In accordance with these schemes a process of the gradual self-realization of the Universal Mind or of an even more perfect unfolding of Ethical Consciousness was envisaged, and therefore not infrequently the summit of their development was conceived of in terms of the period and region of which the investigation was a part. One of the last great efforts in this direction is represented by the 'Völkerpsychologie' of Wilhelm Wundt. But to-day we no longer believe in such one-track schemes of development, nor do we deem it possible to subsume the variety of religious expressions of all times under any one of them. It is significant that in the more recent systematic presentations, Rudolf Otto's *Idea of the Holy*, Gerardus van der Leeuw's *Religion in Essence and Manifestation*, and Mircea Eliade's *Traité de science des religions*, these schemes have been abandoned, and the material has been organized according to a structural order of the elements of historical religion. This indicates progress, though the last word on method and procedure in our field has not been said. In the study of religions we shall have to avoid both extremes, that of historicism and that of making a short cut by uncritically taking as absolute any particular theological or philosophical standpoint. Which then shall be the viewpoints guiding description, selection and presentation? We have said already that in research everything counts, however small the percentage of facts may be which would be of actual interest to the theologian or systematic thinker. Some apparently quite remote instance may prove important. So certain phenomena occurring in the context of a primitive religion geographically far removed from Asia might afford us a better insight into the nature of certain types of men of God in the Old Testament than others geographically more closely related. Neither the Old nor the New Testament scholar will ever be in a position to disregard the results of the labours of the *religionsgeschichtliche-Schule*.

Now even if it be true that everything which is expressive of religious experience is worth knowing and in some degree important, criteria are desirable for the selection of sources and their appraisal, and not only for the actual presentation of the results of the work of the interpreter. The quantitative principle is represented as a regulative norm; the so-called world-religions are more important than less widely spread cults simply because they command a larger number of followers. This fact may justify a more thorough preoccupation with their history and a more intensive investigation of their beliefs. The religions of nations which have played a larger role in the history of the world seem to deserve more careful study than those of less active peoples. But this criterion, which may suffice from a purely historical point of view, is unsatisfactory in other respects. For secular history Eduard Meyer, the great student of ancient civilizations, suggested the criterion of *efficacy* (*Wirkung*) as norm; but the historian of religions cannot assent to this viewpoint. For him a movement, an institution or a custom, a doctrine or a cult will not be important, nor even primary, because it was or is widespread, but because it represents a *specific*, a *characteristic* form of devotion (*Frömmigkeit*). Mohammed, Zoroaster, Mani, the Buddha, and the Jina, though all 'founders' of religions, are personalities very different in character and attitude. They stand each for a definite religious idea which, as it were, they embody. The historian of religions is concerned with the characteristic element in personal religion, in doctrine, worship and fellowship. But his desire is to do justice to the individual and historical as well as to the typical in such concepts as that of salvation, in such rites as that of sacrifice, in such institutions as that of the priesthood. Yet even the notion of the characteristic, much used and stressed by the German theologian Herder, one of the founders of the comparative study of religion, is not quite sufficient; it is too historically conditioned to serve as the principle of organization and articulation. Take the concept of *mana* which is characteristic of all American Indian religions, that of *orenda* which distinguishes the Iroquois, that of *wakanda* which is the Sioux version

THE CONCEPT OF THE 'CLASSICAL'

of this notion. It would be impossible—and unnecessary—to examine all the forms under which this concept can be found here or there (among Primitives generally, among American Indians, Africans, Australians, etc.). Or to chose another example: a characteristic feature of Mahāyāna Buddhism is the belief in Bodhisattvas. Their number is very great. Yet our knowledge of and insight into their nature does not necessarily grow proportionately as each new variant is added. There is always, to be sure, the chance that one of them may help us to perceive or identify some special feature heretofore not known or insufficiently appreciated, but this does not have to be an absolute novelty, however characteristic this feature might be of the individual figure. Chance ought not to determine which phenomena should be adduced to elucidate aspects of our own religion or to figure in a general phenomenology of religions as representative.

We believe that the notion of the *classical* can be helpful here. It may serve the historian of religions well if he will use it with discretion. In distinction from the concept of the characteristic, which is descriptive, the category of the classical is normative. Yet it is, if we may put it paradoxically, a *relative norm* which does not need to do violence to heterogeneous phenomena from a preconceived point of view. There are, to give examples, among the religious leaders of mankind certain figures who stand out as classical founders; of the deities of vegetation known to us from various regions of ancient Western Asia, we can single out some as 'classical' representatives; the seemingly infinite number of mystics of all times and places is reduced by choosing 'classical' figures. There are classical forms of the institution of priesthood and classical patterns of sacrifice and prayer.

What do we mean by 'classical' in all these cases? Negatively, we do not mean those out of a multitude of phenomena which merely happen to be familiar to us, those which show a close resemblance to familiar things, or those which attract our attention first. The phenomena which we designate as classical represent something typical; they convey with regard to religious life and experience more than would be conveyed by an individual instance. We may consider Meister Eckhart, Al Ghazzali, and Shankara as classical mystics because something

51

typically mystical is to be found in their devotion and teaching. However, the notion of the classical does not denote only the representative character which inheres in a phenomenon, but also implies a norm. Out of the multitude of historical personalities, movements and events, thoughts and deeds, some are chosen because we deem it possible to ascribe to them potentially an illuminating, edifying, paradigmatic effect by which they may influence our own religious life. This statement should be taken in a wide sense. It will be granted easily enough that the study of neighbouring fields, such as Gnosticism, Mystery religions, Rabbinic Judaism, or of some single feature of these cults, may yield a great deal of profit to the exegete of the New Testament. Thus a figure like Simon Magus, a rite such as baptism, or the preaching of Jesus with regard to the Sabbath regulations can be better understood in relation—even in contrast—to the aforementioned religious movements. It may seem at first glance that the expressions of Mohammedan, Persian, Hindu or Buddhist religiosity could not possibly offer much that would facilitate the work of Old and New Testament interpreters. Yet the potential significance of classical forms of alien religions quite generally speaking is very great, and it would be a grave error for the Christian theologian or philosopher or even the interested layman to neglect them. The layman has been singled out for mention in this connection with good reason, there being a notion abroad that the layman should be expected to be conversant with all foreign religions as with everything else that may be worth knowing. One of the most acute critics of the educational ideals of the nineteenth century, Nietzsche, attacked, in a rightly famous pamphlet on the advantages and disadvantages of historical knowledge for living, the indiscriminate amassing of information in service to a misconstrued ideal of education. The great danger of an *indiscriminate* appropriation of information regarding remote and exotic phenomena is its threat to our creative powers ('plastische Kraft'). In the realm of religion this power has been greatly endangered throughout modern times, but especially in the nineteenth and twentieth centuries. To deal with the history of religions has come to mean for many, and not without reason, a limitless and hence hopeless relativism or scepticism. This conviction seems to justify the position into which we see those withdraw who believe that it is possible to revert to conditions as they prevailed before the 'fall,' in other words to reject as superfluous and harmful all study of religions except that of one's own faith. Now the influence of which we spoke of foreign religions on our life, which has to be understood in a wide sense, has to be *filtered*. Not all and everything which we may come to know of facts, ideas, usages and institutions connected with alien faiths can or should be significant for and meaningful to us. We shall have in the study of religion, as in other disciplines, to stress the pedagogical viewpoint and to distinguish clearly between what may be *interesting* and what is *essential*. Every phenomenon is potentially interesting, and hence worthy of our attention, our study and our appreciation. Universality of comprehension will ever remain the ideal of this, as of all other scholarly disciplines. But the preservation and cultivation of the creative power, which is in danger of becoming paralysed as an effect of the increase in factual information which the historical age has brought, demands *concentration* upon the essential and the necessary.

We find ourselves to-day in the field of religious studies in a situation like that of the classical philologists who, under the impact of the immense widening of the horizon in the last century, at first ceased to regard as the *classical* the characteristically humanistic concept of the fifth century but are now reconsidering their position (cf. the *Lectures on the Problem of the Classical and Antiquity*, ed. W. Jaeger, 1931). We who have become acquainted with the manifold and variegated forms and figures of the non-Christian world have to develop a new feeling for the specific quality, the value and the significance of classical phenomena in the history of religions. The experience of satisfaction and elation at the successful inclusion of the figures of the world of the Old and New Testaments into the general history of religions, which in turn replaced the desire to defend their absolute value and uniqueness, is yielding to a new attitude in which acquaintance with the variety of historical expression of religious forms is blended with the desire to do justice to the classical among them.

For example: since thorough and painstaking investigations have elucidated their environment and acquainted us with parallels with which earlier generations of scholars could not have been familiar, the figures of the patriarchs and prophets of Israel apppear to-day in an unexpected new light, thus vindicating, as it were, their survival in our historical consciousness. Not merely because of the limitations of the horizon and the conservatism of all the preceding generations who admired and loved them have these well-known figures assumed the patina which for many of the moderns is nothing but dust. There are two things which contribute to cause them to appear as classical not only within the realm of Biblical religion but in that of the whole history of religions, namely, the depth and power of their religious experience and the form in which it is recorded. Abraham, Joseph, Moses, Amos, Isaiah, Job—these names indicate personalities who grow rather than diminish in stature from all that we can make out of the context in which we have to place their lives. They are classical figures. It is an important task of Old Testament exegesis and theology to present them as such. But not only persons, but also events and institutions of which the Old Testament reports possess this classical character. This does not mean that their value is always a positive one. It is well known how much they must appear to a transformed and advanced ethical consciousness as doubtful and objectionable, but the power and intensity of the experience of nearness to or alienation from God as we find it illustrated in these documents not only enlarges but deepens our own knowledge of God, the world and man.

What now of the *selection* of classical phenomena; how do we proceed to isolate out of the wealth of the historical material the light- and life-giving instances? This is not the place for an epistemological analysis of the whole problem of interpretation. It is sufficient to point out that it would not do to proceed by way of abstraction in attempting to isolate the essential by elimination and reduction from a maximum of empirical detail. The essential may well be grasped from a single instance (though, of course, not necessarily from *one* only) rather than induced from the examination of an unlimited number. Such a procedure does not exclude testing and correcting the immediate apprehension of the essential in one historical phenomenon by comparisons. Thus the understanding of the nature of discipleship which we gain from studying the rôle of John in the Fourth Gospel will be enriched and deepened by comparison with that of Ananda, the favourite disciple of the Buddha, as recorded in the ancient texts of the Tripitaka. There is actually, in accordance with the canons of the logic of interpretation, an interplay between the endeavour to illustrate one classical instance by contrast and the attempt to use it as normative in the process of understanding and evaluating the variety of related phenomena. A further question, which, however, cannot be answered fully in this context, is to what extent we can assume some 'foreknowledge' with regard to the nature of spiritual realities which would enable us to evaluate historical instances. Do we 'know' what angels are or what a sacrifice is before we meet in the history of religions with beliefs and rites which illustrate such notions ?

Be that as it may, certain phenomena with which we become acquainted in and through comparative studies impress us as having classical significance. Let us again refer to an example taken from the world of the New Testament: discipleship. The figures of the disciples of Jesus—Peter and John, Thomas and Judas—stand before us very vividly. Nobody can deny that they represent classical instances of highly individual attitudes. Some scholars have spoken of a Pauline and a Johannine version of Christianity, and have traced through its history representatives of both types of devotion: Augustine and Luther exemplifying the former, Fichte and Schleiermacher the latter. It is not feasible to review in the context of a life of Christ figures of all those who were in living contact with Jesus and whose images artists of many generations have brought to life as individuals and as types. Together they form, as it were, a cosmos of classical forms of human existence, positively and negatively determined by the central figure of the Saviour. However, we do not intend by any means to limit the notion of the classical to the world of the Bible, but to apply it in the study of all religions. The concept of taboo, e.g., is classically represented in the religions of Polynesia. After having studied the phenomenon in this region, our sensitivity is increased and our ideas are sharpened so as to detect more readily and understand more fully the various forms under which it appears and lives on even in the higher and the highest religions. Or we may think of the phenomenon known as Shamanism, which has recently attracted considerable attention among students of the history of religions, and which is classically represented in the religions of northeast Asia. Or of the practice of meditation, a discipline of great significance in certain conceptions of the culture of the interior life, of which we find classical examples in Buddhism and Taoism. Finally, of the doctrine of angels, classically represented in the Iranian religion. Quite frequently historians of religion have lately borrowed designations from the language of one area and elevated them to the dignity of a typological category: such terms as *mana, taboo, totem*. This, if done circumspectly, is a justified procedure which prepares us for the recognition and selection of classical phenomena. It is not without danger, however, if it is done with the intention of reducing a phenomenon to something of a lower order (so-and-so is 'merely' so-and-so; 'nothing but') or if it is done without regard to historical individuality. The author has called attention to this problem in his criticism of Max Weber's systematic treatment of the sociology of religion (*Einleitung in die Religionssoziologie* (1930), appendix). The notion of the classical has to be conceived elastically. It is not meant to establish a closed canon of forms, but rather to allow for a steady increase of our awareness of new historical phenomena and their systematic evaluation. In this way we can do justice to the before-mentioned rule of not including indiscriminately any new finding of anthropologists, philologists, or historians in the canon of relevant material without adopting a rigid and inflexible norm (e.g. the Biblical evidence), which prohibits *a priori* an appreciation and use of outside material for the investigation of the religious nature and life of man. This discussion, however, pertains to the methodology of a comparative study of religions; the theological problem of truth is beyond its scope. It is not within the competence of the historian of religions as such to answer the question what religious conviction I in faith should hold. Naturally the Christian theologian will be interested in other classical phenomena of the history of religions than will the Jewish or

Mohammedan theologian. The fact, however, that he sees in Jesus Christ something other and more than a classical figure in that history cannot prevent the student of another faith from viewing him as such (but as such at least).

This last consideration suggests the problem of the relative character of the notion of the classical. It is easy to realize that it is not independent of the subjectivity of the investigator to the same degree as is the recognition of a historical datum. It is a heuristic concept, open to revision and correction in time. But it is not an arbitrary, that is, a purely subjective concept. We can say with some assurance that a given phenomenon will be of classical significance for the student of religion irrespective of the period or community to which he belongs. Thus we see that certain personalities, events and institutions of foreign religions appeared not only as representative but as classical to the historians, geographers and travellers of antiquity or of the Middle Ages, in much the same way as they impress us to-day. The notion of the classical should convince the proponents of subjectivism that not all is 'flux,' but that a gratifying agreement in the judgments of different times and different nations has resulted and has created a tradition which does not lose its meaning even if some doubt its existence or its value. We need to remind ourselves in the field of the study of religion that we must hold on to the principle of relative objectivity, developed in the author's history of hermeneutics in the twentieth century, if we want to escape an anarchical subjectivism which would make all 'Wissenschaft' impossible. Signposts, accents, norms have to be made visible among the mass of 'material' in which the 'positivist' glories, because in this way only does knowledge acquire the value which makes it a part of genuine culture and gives it its truly educational significance.

[B]
HISTORY OF NON-CHRISTIAN RELIGIONS

CHAPTER FOUR

THE IDEA OF MAN IN THE
NEAR EASTERN RELIGIONS (1)

I

IT appears obvious to us that philosophy should begin with
a study of man—of his existence, his nature, his origin,
and his destiny. Especially we moderns, brought up in the
philosophical tradition of the West, as it has developed particularly since the Renaissance, can hardly envisage a more
natural subject for philosophical inquiry than 'What is man?'
Descartes' searching analysis of consciousness has its roots in
man's self-reliance as it began to be formulated with the beginning of modern times. Since Descartes we have become accustomed to base not only the certainty of our existence but also the
idea of God on the examination of our self-consciousness. The
idealistic philosophers of the nineteenth century have regarded
the world as a phenomenon of human consciousness, and the
successors of Schleiermacher and Feuerbach proceeded to
regard God as an illusion produced by it.

But we have to remind ourselves that this development of
Western thought is unique. It is recent too, as Dilthey especially
has shown in his studies *Zur Weltanschauung und Analyse des
Menschen im 16. und 17. Jahrhundert*, though the roots of the
modern concept of man go back to the ancient philosophers of
Greece. It is our contention that, compared to the anthropology
of the West, the Eastern idea of man is characterized by a feature
which in the West has increasingly faded, by the *cosmological
context*. In such a context the Near, Middle and Far Eastern
concept of man is found: the religious anthropology of the
ancient religions of Western Asia and of the founded religions
in this area (Zoroastrianism, Islam), of Brahmanism and of
Buddhism, and the view of man in the teaching of the sages of

China. We shall have to limit our discussion of the concept of the Nature of Man here to Greece and the Near East.

Kant has distinguished two branches of *anthropology*, a physiological and a pragmatic: the former studies man as a product of nature, the latter is concerned with his ideas about himself. It is with the second type of anthropology that we are here concerned.

Man, when he tries to understand and evaluate himself, is never just 'man'; he is the child of his time, the fifth or the fifteenth century, of his culture and his society; he is a member of an ethnic group or nation, a Greek or a Jew, a Mohammedan or a Hindu. Thus anyone who is interested in knowing what man has thought of himself at different times and is thinking of himself under different skies will not be able to abbreviate his studies by simply stating that man is such and such because that is the way I or we conceive of him. What is man? All of us, in saying 'I', seem to know. But what is this 'I'? Is it the physical man, his soul, his mind—or where do we find his true being?

It is one of the great rewards of a comparative study of cultures and their patterns of thought that we begin to realize that the great themes on which man's deepest reflection has concentrated are not unlimited in number and in kind, but actually recur in widely different cultural contexts. *Nature, time, love, death, man's true self* are such themes which naturally stimulate the θαυμάζειν which the Greek thinker declared to be the beginning of philosophy. W. Diltheyin one of his most profound studies, concerned with the nature and development of philosophical thought, has shown that the *homo religiosus*, the artist, the philosopher differ from the average man only in that they are concerned with capturing and rescuing fleeting experiences and impressions, as we all have them, in memory, lifting the meaning or essence of these impressions into consciousness, combining single experiences and observations into general reflections about life and existence, about God, the World and Man. Thus *they* are, though by no means the only, the best-qualified interpreters of man to himself.

We cannot undertake here to show how, where, and when, owing to especially favourable conditions, philosophical reflection became in different parts of the world, apparently independently, emancipated from its religious matrix; why this process got under way in Greece and in some of the cultures which were stimulated by the great religions of redemption, the Hebrew-Christian, Moslem, Hindu, and Buddhist, and finally in China. We also shall disregard here the expression in art of such reflection upon the great riddles of existence, especially in the various forms of literature, though the lyric, epic and tragic poets of the world have hardly a lesser right to be heard on the question of how man has thought about man than the lovers of wisdom, called philosophers. Finally, inasmuch as this lecture is addressed to students of Oriental history, language and culture, we shall forgo reference to the contemporary Western scene, tempting as it may be to allude to the renewed interest in theological and philosophical anthropology in our own midst, an interest which is broad enough to transcend the borderline of physiology, physical and cultural anthropology, sociology, psychology and psychopathology. It will suffice to quote the title of a widely read theological work containing the Gifford Lectures given by Reinhold Niebuhr on *The Nature and Destiny of Man*. This book gives a Christian interpretation. The historian of religions is naturally interested in comparisons. What of the other great faiths and their notion of man? A few years ago Paul Masson-Oursel published his *Philosophie comparée*, a very interesting attempt at a comparative study of epistemology, logic, and metaphysics in various cultures. He did not include in his comparison the doctrine of man. Neither has F. S. C. Northrop, who recently treated us to a comparative study of Western and Eastern thought (*The Meeting of East and West*), set out to tackle this problem, though he rightly stresses the necessity of analysing the basic philosophical and metaphysical attitudes underlying the different cultural expressions of Orient and Occident.

The intellectual expression of man's experience in preliterate and less advanced cultures is cast in terms of myth. Ernst Cassirer has brilliantly analysed the categories of the mythical consciousness, its peculiar notions of time, space, and causality. Different mythical versions of the same theme are not mutually exclusive at first, but in some cultures a tendency towards the systematization of the mythical tradition develops. The priestly centres of Polynesia, West Africa or the ancient Middle

American cultures illustrate this stage. Such systematizing of myths may, if sociological conditions favour it, develop into theological systems, as happened in Ancient Egypt, Babylonia, among the Hittites, in Phoenicia, Syria, Greece, Rome and elsewhere. All these systems of mythological and theological thought treat of the above-mentioned themes: God, the World and Man. The continuity of tradition which they each represent may be interrupted, however, by new and fresh insights, promulgated by prophets or seers or men of God. The founded religions, as distinct from those whose beginnings are lost in a dim past, trace their origin back to such creative religious experiences and impulses. The new religion starts from a specific experience— visions, as we know them from the life of Jesus, Mohammed, Zoroaster, the Buddha—an intuition or revelation which enfolds itself in the nuclear teachings of the founder. As these teachings are developed into a body of doctrines, the communion of the initial circle creates definite forms of worship and begins to organize itself according to a novel pattern. The first topic of the new doctrine is the nature of the Unconditioned, the Eternal, the Deity, its relation to the visible universe and to man (theology); the second is concerned with the universe, the origin and destiny of the world (cosmology); the third topic is the nature and destiny of man (anthropology). Soteriology and eschatology are usually developed from these three basic themes.

Though theoretical reflection is at first limited here to what actually pertains to salvation—even the most philosophical of the great world religions, Buddhism, appears at first restricted to purely soteriological knowledge—the necessity for apologetics and the logic of thought tend to turn theological into philosophical reflection. With cultural, intellectual and sociological conditions favourable, a philosophy of religion emerges, in which epistemological, metaphysical, psychological and ethical problems are discussed and a special technique and terminology created which may be in part original or in part borrowed: in Christian, Jewish and Moslem philosophy from Greek sources; as far as the Manichaean is concerned, from Greek, Christian and Oriental sources; in Buddhism, from Brahmanism.

Thus we find a *concept* of man in religions whose origins are lost in a dim past, like the Egyptian, the Greek, the Hebrew, the Ancient Persian and Indian religions, and a *doctrine* of man in religions of revelation like the Christian, Judaic, Mohammedan, Zoroastrian, Manichaean, Hindu and Buddhist. The theological and philosophical concepts in the religions of revelation are interpretative; they develop the theological, cosmological and anthropological implications of the founder's message by applying methods and categories evolved in earlier thought. Thus the Christian interpretation of human nature tries to outline Jesus' concept of man from the records of his attitude and teaching, by using the categories of Hebrew and Greek anthropology; and Mohammedan thinkers concentrate upon the exposition of the Koranic anthropology with the help of thought-forms developed by Greek, Jewish and Christian thinkers.

In the mythological stage thought is primarily directed to theology and cosmology, as in most preliterate cultures and in the ancient cultures of the East. A comprehensive world-view is centred in a concept of a *cosmic ·moral and ritual law*, on which the course of nature, of human life and society depend and towards which they are oriented. R. Callois has demonstrated this theme for the preliterate cultures, O. Franke and P. Granet for the Chinese, Jane Harrison for the Greek, William Robson in his book on *Civilization and the Growth of Law* for the West. The founded religions naturally bring a greater emphasis to the anthropological theme and, preoccupied as they are with the salvation of man, yet in practically all of them is safeguarded the cosmic aspect, according to which man is assigned his place in the chain or hierarchy of being. Anthropocentrism is practically unknown in the East. That is certainly true of the *Weltanschauung* manifest in the Near Eastern religions of revelation, but it is also true in India of Samkhya and even Yoga, and in Confucianism and Taoism. Greece seems to be the great exception. Let us, therefore, briefly glance first at the development of Greek anthropology.

II

In the Ionic philosophy of nature the cosmological interest still prevails, though the sayings of the sages betray their interest in moral and psychological problems. Heraclitus appears attracted to the study of man and of the Logos that made him think, and so does Pythagoras, who followed the soul through the cycle of existences, both within the framework of their metaphysical theories. Pythagoras' ascetic anthropology has all the characteristics of Oriental soteriology. With Empedocles' philosophical system, resting on his theory of basic elements and basic forms, a new impetus is given to the study of man: his bodily constitution, the elementary composition of his bones and flesh, the process of respiration, sensory perceptions and the acquisition of knowledge are carefully studied by the philosopher of Agrigentum. The naturalist school of Leucippus and Democritus, who were to become the ancestors of all later Western naturalism, in its theory of atoms combines metaphysical speculation with a naturalistic anthropology: here we have the first Western materialistic theory of the soul. It consists, according to Democritus, of round and smooth-faced atoms—that is ultimately of fire—distributed through the whole body. Yet we can see how closely cosmological and anthropological motives are still interwoven, in the contention that the air must contain much $νοῦς$ and $ψυχή$ since otherwise we humans could not receive it by our breathing. It is significant that our thinking is explained by Democritus as a subtle elementary change of the soul-elements. It is only logical for him to lean to a pessimistic view of man's capacity to know. His ethics, the first of its kind in the Western world, makes man's happiness dependent on the balance of his inner state ($μετριότης$ $τέρψιος$ $καὶ$ $βίου$ $συμμετρία$). We are well on the way in the direction of the anthropocentrism of later times.

In his anthropology, Anaxagoras, who attributes to the $νοῦς$ so important a rôle, agrees with Democritus: true knowledge is accessible to man only through his $νοῦς$. The cosmological background which is so characteristic of pre-sophistic Greek anthropology fades with the Sophist teachers of the fifth century: Anaxagoras and Empedocles had still been theologians, attributing to man a relative position in the hierarchy of the cosmos. πάντων χρημάτων μέτρον is, according to Protagoras, ἄνθρωπος. Protagoras drew these radical consequences from Heraclitus' metaphysical theories of change and of the coincidence of opposites, and from Leucippus' subjective theory of perception. Hippias and the younger Sophists applied the new anthropology to ethics, developing the idea of the contrast between νόμος and φύσις. In the name of the latter, φύσις, man was urged to fight the former. Man-made conventions, parading as custom, law or religion, were to be abolished by men. Force or power, as only man, or superior man, can wield it, secures to man his unchallenged position according to these new emancipated views.

We are accustomed to trace the ideology of the West to the metaphysical and anthropological foundations which Socrates, Plato and Aristotle laid. Yet the trend of pre-Socratic philosophy was to have a profound effect upon the intellectual orientation of the West. Plato and Aristotle were, in part, acceptable to the East. *Socrates*, who is tied to the Sophists by more than mere antagonism, was not. Plato and Aristotle could be claimed as saintly heathens ('maestri di color che sanno') by Christian, Jewish and Arab thinkers. Socrates remains ambiguous. It was his great pupil who laid the foundation for the theory of *paideia* in which recently W. Jaeger has found a leit-motiv for his history of Greek thought and culture. The free play of human reason in which we see Socrates engaged with his interrogators is not conceivable without the task of emancipation carried through by the Sophists; this play of the free spirit was to exercise considerable fascination on later ages in the West. The East has never openly welcomed it. There is nothing like it, except, superficially seen, in China, where, however, man could never be regarded as the centre of the universe. Man was not so regarded by Confucius and certainly not by Lao-tse.

The reason why Plato, Aristotle and even more their later interpreters became eminently acceptable to the philosophy of the great religions of revelation while other earlier and later thinkers won influence only in small groups (Atomists in Islam), is precisely because their anthropology appears reinterpreted in a cosmological and theological framework. There can be no doubt, in spite of contradictory statements, that *Plato* drew from Oriental sources, though it will be difficult to explain exactly where, when and what. But a sound instinct was guiding the earlier Christian, Jewish and Moslem theologians and philosophers when they tried to work out with the aid of Platonic (or Neoplatonic) and Aristotelian and Stoic categories their doctrine of man. Plato's interest in myths is not accidental. It is not a naïve conservatism which makes him use mythological language when he discusses the most crucial problems of cosmic and human existence; for, reinterpreting the traditional myths, Plato sketches a cosmological and theological background for his concept of the nature and destiny of man.

Plato was the first Occidental to develop a complete doctrine of the human soul. It was he, not Socrates, who became the founder of the typically Western doctrine of man. The basic dichotomy of body and soul is one of the Oriental elements in Plato's anthropology and one of the great motifs in his *receptio* by Christians, Jewish, and Moslem thinkers. This dichotomy is qualified by his concept of hierarchical powers in the soul ($\epsilon\pi\iota\theta\upsilon\mu\iota\sigma\tau\iota\kappa\acute{o}\nu$, $\theta\upsilon\mu\omicron\epsilon\iota\delta\acute{\epsilon}\varsigma$, $\lambda\omicron\gamma\iota\sigma\tau\iota\kappa\acute{o}\nu$). It is the role Plato attributed to the last-mentioned element ($\nu\omicron\hat{\upsilon}\varsigma$) which makes him the genuine successor of Heraclitus, Parmenides, Anaxagoras and Socrates. But he leaves his predecessors, except Anaxagoras, behind in his teachings on the *divine nature* of the $\nu\omicron\hat{\upsilon}\varsigma$ which, according to Plato, is united with the body only with its entrance (the myth of 'Phaedrus' alone envisages a pre-existent body) and by his theory of *eros* as the longing of the mortal for the eternal, of the phenomenal for the noumenal, of the individual for the contemplation of the ideal world. In assigning the highest place in his rich and typically Greek theory of *paideia*, which leads through character formation by music and athletics, by mathematics and philosophy, to dialectics and with it to the contemplation of the Good, Plato makes room for his highest vision : man through insight and virtue becomes $\theta\epsilon\omicron\epsilon\iota\delta\hat{\eta}\varsigma$. Thus his anthropology culminates in the soteriology which, especially in the interpretation of Neoplatonism, came to have so profound an appeal to the philosophy of Christianity, Judaism and Islam.

Greek philosophy and, with it, its concepts of the nature and the destiny of man originated, as we have seen, in the mythological stage. Under the influence of metaphysical and especially cosmological notions, it came to raise specific questions as to the physical, mental and spiritual contribution of man and to develop methods of thought in which the Greek attitude towards life could find its genuine and adequate expression. The soteriological ethics of Plato was his solution of the problem of the destiny of man. It was to be the closest approximation of Western to Eastern anthropology, if we leave aside the Neoplatonic anthropology, in which Oriental elements predominate.

Less speculatively inclined than Plato, *Aristotle*, the great systematizer, eliminates the mythical element from his model of the cosmos and of man: his metaphysics, also, is concerned with the ultimate, which, however, he envisages not as a ἔν παρὰ πολλῶν but as a ἔν κατὰ πολλῶν. Only to the extent to which the individual participates in movement and actuality, to the extent his νοῦς is actualized, does he approximate to the highest goal, because life can be defined as the capacity to move by itself. Only the νοῦς, according to Aristotle, which enters θύραζεν into the soul of man, enables him to realize his final destination. The ἐπιθυμία, originating in the lower soul, controlled by the νοῦς, becomes the will. The will of man is, according to Aristotle, free. It is in true wisdom, that is, in the preponderance of the theoretical over the practical, that Aristotle places the realization of the aim and goal of human life: εὐδαιμονία. The great systematic force, the empirical bent and the strong rational emphasis of the philosophy of Aristotle had a tremendous appeal for Greek, Christian, Jewish and Moslem thinkers alike. But, in being more rationalistic and anthropocentric than that of his teacher, the philosophy of the Stagirite was difficult to reconcile with the presuppositions of the religions of revelation. Not εὐδαιμονία but the salvation of man's soul is their goal. Hence only an intellectual élite, frequently bordering on heterodoxy, could identify itself with this teaching.

Human reason is exalted even higher in *Stoicism*. Zeno reverts to Heraclitus' monistic concept of the cosmos and of all-pervading cosmic law, finding its nature in a materially conceived pneuma. Reasonableness means pneumatic purity. All living beings are divided by the Stoics into four classes according to the amount of pneuma active in them. In man it becomes the rational soul, which is active from its centre, the human heart. In subduing the affections as νόσος ψυχῆς, the sage realizes the aim of ἀπάθεια. Happiness is moral and intellectual perfection. It was in the gnostic systems that this anthropology was re-absorbed by Oriental cosmological and soteriological mythology.

III

Nowhere in ancient Near Eastern thought do we find the emancipation of the *logos* from the *mythos* which characterizes the development in Greece. The systems of Egypt and Asia Minor, Babylonia, Phoenicia, Syria and Persia share a cosmocentric and hence a theocentric orientation. The origin of the world and its destiny, the nature and history of the gods, the creation of man, his true being and his destiny are here as everywhere the great topics of mythological lore. Within this framework, in proverbial wisdom, man is advised how to assess life and to guide his own, and how to regulate his relations to the higher powers as well as those to his fellow-men. Here he is told the sum of what he may expect of this life. He is reminded of its brevity and his own insignificance. In each of these cultures we find a growth of moral discernment and a growing realization that man becomes more pleasing to the deity and thus truer to his destiny the more he learns that ritual or ceremonial purity is less important than moral righteousness. None of these religions limits man's existence to this world: they all—perhaps with the exception of the Mesopotamian—hold out the distant goal of an after-life in which the believer will be with or become somewhat likened to the deity that made him. It is significant that the Egyptians, whose ethics exhibited so distinctly an immanent character, were very profoundly motivated by the thought of the hereafter. In Egypt we find differentiated concepts of the mental and spiritual equipment of man, concepts which are not startlingly different from those of other early cultures but which lend themselves to a more profound reinter-

THE IDEA OF MAN

pretation in Hellenistic times (Hermetic literature). H. R. Willoughby has studied the documents witnessing to the deeper experience of the rebirth of the soul in his *Pagan Regeneration*.

Even in Babylonia, where priestly wisdom constructed one of the most comprehensive and unified theories of the cosmos known to man, a theory according to which an exact correspondence between macrocosm and microcosm permitted man to orient himself (divination) and to propitiate the powers which hold him captive—even in Babylonia a soteriology developed with the moralization and spiritualization of the concept of human perfection which was to culminate in the idea of man's redemption. We have a parallel development in the religions of Syria. The ideas of the physical cycle of life, growth and decay in nature, and the concept of the celestial order to which man finds himself bound, as are the divine figures who symbolize this cycle, produced the intense longing for redemption and a redeemer which later on characterizes the devotees of the Syrian gods.

In none of these contexts do we find anything comparable to the anthropological theory of the Greeks which we have previously tried to outline. But we have, as yet, not mentioned the source upon which the anthropology of the great religions of revelation came to depend beside the Greek: and that is the *Hebrew*. Careful studies have been devoted to the doctrine of man in the Old Testament. It has been shown how much primitive Hebrew psychology has in common with the preliterate view of man: the quasi-physical concept of the soul-breath, the demonological notion of the influence of spirits and their entrance into the human body otherwise than through the senses, and, finally, the concept of corporate personality which Robertson Smith and H. Wheeler Robinson have so ably illustrated. All this explains the analogies which exist between the Hebrew's concept of his world and those of the peoples surrounding him. In both the life of man is precarious, endangered by influences for which his belief in a benevolent deity leaves ample room, influences which hinder him in the pursuit of the good life that is required of him by his creator, and in both he employs means to combat these influences (magic, divination). But there is also a difference:

Israel and Israel alone in the ancient world evolved a more and
more refined and spiritualized notion of the deity and its transcendence. The degree of intensity and intimacy which in Israel
characterizes the communion between God and man (notwithstanding his shortcomings) has no parallel. True, the ancient
Hebrew's notions of human physiology were deficient: the
brain, the lungs, the nerves were not known to him. With
other peoples he believed that the physical organism (or a
group of organs) draws its life-energies from the breath (which
may also be in or identical with the blood) and that the breath-
soul is actually the principle of life. The terms *neshamah*,
nephesh, *ruach* were used to connote this breath-soul. No sharp
division separates its expressions in *either* soul or body. But again
characteristic of ancient Hebrew anthropology is the close
relation of the spirit in man to the spirit of God. ('Thou shalt
love Yahweh, thy God, with all thy heart and with all thy
nephesh and with all thy might.') Especially could the *ruach* in
man be touched by and enter into association with the *ruach*
of God. It is well known how profoundly the Hebrew concept
of personality was deepened by the prophets; how especially
in the teachings of Jeremiah, Isaiah and Ezekiel the notion
of individual responsibility was developed in the ancient world.

While later on Israel wrestled valiantly with the concept
of retribution, the Hebrew did not develop a satisfactory
doctrine of a future life. Faith transcending death, the 'I
know that my redeemer liveth,' was, as we saw, by no
means an exclusively Hebrew notion; but the profundity with
which the Psalmist expresses his confidence bears witness to the
spiritual depths of the Hebrew view of the nature of man.
'Nevertheless I am continually with thee: thou hast holden me
by my right hand. Thou shalt guide me with thy counsel and
afterwards receive me to glory. Whom have I in heaven but
thee? and there is none upon earth whom I desire beside thee.'
Finally, it is the concept of sin which determines the Hebrew
view of man. Superficially seen, there seems to be again an
analogy to the development in other religions from ritual
uncleanness to a moral notion of what the deity asks of man, but
as Rudolf Otto has rightly shown, in his relation to the numinous
Lord of Israel, man comes to a fuller realization of his 'numi-

nosen Unwert.' 'Thou alone art holy.' The history of the growth
of this insight is illustrated by the development of the idea of
propitiation into that of redemption. Israel came only late to
distinguish between a deed sinful because of its effect and a
deed for which the doer was to feel responsible because of his
intention (objective liability and subjective guilt). It is illus-
trative of the realism of the Hebrew view of man that his sinning
is not regarded as accidental: 'Behold, in iniquity was I brought
forth and in sin my mother conceived me' (Ps. li, 5) or (Isa.
xlviii, 8) 'Rebellious from birth art thou called.' Yet Hebrew
anthropology is anchored in the conviction of the goodness of
man and his responsibility (Gen. iii). He is made in God's image
and knows himself to be in the guiding and controlling hands
of his Creator who upholds him with his spirit (*ruach*). Theology
and anthropology are closely intertwined: in the images of the
king and of the *father* the Hebrew idea of the relation of man to
his God finds its most adequate expression.

In the days of Alexander, East and West began to mingle as
they never had before. Syrian, Egyptian, and Anatolian
thinkers developed at the beginning of our era the soteriological
speculation which is known as *Gnosticism*. It is the answer to
the longing for redemption in the late Hellenistic and early
Christian age in East and West. In reinterpreting the theological
and cosmological myths of the traditional tribal religions of
Syria, Egypt, Asia Minor and Persia as well as Jewish and
Christian theology and Greek philosophical concepts, the
Gnostic teachers built up their elaborate soteriological systems,
treating of the history of the world, of mankind and of the
redeemer who repeats in his own development that of the world,
and of the single human being who suffers, dies, and rises again,
of world, mankind and the redeemer. According to this theory,
man, placed as a microcosm in the graded hierarchy of being,
is able by acquiring the saving knowledge ($\gamma\nu\hat{\omega}\sigma\iota\varsigma$) to liberate
himself or the divine particle in him for the benefit of the
redemption of the world. The well-known division of men
into hylic, psychic and pneumatic, reflecting the cosmological
and anthropological gradation of *nephesh*, soul and spirit, is
strictly predestinarian. The soul of the pneumatic alone may
enter, after trials, the pleroma ($\pi\lambda\acute{\eta}\rho\omega\mu\alpha$).

The Greco-Roman civilization came to its end, not without bequeathing its intellectual heritage to the emerging cultures which were to draw their inspiration from the three great monotheistic religions.

IV

Through the three religions of revelation, Christianity, Judaism and Islam, a philosophical renaissance occurred in the early Middle Ages in West and East, and, with it, a renewal of interest in the discussion of the doctrine of man. *Judaism* had, since the destruction of the Temple by Titus, concentrated upon the task of interpreting its holy heritage by means of the method of rabbinical exegesis. No philosophical problems had beset the teachers of the Halakha and Haggada. They did not engage much in apologetics between the second and the eighth centuries. The last teachers of wisdom had emigrated from Greece to seek new homes in Rome and Persia. Their wisdom was gathered to be transmitted in Latin in the West and in Syriac in Edessa and Nisibis, Harran and Gondeshapur, where from the fourth to the eighth century a chain of Syrian translations from the Greek was made. Neither the Romans nor the Syrians were great philosophers.

The first generations of *Christians* were concerned with safeguarding the integrity of the pure message of Jesus Christ. Following the example of their great missionary, Paul, they were anxious to win souls. While some were prone to emphasize the basic difference between the gospel to be received by faith and knowledge gained by human understanding and reasoning, others, among whom were those who had been brought up in the thought-world and with the learning of the classical civilization, attempted to effect a reconciliation either by applying merely traditional techniques or by an interpretation of the new basic experience in the light of ancient philosophumena. While the separation of Christianity from Judaism and Oriental gnosis had to be justified on theological grounds, that from antiquity had to be argued in both philosophical and theological terms. The first phase of the history of the Christian Church saw the elaboration of Christian doctrine; it continued through the first seven centuries. Only one really great Christian philosophical thinker of originality is to be found in this period: *St. Augustine.*

Whereas the main teachings of the Church concerning God and the Redeemer, his nature and work, were the result of the combined efforts of the fathers and of the councils, the Christian doctrine of Man, as the West has accepted it, is pre-eminently the work of this one man, St. Augustine. His teachings on the soul and on immortality, on sin and grace, on the communion of saints and the meaning of history defined for the early Christian Church the ever-recurring themes of a Christian anthropology. Attempts to safeguard the truly Augustinian understanding of the nature of sin and grace against all Pelagian or semi-Pelagian attenuations have been repeated throughout the history of Christian theology to this day. The soteriological limit to his speculative interest the great Church father has himself indicated: 'Deum et animam scire cupio. Nihilne plus? Nihilne minus.'

The centuries of profound unrest into which the Western world was to fall after the decline of the Roman Empire, and the beginnings of which the great Christian philosopher had himself witnessed, came to a close with the establishment of a central power in Europe in the eighth century. Meanwhile the new religion of revelation which originated in the Arabian peninsula in the seventh century had conquered the greater part of the Near East. The message of the *Arab* prophet was centred in a new vision of God, the maker and judge of man, whom he has created and ordained to his service. It was with the most intense devotion that the divine book containing this revelation was read and interpreted by the early generations of Mohammedan followers. With the contact established by the conquest of the culturally and religiously highly developed countries of the Near East, Syria, Mesopotamia, Egypt, Persia, and the rise in the intellectual and cultural level of the Arab States, a process which G. von Grünebaum has attractively described in his studies in *Medieval Islam*, the necessity for greater familiarity with the forms of thought and the teachings of other peoples made itself increasingly felt. Syrians were commissioned during the eighth to the tenth centuries to translate from the Greek into Arabic innumerable works of a scientific and philosophical nature. Although the Koran had not much to say on the nature of man, curiosity had to be satisfied, and it is characteristic that one of the few treatises of this period extant is a study of the difference between soul and spirit (by Qosta ibn Luqa). The spirit of man, according to him, is material, the soul immaterial, simple and imperishable. The role of the spirit is merely that of mediator between body and soul. This distinction did not find favour for long, because, with the increase of interest in the study of Aristotle, it was not upheld but replaced by that between soul and *nous*. The soul was held by these Moslem thinkers to be subject to the affections, the *nous* alone truly imperishable and sovereign. This is not the place for a review of the reception of Greek thought by the Moslem. We shall mention only the circles of the secret societies, such as the Carmatians and the *ichwan as-safa* of the tenth century. Neopythagorean and Neoplatonic teachings were popular. Their psychology is soteriological: the human soul is capable of transcending the limitations of sensual existence and of uniting with the Universal or World-Soul.

It should be emphasized that no mere chance or taste guided the Islamic thinkers in their preferences. If the prophet himself was credited with having uttered the well-known '$\gamma\nu\tilde{\omega}\theta\iota\ \sigma\epsilon\alpha\nu\tau\acute{o}\nu$,' this goes to show how much Mohammedan man was interested to know his true nature and how differently from the ancients he would interpret the Pythian-Socratic saying. The lack of precise knowledge of the author's identity in the case of many writings did much, of course, to confuse these pupils of the Greek. Needless to say that the 'Aristotle' of the earlier period was so enthusiastically received and absorbed only because of the Neoplatonic substance of the writings current under his name.

No *Jewish* philosophy existed before the tenth century, except for the syncretist-eclectic speculative system of *Philo*, who in his anthropology combined Platonic-Stoic with Hebrew notions (man consists of the earthly body and the ethereal soul whose highest function is reason, by means of which man can in ecstasy contemplate the divine). Around the tenth century two different philosophical schools emerged: the mystical Kabbala, and the non-mystical philosophy which began in the Gnostic circles. In both, one of the basic problems is the question: what is man? On the pretext of a mystical interpretation of the account in Genesis (*maaseh berešith*), the Kabbalist masters, drawing on Neoplatonic and Gnostic ideas, speculate on the reflection of the macrocosm in the human microcosm, the transmigration of souls, and dream of perfecting human knowledge to make it God-like. Jewish scholars like Isaac Israeli (845–940) had translated and collected the writings of Greek physicians, but it was the example of Christian and Moslem theology which started the second school of Jewish philosophy. John of Damascus (eighth century), the greatest theologian of the Christian Church of the East, had, in his Πηγή γνώσεως, provided a comprehensive system of Christian doctrine. Its significance has been greater than is generally realized. John justifies his use of philosophy—the introduction gives a sketch of Aristotelian and Porphyrian logic and ontology—by the remark that the profane studies are subservient to theology. Anthropologically interesting is his theory of the πάθη (passions) and the freedom of the will. The Mohammedan scholars, as C. H. Becker especially has shown, learned from the Damascene as they did from other Christian predecessors. They learned two things: one, an acquaintance with some of the basic problems which have to be discussed on the basis of revealed truth (including the doctrine of man, his nature, sin, freedom and destiny), and, second, the method of systematic exposition. The *mutakallimun* were the counterpart of the Christian dogmatists. An anthropological topic, the question of the freedom of the will, which had so much occupied the mind of the protagonists in the Christological controversies, came to be the first major issue between the conservatives on one side and the Qadarites and Mutazilites on the other. Al-Allaf, an-Nazzam, Jahiz and Muammar agree in attributing to man freedom and responsibility. The great and unorthodox confidence in human reason which characterized the *Mutazilites* brought them into conflict with strictly scriptural theology. Because this was not Attica in the fourth but Baghdad in the tenth century, it was the mediating doctrine of al-Ashari which carried the day. According to him, man can actually appro-

77

priate—this is his freedom—the acts which God creates. Man knows God with his reason but only through God's revelation, the unique source of such knowledge. Meanwhile, a Jewish thinker, Saadya Gaon (892–942), influenced by the Kalam, had taken up the same problems and answered them roughly along Mutazilite lines.

We cannot here trace in detail the discussions which, under the impact of growing and deepening acquaihtance with Greek philosophical and scientific writings, developed in the following centuries among Christian, Jewish and Arab thinkers concerning the nature of man. Plotinus and Porphyry, Proclus, Plato and Aristotle, Hippocrates and Galen in the East, Boethius in the West, were widely influential. While the doctrine of the three religions of revelation, with its insistence upon the creatureliness of man and his dependence upon God, his sinful nature and his responsibility, provided the framework for the anthropological quest of the thinkers, certain main trends became visible in their argument. One school—and each has its representatives in each of the three faiths—tended to yield to the double suggestion of the Greek method of rational analysis and concentration upon certain cardinal issues (relation of higher and lower powers in man, eternity of the world, unity of the intellect) in philosophical thought. Another is concerned with safeguarding the specific insights of the prophetic revelation against the inroads of rational doubt. A third school includes those who, of themselves or influenced by others, endeavour to deepen traditional religion and philosophy along mystical lines. The implications for the doctrine of man are obvious. In the first case, they may consist in the filling out of the traditional, that is, the scriptural framework, or in bending it so as to accommodate the picture of man which the Greek physicians and naturalists or which Neoplatonist, Aristotelian or Stoic thinkers had constructed. While in the former case the main interest appears focused upon the physiological constitution, in the latter it is concentrated on the mental and more especially the rational capacities of man. Examples of the first (naturalism) are the physician Isaac Israeli, or the author of *Microcosm*, Joseph ibn Zaddik (1149), in Judaism; ar-Razi and at-Tusi or Ibn al-Haitham in Islam; of the second (intellec-

THE IDEA OF MAN

tualism), Saadya and Abraham ibn Daud, Maimonides and
Gersonides (1344) in Judaism; al-Kindi and al-Farabi, Ibn
Sina and Ibn Rushd, Ibn Miskavaih, Ibn Badja (1138), Ibn
Tufail (1185) in Islam; Berengar and Anselm, Albertus and
Thomas, Scotus and Occam among the Christians. The second
school, representative of fideism with its stress upon the nature
and growth of faith within man, would include the Jewish
philosophers Bahya ibn Pakudah (1106–43) and Jehuda ha-
Levi (1080); the Moslems al-Ashari (935) and al-Maturidi
(944); and the Christians Petrus Damianus, Otloh, and Mane-
gold. The third, a mystical group, comprises Bernard and the
Victorines, Bonaventura and Meister Eckhart among Christian
theologians; al-Muhasibi and al-Junaid, al-Ghazzali and
Ibn ul-Arabi among Moslems; Ibn Gabirol and Isaac Lurya
among the Jewish thinkers.

Time does not permit of a detailed comparison of the picture
of man in Christian, Jewish and Moslem naturalism, rationalism,
fideism and mysticism. It was the one-sided emphasis on his
physical nature which again and again called for a stress upon
his rational capacities, and it was to defend the mystical spark
in man against fideism and intellectualism that the former
doctrines were approved.

West and East still face the task of working out a doctrine of
the nature of man which rightly balances body and mind, soul
and spirit, revealing, to quote a modern theologian (Brunner),
'a true knowledge of his responsible existence.'

CHAPTER FIVE

SPIRITUAL TEACHINGS IN ISLAM WITH SPECIAL REFERENCE TO AL-HUJWIRI

I

CHRISTIAN theologians and Christian laymen are still little acquainted with the non-Christian religions at their best, although Orientalists have put at their disposal a wealth of material, including numerous translations of important documents of the various Eastern faiths. The question is where to begin and how to make use of this material in an intelligent way. Some are weary, and rightly so, of the attempts of certain Western writers to pick and choose isolated 'nuggets' out of the context of a religious text in which they belong. There is a difference between selecting passages one happens to like for one's personal scrapbook and promulgating a *philosophia perennis* arrived at by a more or less arbitrary fiat. For the study of non-Christian religions, some reach for the nearest manual or compendium which enumerates the basic tenets and lists the basic practices of the major world faiths. There is usually a choice between a presentation which concentrates more or less exclusively on beginnings and one which stresses contemporary aspects. This rather unsatisfactory state of affairs is reflected in the one-sided picture of some of the major religions in the minds of a large number of people, theologians and laymen alike. Islam, for example, means to many the personal teachings and practices of Mohammed, or a somewhat austere, other-worldly, fanatical faith accompanied by rigid sanctions. Buddhism is understood either as a lofty, highly rational ethical ideal supposed to have been taught by a twin brother of Socrates, or as the thinly veiled polytheism of the masses of the North and East Asiatic peoples. Hinduism, for which it seems so difficult to find any constitutive features, appears as an enormous mass of heterogeneous concepts and idolatrous practices, though some may feel inclined to identify it altogether with either an ancient or a modern version of the monistic metaphysics of the Vedanta school. Confucianism, seen most frequently as the application of a faithfully kept body of the sayings of the great sage, is conceived as a replica of modern Western 'humanism,' purged of all that smacks of 'metaphysics' and 'superstition.' Granted that this characterization of widespread notions of non-Christian religions is something of a caricature, who can deny that it possesses some validity? In another paper (above, Chap. I), it was argued that neither the theologian nor the layman can afford nowadays not to inform himself concerning the non-Christian religions. Even if political, economic, and technological considerations did not urge this understanding upon anyone seriously concerned with orienting himself in the world in which he lives, some of the recently published best-sellers presuppose on the part of the reader a not inconsiderable knowledge of religions other than our own. Toynbee's *A Study of History* and Northrop's *The Meeting of East and West* are instances (1).

The historian of religions will have to rise to this challenge. He will have to supply the educated layman, the philosopher, and the theologian with well-chosen, representative material that will be of use and significance for any attempt to formulate new answers to the age-old quest for truth. He will have to be on guard not to thrust random florilegia upon the unprepared Western reader nor to attempt to proselytize on behalf of a genuine Eastern cult, a hybrid substitute, or a hastily fabricated 'world faith.'

II

Islam (2), like other religions, has developed a body of doctrine, forms of worship, and principles of organization (3). It is with the first, with Mohammedan teachings and their application, that we are here concerned. Among those who have contributed to the formulation of such principles we can distinguish (*a*) theologians proper, (*b*) canonists, (*c*) philosophers, and (*d*) mystical and spiritual leaders. To the extent that they were true Moslems, they have all recognized as binding the revelation afforded to Mohammed and laid down in the Koran, and some form of tradition, variously as its nature and meaning may have been interpreted (4). All these interpretations have been affected to a larger or smaller degree, directly or indirectly, consciously or unconsciously, by outside (Greek, Jewish, Christian, Persian, Hindu) notions. There has also been an appreciable amount of mutual influence between the 'schools,' though we find in each group more or less typical and individual systems of thought which show a minimum of such cross-fertilization. To regard any group as exclusively representative of the whole of the Mohammedan community would be a mistake. Actually each has yielded its characteristic contributions and helped to make Islam what it is.

We propose in the following pages to concentrate upon the fourth group of Moslem thinkers, the mystical and spiritual. Of all the four 'schools,' this one has affected more broadly and probably also more profoundly than any other the lives of the members of the Moslem body (5). Impressive and influential as the figures of some of the great theologians, canonists, and philosophers have been in shaping the minds of the more highly educated throughout the history of Islam, the real saints of the faith have not been these men. Our concern is with the practical implications of the Moslem faith as articulated and lived by those seekers after God whose wellnigh uninterrupted line of succession reaches back into the first century of the history of Islam. Though we might be accused of partiality, owing to the relative closeness of this type of Moslem piety to our own Christian type, we feel justified in stressing this contribution, because to examine it will help to correct the one-sided picture of Islam as a legalistic religion to which we referred above. We need to learn about Moslem saints whom we can compare with St. Augustine, St. Bernard, St. Francis, St. Bonaventure, Tauler, St. John of the Cross, so that we can do justice to the spiritual riches to be found in a non-Christian tradition, rejoice in the nearness of its spirit to that of our own faith, and, by comparison, learn to know better and love more deeply the treasures hidden in the teaching of the great Christian counterparts of the Moslem seekers (6). However, it is important to remember that the teachings of these Moslem leaders cannot be isolated from the *tradition* in which they developed and which gives them their character. This tradition is not only the 'golden chain' of its own masters but the development of the religion as a whole all the way from the initial experience of its founder. Sufism arose, according to R. A. Nicholson, during the second and third centuries after the Prophet's death out of what was originally an ascetic revolt against legalism, scepticism, and worldliness in high places (7), and spread rapidly through Syria, Egypt, Mesopotamia, and Persia (8). Only if we could give a full account of the history of Sufism (9) here would it be possible to convey to the reader a notion of the variety as well as the unity of this vital branch of Moslem devotional thought and practice (10). That, however, is not possible within the limits of this paper. We shall present, therefore, the content of one of the representative texts on Sufi theory and practice, one which is easily accessible in a readable translation. Since this book includes the words and acts of a great many of the earlier and later 'masters,' it will prove useful to any reader who, not satisfied with a single author's presentation, would like to gain a wider knowledge of Sufi teachers and teachings.

III

There have been greater Sufis than al-Hujwiri, whose book, *The Unveiling of the Veiled*, we propose to discuss here (11). There is the martyr-saint al-Hallaj (d. 922), whom the eminent Louis Massignon has chosen as the subject of his two-volume biography (12); there is al-Muhasibi (d. 857), whose theology has been studied by Margaret Smith; there is al-Junaid (d. 911), the teacher of many spiritual leaders in Islam (the 'Peacock of the Divines' (pp. 188–9)) (13); there is Ibn ul-'Arabi (d. 1249) (14), whose importance has become known to us through Asin y Palacios, Nicholson, Nyberg, Schaeder, and Affifi; and there is the most influential and best known of all, the 'church father' al-Ghazzali (d. 1111) (15). Yet we have chosen the treatise of al-

Hujwiri (16) because (a) it is available in the translation of R. A. Nicholson, one of the greatest European students of Sufism; (b) it is both a historical and a systematic work; and (c) it comprises both the theory (philosophy and theology) and the practice of Sufism (17).

The work consists of twenty-five chapters, of which Nos. vii to xiv treat of the lives and teachings of earlier and con-temporary masters (18), while those that follow deal topically with central tenets and practices of Sufism. All through the book opinions and *apophthegmata* ('sayings') of authorities are cited, and anecdotes are narrated to illustrate the theories of al-Hujwiri himself or those of older Sufis (19). Such fundamental notions as those of knowledge, of poverty, and of 'blame' in Sufism are taken up first (chaps. i–vi), while the main body of the theoretical section is arranged in chapters dealing with the successive 'uncovering of veils,' of which there are eleven (xv–xxv) (20).

The author says that he has composed his book for 'polishers of hearts' who 'are infected by the veil of cloud-ing' (while the veil of 'clouding' can be quickly removed, that of 'covering' can 'never be removed'), in whom, however, 'the substance of the light of truth exists, so that they may find their way to spiritual reality.' This way, al-Hujwiri states, is difficult to travel except 'for those who were created for that purpose' (p. 4). Because all human action and inaction is the act and creation of *God*, it is necessary to invoke his help (p. 6). We are reminded that Sufism has already a *history* of several centuries behind it, though the times seem unfavourable for accepting its teachings. 'Nowadays true spirituality is as rare as the philosophers' stone' (p. 7). 'Everyone makes pretensions, none attains to reality.' An older authority (al-Sayrafi (d. 961)) is quoted by al-Hujwiri: 'The depravity of men's hearts is in proportion to the depravity of the age' (p. 16). Men are deeply 'veiled' by their gross views; 'substances, accidents, elements, bodies, forms, and properties,' the favourite terms of the philo-sophers, are but 'veils.' Therefore the author sets himself the task of explaining the 'veils,' the stages and the 'stations' by which the spirit is freed and the way to God is opened (Introduction).

Like those of the other religious communities mentioned, the

Moslem contemplatives have differed in their estimation of the nature and value of *knowledge* (21). Al-Hujwiri, conscious of the fact that knowledge is 'immense and life is short,' is of the opinion that it is obligatory only in so far as it is requisite for acting rightly (p. 11). He refers to the Scripture (Koran, ii, 96): 'God condemns those who learn useless knowledge.' Knowledge and action cannot and should not be separated. The Prophet's saying is quoted: 'The devotee without divinity is like a donkey turning a mill,' and reference is made to the ignoramuses among the Sufis who 'graze in the fields of heedlessness and imagine that it is the field of sainthood' (p. 148). We are reminded that for knowledge without action there will be no heavenly reward (p. 12). According to an older master, whom our author quotes, those who are satisfied with disputation about knowledge and do not practise discipline become heretics; and those who are satisfied with the study of canon law and do not practise abstinence become wicked (p. 17; cf. also pp. 95–6 and 132). Al-Hujwiri distinguishes divine and human knowledge, of which the former is infinitely superior. An earlier Sufi is quoted who said that he had chosen four things to know, discarding all other knowledge: first, that his daily bread was apportioned to him, and, since it would neither increase nor diminish, he would cease seeking to augment it; second, that he owed to God a debt nobody else would pay for him and which he therefore was occupied with paying; third, that he was pursued by One (death) whom he could not escape, hence he had prepared to meet him; fourth, that God was observing him, wherefore he was ashamed to do what he ought not (p. 130).

Any Moslem, like any Christian or Jewish theologian, would agree with al-Hujwiri's definition of the object of human knowledge: to know God and his commandments. Al-Hujwiri recalls a typical Sufi doctrine when he stresses the necessity of the knowledge of 'time' (*waqt*), that is, of the actual spiritual state of a person. Man is determined and can be judged, says our author, according to his 'achievements,' which are, first, external profession of faith and internal attainment of true knowledge, and second, external practice of devotion and internal seriousness of intention. The external and internal aspects are declared to be inseparable, an indication that al-Hujwiri steers a middle course between the formalism of the *opus operatum* and the antinomianism characteristic of the extreme spiritualists. Knowledge of the law (*shari'at*) is as indispensable as knowledge of the truth (*haqiqat*) (on the identity of the two see pp. 139–40). Both are tripartite, the former including knowledge of the Koran, *Sunna* ('tradition'), and *ijma'* ('consensus'); the latter, knowledge of the essence and unity, of the attributes, and of the actions and the wisdom of God (p. 14). The views of the 'sophists' who negate knowledge are expressly refuted by al-Hujwiri. He agrees, however, with one of his most famous predecessors among the Sufi teachers, al-Bistami (d. 875), whom he quotes as saying: 'I strove in the spiritual combat for thirty years, and I found nothing harder to me than knowledge and its pursuit' (pp. 17–8) (22). In the chapters devoted to the 'uncovering' of the first three 'veils,' al-Hujwiri expounds his doctrine of God under the headings of 'Knowledge of God,' 'Unification,' and 'Faith.' He refers to a saying of Mohammed: 'If ye knew God as he ought to be known, ye would walk on the seas, and mountains would move at your call' (p. 267). Theologians, canonists, and others regard right cognition of God (*'ilm*) as the true knowledge; the Sufi masters, according to al-Hujwiri, call right 'feeling' (*hal*) by this name (p. 267). Our author distinguishes between the cause and the means of true knowledge; soundness of reason and regard for evidence are *means*, whereas God alone, as man's 'only guide and enlightener,' is its *cause* (p. 268). It is a mistake to assume that any created being is capable of leading anyone to God by demonstration. Even Mohammed or Jesus could not do this (p. 273), as al-Hujwiri makes plain. He expressly rejects two other theories of how true knowledge is brought about: that of inspiration, which he illustrates by the teaching of the Brahmins, and that of intuition (cf. the definitions of older masters on true knowledge on pp. 274 ff.). With regard to 'Unification' (*tawhid*), a notion of central importance in the teachings of all Sufis (the various Sufi groups which are surveyed in chapter xiv are said to differ from one another in devotional practices and ascetic disciplines but to agree in the fundamentals and derivatives of religious law and of unification (p. 176)), al-Hujwiri holds that it implies two things: assertion of the unity of a thing and perfect knowledge of it (p. 278). In the case of God's unity these are: first, God's own knowledge of his unity; second, the creation of the notion of unification in the human heart; and, finally, men's actual knowledge of the unity in God. A realization of God's unity enables the true knower (*muwahhidun*) definitely to predicate certain attributes of the Divine and their eternity. Any form of separation or dualism is thus excluded. The views of the 'Magians,' of the philosophers of nature, of the astronomers, and of the rationalists (*Mu'tazilites*) are repudiated, since they affirm (several) 'creators' and 'artificers.' As to the nature of faith (*iman*), al-Hujwiri reminds us, different opinions have been set forth by Moslem theologians: the Mu'tazilites (rationalists) include practical devotion under this term; some consider it to be simply a verbal profession; for some it is only knowledge of God; and for others mere verification. Even Sufi masters are divided on the question whether, in addition to verbal profession and verification, it is also practice (p. 286). However, al-Hujwiri sees theologians and Sufis agreeing in the assumption that faith has a principle ('verification in the heart') and a derivative ('observance of the divine command'). The first without the second 'does not involve security' (p. 287). The longing of the heart for God is a manifestation of love; faith and true knowledge are signs of love, as is obedience. Al-Hujwiri repudiates all antinomianism: 'I reply that when you know him, the heart is filled with longing and his command is held in greater veneration than before' (p. 288). It is not correct to say either that faith is man's work or that it is exclusively God's work; 'the doctrine of unification is less than compulsion (by God) and more than free will (on the side of man)' (p. 288). Rather is it held that inclination to believe is the guidance of God, while belief is the act of man (cf. pp. 36–7).

IV

With the theologians and canonists, al-Hujwiri believes in God's *predestination*. Of a human being two things are expected; one is theoretical, the other practical. The first is to understand that all good and evil is preordained; the other is to obey

God's commands. 'Predestination can never become an argument for neglecting these' (p. 104). Predestination, in other words, does not preclude the exercise of man's will. In order to understand al-Hujwiri's position on this question which has been so heatedly discussed in Moslem theology, we have to consider his theory of 'states' (23). Blending notions developed by his predecessors and anxious to avoid certain extreme consequences which some of them had drawn, owing to an over-emphasis upon one of these notions, al-Hujwiri distinguishes between 'Time' (*waqt*), 'Station' (*maqam*), and 'Favour' (*hal*) (pp. 367 ff., 180 ff.). The first, which we might paraphrase by the Greek term *kairos*, denotes a fleeting realization of the 'unity' wrought by thought and 'made possible by God's grace.' When a man's power of volition is cut off from him, whatever he does or experiences is the result of time (*waqt*) (p. 368). It is therefore called a 'sword' because it cuts the roots of the future and the past. Now Time needs Favour to stabilize it, 'for when someone has *waqt* without *hal* he may lose it, but with *hal* all his states become *waqt*, and that cannot be lost' (p. 369). Jacob was a possessor of *waqt*, 'now blinded by separation, now restored to sight by union.' Abraham possessed *hal*: 'The sun and moon and stars contributed to his *hal*, but he, while he gazed, was independent of them: whatever he looked on, he saw God only, and he said: "I love not them that set"' (Koran, iv, 76) (p. 370). Station (*maqam*) (24) is 'a stage on the way to unification reached by fulfilment of one's obligations with strenuous exertion and pure intention.' The examples of *maqamat* which al-Hujwiri gives are: repentance like Adam's, resignation like Abraham's, sorrow like David's, hope like Jesus', praise (*dhikr*) like Mohammed's. The clearest definition of the difference between *hal* and *maqam* is suggested by al-Hujwiri in connection with his discussion of al-Muhasibi's views: 'The term *station* (*maqam*) denotes the way of the seeker and his progress in the field of exertion and his rank before God in relation to his merit; the term favour (*hal*) denotes the favour and grace which God bestows . . . without any mortification on the seeker's part' (p. 181).

The 'formalists,' on the one hand, are satisfied with the distinction between the knowledge that this world is perishable (relative concept of annihilation) and the notion that the next is everlasting (concept of subsistence) (p. 242). Certain radical Sufis, on the other hand, contend for total annihilation. Our author holds that the terms 'substance' (*baqa*) and 'annihilation' (*fana*) (25) do not refer to knowledge or state, but rather to the degree of purification of holy men who have overcome these and have 'purposely' become 'annihilated in the object of desire and in the very essence of desire have lost all desire of their own' (perfect subsistence) (p. 242). 'In annihilation there is no love or hate, and in subsistence there is no consciousness of union or separation.' In this connection al-Hujwiri directs his polemic against the Syrian Christians, who believe, according to him, that Mary by self-mortification annihilated all attributes of humanity and that the divine substance became attached to her and through her was transmitted to Jesus, whose subsistence is supposed to be produced by the realization of the subsistence of God (p. 244). Man's will is phenomenal; it is an attribute by which he is veiled from God. God's will is eternal. When it becomes subsistent with regard to man, man's will is annihilated (pp. 171, 245). Then 'he is made divine (*rabbani*) in the disappearance of humanity,' and 'gold and earth are the same for him.' Al-Hujwiri adds a quite characteristic observation: 'The ordinances which others find hard to keep become easy for him' (p. 33).

The theory of annihilation is, of course, most intimately connected with the concept of the aim and goal of the religious life. Again al-Hujwiri steers a middle course between the definition of the 'formalists' and the claims of the radical Sufis. The two terms which he sets out to clarify here are 'union' (*jam'*) and 'separation' (*tafriqa*) (26). According to him, the real mystery of union is 'the knowledge of the will of God,' while separation is 'the manifestation of that which he commands and forbids.' 'Union is that which he unites with his attributes, and separation is that which he separates by his acts' (p. 33). Again the criterion is introduced by which our author distinguishes between station and favour, between God's grace and man's striving: 'Whatever is gained by mortification is "separation," and whatever is solely the result of divine favour and guidance is "union"' (p. 254). When he says that 'it may happen that God's love holds absolute sway over the hearts of his servants' and that his servants' reason and natural faculties are too weak to sustain its rapture and intensity and man loses all control over his power to act (p. 254), he seems to make concessions to an extreme definition of 'union.' Yet the author of the *Kashf al-Mahjub* is at pains to repudiate the ideas of those who defend a *unio substantialis* as it is implied in the terms 'mingling' of substances (*imtizaj*) or identification (*ittihad*)—with his creation—or incarnation (*hall*) (p. 254; cf. also pp. 260 ff.). God is exalted far above that and 'far above what the heretics ascribe to him' (p. 254). In a very significant phrase al-Hujwiri states that 'we live through his creation, not through his essence and attributes' (p. 268). To say that the saints of God are 'united' by their inward feelings and 'separated' by their outward behaviour means that 'the internal union strengthens their love of God and the external separation assures the right fulfilment of their duties towards him as his servants' (p. 255; cf. p. 131). It is only logical, therefore, that al-Hujwiri takes sides in this controversy with those who prefer to characterize the rapture of love for God by 'sobriety' (al-Junaid) and against those who favour 'intoxication' (al-Bistami and al-Hallaj) (pp. 184 ff.). Intoxication, al-Hujwiri says, is 'to fancy oneself annihilated while the attributes subsist, and this is a "veil."' Sobriety, on the other hand, is the vision of subsistence with the attributes annihilated, and that is actual revelation (p. 187).

The interpretation of the notions of 'Presence' (*hudur*) and 'Absence' (*ghaybat*) corresponds to his general principles (27). The former is defined by him as 'presence of the heart,' meaning that that which is 'absent' (God) has the same force as that which is visible to the heart, while 'absence is absence of the heart from all things except God' to the extent that the heart becomes 'absent from its own absence.' Absence from one's self therefore is presence with God and vice versa (p. 248; cf. p. 144).

There is an intimate connection between the ideas of 'Presence' and of 'Preference' (*ithar*). The lover of God prefers him to anything else. Two kinds of preference are identified by the author of the *Kashf al-Mahjub* (pp. 190 ff.): that of love, in which there is 'nothing but pleasure and delight,' and that of companionship, which is more demanding. The latter consists in maintaining the rights of the person with whom one associates and in helping him (pp. 190 ff.). The 'Uncovering of the Ninth Veil' is concerned with the rules which follow from his principles (cf. below, Sect. VII).

V

We are now ready to consider al-Hujwiri's understanding of the practice of Sufism. He does not want to quarrel about the right name or designation: 'Ideas are unrelated to things which bear names.' However, to deny the essential ideas would be tantamount to a denial of the 'whole sacred law of the Apostle' (p. 44). Al-Hujwiri follows his usual method of examining the *apophthegmata* of older masters and some among contemporary practices, indicating his approval or disapproval without developing a comprehensive theory of his own. We have referred already to the complaint that in his time God seemed to have 'veiled,' as al-Hujwiri says, most people from Sufism and its followers, concealing its mysteries from their hearts (p. 31). So the outward forms are taken for the real thing, and they are condemned all too often because of a lack of understanding of their true meaning (cf. p. 86).

With all the great Christian, Jewish, Hindu, and Buddhist spiritual leaders, our author considers purification as a first and indispensable step. 'The true Sufi is he who leaves impurity behind' (p. 32). An older authority is quoted to the effect that the 'combination of the light of the sun and moon when they are in conjunction, is like the purity of Love and Unification when they are mingled together' (p. 33). In Platonic fashion al-Hujwiri refers to purity as 'a resplendent and manifest idea of which Sufism is an imitation' (p. 35). There are three grades of aspirants: those who copy for external advantage the ways of the Sufi; those who try to reach perfection by self-mortification; and the true Sufis, who are dead to self and, living by the Truth, having escaped from the grip of human frailties (p. 35). In his discussion of the teachings of a contemporary Sufi who stressed mortification (Sahl al-Tustari), al-Hujwiri develops his notion of the 'lower soul' (28) as a 'veil' and of the nature of the passions, of which 'lust' is the foremost (pp. 196 ff., 207 ff., 135 f.). The 'uncovering' of the fourth 'veil' (chap. xviii) entails an analysis of what is meant by *purification*. There is an outward and an inward kind (p. 291). The cleansing of the body which the law requires is the precondition of prayer; purification of the heart is required for true knowledge (on the respective merits of poverty and purity see chap. v). The Sufis, says al-Hujwiri, are always engaged in purification outwardly and in unification inwardly. Of one of his great predecessors (al-Shibli (d. 945)) he reports that, while purifying himself before entering a mosque, he heard a voice crying, 'Thou hast washed thy outward self but where is thy inward purity?' (p. 293). Of the same *shaikh* he tells the following moving experience. While purifying himself, al-Shibli heard a voice whispering in his heart: 'Art thou so pure that thou enterest my house with this boldness?' He turned back, but the voice asked: 'Dost thou turn back from my door? Whither wilt thou go?' He uttered a loud cry. The voice said: 'Dost thou revile me?' He stood silent. The voice said: 'Dost thou pretend to endure my affliction?' Shibli exclaimed: 'O God, I implore thee to help me against thyself' (p. 294).

To purification corresponds repentance (29). According to a traditional saying attributed to Mohammed, there is nothing God loves more than a youth who repents. Repentance implies three things, namely, remorse for disobedience, an immediate abandonment of sin, and a determination not to sin again (p. 294). For contrition three causes can be listed: fear of divine chastisement, desire for divine favour, and, finally, shame before God. The first is the station of the mass of believers, the secon of the saints, and the third that of the prophets and apostles (p 295). For al-Hujwiri the repentance of fear is caused by the revelation of God's majesty; that of shame, by the vision of God's beauty (p. 299). The deepening of spirituality which we notice in comparing the Sufi teachings on repentance with those of the legalists is reflected in the notion of progression: 'from what is wrong to what is right,' 'from what is right to what is better,' 'from self-hood to God.' It is beautifully expressed also in a verse of one of the most eminent of all Sufis (al-Junaid):

'When I say: What is my sin? she always says in her reply: "Thy existence is a sin with which no other sin can be compared"' (p. 294). This interpretation comes close to the understanding of the greatest of Christian theologians.

The notion of love so familiar to the Christian from the teachings of his Master and from those of the great Christian teachers from St. Augustine down the ages, and to the Hindu through the doctrine of the masters of *bhakti*, is equally fundamental in Sufism (30). Following his predecessors, especially Rabia, al-Bistami, al-Hallaj, and al-Junaid, al-Hujwiri regards love as a cardinal tenet of Sufism (31). There are, basically, two forms of love (*mahabbat*), the author of the *Kashf al-Mahjub* holds: that of like towards like, 'a passion of the lower soul with the aim of achieving union with the essence of the beloved object by means of sexual intercourse', and that of one who is unlike the object of his love. We can also distinguish three derivative kinds of love: first, the restless desire (passion) of man for the object, that is, created beings; second, God's beneficence by which he imparts the gifts of his grace; and third, the 'praise bestowed by God on man as reward for a good action' (p. 306). The love of God, in the second meaning, can be regarded as a qualification of his *will*, and by the same token, in the third, as part of his *word* (*kalam*). The love of man for God can never be of the first kind. It consists in 'veneration' and 'magnification,' grows with the 'remembrance' of him (*dhikr*) to the exclusion of anything else (avoidance of idolatry (*shirk*)), and is restless in its desire for the vision of him (p. 307). (The argument that when a man is overcome with love for the 'Doer' he no longer sees his act but only the 'Doer,' as one sees only the painter when looking at a picture (pp. 91, 127), reminds us of Augustine's *Confessions*.) The typically Sufi notion of love comes into its own with al-Hujwiri's division of believers into those 'who are led by the contemplation of God's beneficence to a love of him' and those 'who are so enraptured by love that they regard all favours as a veil between themselves and God' (p. 308). Realizing the difference between the Sufi notion of love, as defined in this second alternative, and the traditional theological and legal teachings, al-Hujwiri is anxious to make clear that he does not intend to follow the extremists among the Sufi exalters of excessive love (*'ishq*) and total annihilation (pp. 310 ff.). He takes issue with al-Hallaj (quoting the famous statement, 'It is enough for the lover that he should make the One single,' which brought this mystic to the scaffold), though he exculpates him and wants judgment on him to be suspended because 'a person overcome with rapture has not the power of expressing himself correctly, so that the meaning of his words could be easily misunderstood' (pp. 150 ff.). But it is sheer heresy, according to al-Hujwiri, to declare, as some have done, that when a certain degree of love has been attained obedience is no longer required (p. 312). The law is never abrogated, he says. But he is inclined to agree with the statement of an older Sufi to the effect that 'tranquillity is unlawful to the saints of God' because 'they are not permitted to rest here, absent from God, nor there, because of the rapture of joy in the beatific vision,' wherefore al-Hujwiri does not hesitate to conclude that 'the annihilation of the lover in the everlastingness of love is more perfect than his subsistence through the everlastingness of love' (p. 107).

VI

The gap that seems to exist between the Islam of the highly spiritualized aphorisms of the Sufi saints and that of the ordinances of the traditional religion (32) as interpreted by the theologians and canonists (cf. p. 132), is bridged by the method of exegesis which is employed in the *Kashf al-Mahjub*. Quoting an elder who had said, 'Sufism is good nature,' al-Hujwiri proceeds to interpret this aphorism as requiring rectitude in three kinds of attitudes: that towards God by fulfilment of his commandments without hypocrisy; that towards men by showing respect towards one's superiors, kindness towards inferiors, and justice towards one's equals; and, finally, that towards one's self 'by abandoning the flesh and the devil' (p. 42). He agrees with one of his predecessors that 'Sufism consists entirely of *behaviour*' (cf. p. 148) (33). Practices and 'sciences' are not enough, as they can be acquired by effort and instruction; moral principles are needed with which actions have to accord. Moslem theologians have always stressed sincerity (pp. 86–7) and intention. The author of the *Kashf al-Mahjub* also considers it a necessary preliminary to every act. Hunger serves as an example. No reward is given for it in the next world, but, if it is preceded by the intention of fasting, one becomes 'one of the favourites of God' (p. 4). Hardly any other virtue is extolled as highly among Sufis as poverty. Innumerable sayings praising true poverty have been handed down. Al-Hujwiri refers to quite a few of them (chaps. ii and v). He distinguishes between its 'form,' which is 'destitution and indigence,' and its 'essence,' which he defines as 'good fortune and free choice' (p. 20). The belief that worldly possessions hold back the friend of God from contentment, al-Hujwiri shares with the ascetics of all ages. Yet there have been some who have expressed different views, regarding wealth as a gift of God or as a trust which increases responsibility. But what is really involved, al-Hujwiri insists, is not 'acquisition of the Benefactor' (p. 22). 'The rich man is he who is enriched by God' (p. 23). True wealth is not compatible with 'the survival of any attribute'; it involves the 'annihilation of attributes' (pp. 23, 127). Thus the statement of a contemporary sage is to be understood to the effect that 'the poor man is not he whose hand is empty of provisions but he whose nature is empty of desires' (p. 25). The celebrated Junaid is credited by our author with this summary: 'People have spoken much concerning poverty and wealth, and have chosen one or the other for themselves, but I choose whichever state God chooses for me and keeps me in; if he keeps me rich I will not be forgetful, and if he wishes me to be poor I will not be covetous and rebellious' (p. 24).

In the same way in which Sufism spiritualized the notion of poverty, its masters have been concerned to reinterpret the basic ordinances ('pillars') of the Moslem faith: prayer, alms-giving, fasting, and pilgrimage. Al-Hujwiri treats of these in the nineteenth to the twenty-second chapters of his work. Reference is made to a saying ascribed to the Prophet: 'In prayer lies my delight' (p. 302). Our author holds that for novices the whole way to God is included in the term 'prayer' (34). In it their 'stations' are revealed. What repentance is for the adept, purification is for the novice; the place of meditation (*dhikr*) is taken by the reciting of the Koran, that of humility by the bowing of

95

the head; instead of ascertaining the *Qibla* (direction of prayer), the novice depends upon the guidance of a spiritual director; salutation takes the place of detachment from the world, etc. (p. 301) (35). It is customary among some Sufis to perform the obligatory prayers openly while concealing the supererogatory for fear of ostentation or hypocrisy (p. 304). Any benefit received from God, not only property, should lead, according to al-Hujwiri, to 'thanksgiving,' that is, giving of alms (p. 314). Hence this ordinance is binding on rich and poor alike. It calls for generosity because 'infinite blessings call for infinite, not just statutory, thanks.' To refuse to accept alms, as some Sufis have done, is not right, since they should be regarded as a chance of relieving a brother-Moslem of his obligation. God, al-Hujwiri says, 'afflicts the dervish with a slight want in order that worldlings may be able to perform what is incumbent upon them' (p. 316). Liberality is thus so important that it might be called the first step in Sufism (cf. pp. 190 ff., 114–15, 124–5). It means that one should follow one's first thought and not yield to the second, which may be inspired by avarice—a vice detestable to the 'friend of God'—'for the first thought is unquestionably from God' (p. 318). As Christian and Hindu ascetics are fond of telling us, hunger, though an affliction of the body, may 'illuminate the heart and purify the soul.' Al-Hujwiri quotes Junaid again to the effect that 'fasting is half of the way' (p. 320). It is not difficult for him to recall numerous anecdotes illustrating the not infrequently excessive practice of abstinence among Sufis (chap. xxi). Because the 'lower soul' becomes stronger by nourishing the 'natural humours' and the diffusion of passions produces in every man 'a different kind of veil,' those desirous of penetrating into the mysteries of God have to strengthen the powers of reason, which is done by abstinence (p. 325). The spiritual interpretation applied to the other requirements of faith is used by the Sufis with respect also to the pilgrimage. According to the rules of typology, Abraham is regarded as having had two 'stations': Mecca as that of his body, and 'friendship'—he is the friend of God (*khalil Allah*)—as that of his soul (p. 326). 'To enter the bodily station is to be secure from enemies and their swords, but to enter the spiritual station is to be secure from separation (from God) and its consequences' (p. 327). Al-Hujwiri draws a detailed parallel between the various prescribed steps in the pilgrimage as required by the law and the corresponding inner states of contemplation (cf. pp. 329 ff. on contemplation). Because there are these two kinds of pilgrimage, that in the 'absence' and that in the 'presence' of God, 'anyone who is absent from him at Mekka is in the same position as though he were absent from him in his own house, and one who is present with God in his own house is as if he were present with God at Mekka' (p. 329).

We saw that Sufism is defined *pars pro toto* by some of its exponents as behaviour. Islam has developed a special discipline, called *adab* (36), concerned with rules of proper conduct. For all 'stations' there are such *adab*: 'for men in general they consist in the observance of "virtue"' (*muruwwat*) (37), 'for the religious in that of the Sunna, for those inhabiting the realm of love in that of respect' (pp. 334, 341). The rules of discipline are threefold, regulating attitudes towards God, towards one's self, and in social intercourse (38). These go into great detail especially with regard to 'companionship.'

VII

'The Uncovering of the Ninth Veil' is concerned with the principles and rules of companionship (chap. xxiii), a topic highly popular in both traditional and Sufi theology and ethics (cf. p. 338) (39). Al-Hujwiri insists that companionship must be for God's sake, not for the gratification of the 'lower soul' or for selfish interests (pp. 337, 339). 'Whoever is detained by a created thing from that which is uncreated is without worth and value' (p. 107). Solitude has its dangers, as a traditional saying of the Prophet indicates: 'Satan is with the solitary but he is farther away from two who are together' (p. 338). It is interesting to note the difference between Sufism, on the one side, esting to note the difference between Sufism, on the one hand, and Hindu and Buddhist notions on the other, in this respect. The latter have always encouraged the solitary search for truth (Yogin, Pratyekabuddha). Al-Hujwiri enunciates as the principle of Sufi companionship the rule of treating everyone according to his 'degree' (p. 339: cf. above on 'states'). The aspirant should associate either with one who is superior or with one who is inferior to him, so that a definite benefit from such an association is assured for at least one, or for both those involved.

According to al-Hujwiri's typology, there are 'cultured' people and those without culture (cf. above on *adab*). Among the former are found three classes: (*a*) 'worldlings,' (*b*) the religious whose culture consists in disciplining the 'lower soul' and observing the legal ordinances, and (*c*) the elect (Sufis), who 'keep watch over their hearts' and are 'guarding the state they are in.' Like other treatises devoted to Sufi practices, the *Kashf al-Mahjub* includes not only general rules of behaviour but develops 'middle principles' which regulate the application of the former to concrete situations (casuistry). We cannot go very deeply into these interesting matters here. Suffice it to note that detailed rules are given for the conduct of the 'resident' as well as the travelling 'dervishes' (Sufis) for eating, walking, sleeping, and speech (pp. 340 ff.). It is interesting to compare these with the precepts laid down by Clement of Alexandria concerning the very same matters (*Paedagogus*, ii) (40). Only two issues need comment. One is marriage; the other is 'audition.' Regarding the first, al-Hujwiri develops views which indicate his usual disinclination to follow either the 'formalists' or the extreme ascetics. He is in agreement with traditional Islam when he stresses that 'no companionship is equal in reverence and security to marriage when husband and wife are well suited to each other,' adding, however, that 'no torment and anxiety is so great as an uncongenial wife' (p. 361). He says that 'in our time it is impossible for anyone to have a suitable wife, that is, one whose wants are not excessive and whose demands are not unreasonable,' so that many have adopted celibacy mindful of the *hadith* (tradition): 'The best of men in latter days will be those who are light of back' (p. 363). The dervish therefore must first consider what he is doing and clearly envisage the evils of both marriage *and* celibacy, the former danger being 'preoccupation of the mind with what is other than God and distraction of the body for sensual pleasure,' and the latter 'the neglect of the "apostolic" custom and the fostering of lust in the heart with resulting dangers' (p. 363). Wisely our author remarks that a man is not ruined by marriage or by celibacy but that the mischief consists in 'asserting one's will and in yielding to one's desires' (p. 365).

Whereas in other manuals of Sufi theory and life the relation of the spiritual guide (*pir*) (41) to the disciple (*murid*) is expounded at some length (42), al-Hujwiri discusses it only in passing (pp. 54 ff., 85, 118, 104, 128–33, 194). An elder is quoted by him to the effect that 'it is better for a novice to be under the authority of a cat than under his own' (p. 104). The novice should undergo three years of spiritual discipline under guidance before he is admitted to the path (*tariqa*): the first year he must serve the people; the second, God; the third, he must 'watch over his own heart' (p. 54). Upon achieving detachment from 'heedlessness and selfishness,' he is ready for investment with the 'garment of piety' (*muraqqa'at*) (the Sufi garb). This investiture can be performed only by one who has travelled the whole path, has experienced the 'states,' knows the 'nature of actions,' and is familiar with both divine majesty (*jamal*) and divine beauty (*jalal*) (pp. 177, 376). As 'physicians of souls,' the Sufi masters know the 'treatment' the disciple needs. Like the spiritual guides in the Christian, Jewish, Hindu, and Buddhist traditions, the Sufi *shaikh* has an immediate, intuitive insight into the inner status of the disciple (*firasa*) (pp. 129, 130) (43). Of one such *shaikh* (Nuri), al-Junaid said: 'He is the spy on men's hearts' (p. 194). Because of the variety of 'states' mastered by different preceptors, al-Hujwiri considers it permissible for a novice to associate successively with several ('six or more') spiritual teachers (p. 134). The human element of jealousy is thus overcome also (pp. 133–4). The master will examine the disciples' states and judge what point they will ultimately reach. Knowing that some will abandon the path, he must dissuade them from continuing. If they are promising, he must give them 'spiritual nourishment' (p. 55). Once invested with the garb, the novice should never let it be torn save under physical duress. So great is the mystical power believed to reside in the spiritual director that a candidate whom he accepts will necessarily become a saint (p. 57) (44).

The 'Uncovering of the Eleventh Veil' (chap. xxv) is concerned with a peculiarly Mohammedan issue, that of 'audition' (*sama'*). Generally speaking, it might be treated in the context of the theory of knowledge (cf. above), inasmuch as hearing is one of the five senses through which we gain knowledge. However, it is also related to the doctrine of the Word, and to the extent to which it is so, it has its place in any theological (dogmatic) exposition of the Moslem faith. But inasmuch as we hear not only God's word ('the most beneficial audition to the mind and the most delightful to the ear' (p. 394)) but also other speech, music, etc., the question arose as to where the limits should be drawn in approving of audition. Among radical Sufis practices were adopted which appeared so dangerous to some authorities that they felt compelled to prohibit any audition except that of the divine word. A casuistic discussion of right and wrong audition developed (45), and to it al-Hujwiri contributes in his usual moderate and sagacious way. He goes a great part of the way with the traditionalists who consider 'hearing' superior to 'seeing'; his motivation is that 'it is hearing that makes religion and its ordinances obligatory' (pp. 393-4). 'All Muslims are obliged to listen to the Quran' (p. 396). A criticism of formalists and radical Sufis is implied in his reminder that anyone who denies audition denies the entire religious law. On the other hand, a 'middle principle' is necessary to determine what kind of hearing is inadmissible. Al-Hujwiri establishes a pragmatic one in stating that the lawfulness of hearing depends on the effect it produces (p. 402). He discerns between two classes of 'auditors'; those who hear the spiritual meaning and those who hear the material sound of utterances. Both kinds of auditors have their assets and their dangers. The reason, al-Hujwiri feels, why men are seduced and their passions excited by listening to music is that 'they hear unreally.' If their audition corresponded with the reality, they would escape from evil consequences (p. 403). Even to hear the word of God may be without profit to some, while the true Sufi perusing a poem may 'regard the Creator of the poet's nature and the Disposer of his thoughts, and see in the act an evidence of the "August"' (p. 403). Al-Hujwiri seems to agree with an older Sufi (Shibli) that 'audition is outwardly a temptation and inwardly an admonition' (a reminder of the Creator). Temptation means 'to be arrested by the medium or mediator' (the reciter), hence al-Hujwiri calls mediated audition a 'faculty of absence', while immediate hearing of 'the Beloved' (God) is a 'faculty of presence' (p. 406; cf. above) (46).

The theory of 'states,' which has been discussed previously, affords the possibility of discerning grades in the 'reality' of audition. Each Sufi, according to our author, has a particular grade, and the feelings which the hearing evokes in him are proportionate to his grade, so that whatever 'penitents' hear augments their contrition, what 'lovers' hear impels them to abandonment, and whatever the spiritually deficient hear 'increases hopelessness.' Audition is compared to the sun, which 'burning, illuminating, and disclosing, shines on all things, but affects them differently' (p. 407). Beginners upon whom the Divine influence begins to work are at first not able to absorb it: 'novices are agitated but adepts are tranquil in audition' (p. 408). There is great wisdom in al-Hujwiri's statement that, when an anchorite goes into a tavern, the tavern becomes his cell, and that when a haunter of taverns goes into a cell, the cell becomes his tavern (p. 409). 'Audition' in the deeper sense of inviting the Divine Presence, he thinks, should not be made a habit but should be practised only infrequently so that 'it may ever be held in reverence' (p. 419). On these principles al-Hujwiri's casuistry of 'hearing' is based. With regard to the hearing of poetry and instrumental music, as well as participation in the sacred dance (raqs) (and the ecstatic 'rending of garments' which may accompany it), the presence or absence of the desire for 'spiritual advantages' (p. 401) is the criterion. 'Anyone who says that he finds no pleasure in sounds and melodies and music is either a liar and a hypocrite or he is not in his right senses, and is outside the category of men and beasts' (p. 401). Our Sufi is not a Puritan. But he is also no Epicurean or antinomian: 'In the present age some people listen to music, yet they say, "We are listening to God," and the wicked join with them in the audition and are encouraged in their wickedness, so that both parties are destroyed' (p. 409; cf. pp. 416–7 and 171). The Koran forbids all 'idolatry' (shirk). It is a long way from this general injunction to al-Hujwiri's special admonition that 'there is nothing in the two worlds that is sufficiently important to hold man back from God' (p. 113).

VIII

These are, in broad outline, the views of the author of *The Unveiling of the Veiled*, a compendium of Sufi teachings and practices of the eleventh century. To the Christian reader not familiar with this type of attitude in Islam, al-Hujwiri's book will be of interest mainly for two reasons. First, it will introduce him to a different devotional and mental atmosphere from that of traditional Mohammedan theology. Yet it does not reflect the heterodox climate of the more extreme Sufi teachings, but represents, as it were, the aspirations of moderate Sufism, whose function could be characterized as that of a leaven in the dough of the Islamic community. But the Christian student will, secondly, also note with interest the resemblances to teachings in his own religion. He will find it easy to parallel al-Hujwiri's notions of knowledge, of faith, of love, of virtue, and of companionship, with the utterances and statements of Christian theologians through the ages. He will, however, not be surprised to find so much that is familiar to him if he is aware of the profound influence which early Christian thought and practice actually exerted upon early Islam. More recent scholarship especially has proved this to have been the case, as we had opportunity to point out above.

There is one more question, however, which has not as yet been discussed at length in the literature on the subject, but which is of the greatest interest to the historian of religion. How was it possible for Mohammedanism to absorb so many foreign ideas and practices in relatively so short a time without losing its identity? It is true, of course, that Jewish, Christian, and, to a lesser extent, Iranian notions had already been absorbed by the founder of Islam. But they had been moulded by him into an independent, highly original, and forceful religion. It is easy to overlook the spiritual depth of Mohammed's vision if attention is concentrated upon the credal and legalistic aspects of its development. Yet there has always been in Islam from the beginning a strong element of protest against all enshrining of the spiritual in the material. Though the sharp emphasis upon God's transcendence became mitigated in some of the later theological and philosophical teachings under foreign influences, the notion of 'unification' and the dread of *shirk* (idolatry) acted as constant reminders that God is Spirit and that he is One. This emphasis has prevented Islam from becoming, to the degree to which Hinduism and Mahāyāna Buddhism became, the receptacle of highly divergent ideas and practices and from enshrining the invisible in the visible. For the localization and materialization of the holy there was never much room in the religion of Mohammed. The idea of 'incarnation' remained repulsive to all but the most extreme among his followers. This meant that it was not difficult for spiritually and mystically inclined Moslems to reinterpret the basic tenets and ordinances of their religion so as to stress the otherness of the holy and the inwardness of all acts by which man communicates with it. It is characteristic that even in Sufism there has never been room for a mysticism of nature as, notwithstanding the traditional stress on the transcendence of God in Judaism, we find it in Hasidism. By the same token it is no accident that, in some of the modern reform movements in Islam, 'Puritanism' (*Wahhabi*) and Sufism have coalesced and have both contributed to a constructive criticism of traditionalism. With all this we do not mean to imply that the foreign influences which have been absorbed into Islam have acted only to reinforce existing tendencies and dispositions. A careful study of the theology of Sufism, tenet by tenet, will easily show deep-reaching transformations, changes, and deflections (cf. especially the influence of the Christian notion of love and its reception in Islam). But we do wish to point to the power of the initial insights with which this religion started and which enabled it to reform and rejuvenate itself and yet to preserve, wherever it remained genuinely Islamic, its essence and genius in spite of all borrowing.

This is not the place to treat more fully a last problem which these considerations may suggest: the problem of the classifica-tion of a theology such as that of al-Hujwiri. A great deal of con-fusion reigns in the field of the history of Christian thought with regard to the use of the terms 'spiritualism' and 'mysticism.' We badly need some clarification as to terminology. It will depend upon the definition of these two terms—and we hope to come back to this question very soon—how we feel that the teachings set forth in *The Unveiling of the Veiled* should be classed.

CHAPTER SIX

THE STUDY OF MAHĀYĀNA BUDDHISM

I

ONE of the most difficult tasks confronting the student, and—more especially—the teacher of the history of religions is the study of Mahāyāna Buddhism (1). Let us consider wherein the difficulties lie. Buddhism originated in India, and Indian thought is different enough from our ways of thinking to pose serious problems to the Western scholars. In a stimulating little book, B. Heimann has shown how different is the basic approach in theology, ontology, ethics, logic, and aesthetics in the two parts of the world (2). Hīnayāna Buddhism, on the whole much better known in Europe than Mahāyāna (3), differs just enough from Brahmanism, from which it evolved, and from orthodox Hinduism, to warrant the most careful examination. It uses a terminology which shows considerable independence of that employed in the so-called classical six systems, and in its epistemology, psychology and philosophy Buddhism is different enough to prevent us from regarding it, as some have suggested, as a Hindu sect (4). We have not as yet been able to ascertain with all the accuracy desirable the definite meaning of such central notions as that of Nirvāna (5) or Dharma (6), or to form a clear picture of the teachings and the historical development of the earlier philosophical schools in Hīnayāna Buddhism (7). A British scholar presented us recently with a comprehensive publication in which, grouped according to topics, a number of important texts of the Southern branch of Buddhism are newly translated, and a great number of cross-references enables the student to compare pertinent passages (8). The tireless work of a number of older and younger Pāli scholars has by now made available to the Western reader translations of practically all the canonical and several—though not by any means all—extracanonical writings and commentaries. One of the results has been to correct the once widespread notion of a sharp division between Hīnayāna and Mahāyāna Buddhism. The beliefs and practices of Ceylonese, Thai, and Burmese Buddhists are by no means identical with those of the early *samgha* (community) (9). The last comprehensive study of contemporary Buddhism in these countries by a competent Western visitor-scholar (10) is twenty years old.

The study of Mahāyāna Buddhism presents great additional difficulties for anyone familiar with the 'Little Vehicle.' The territory which it covers is vast and the peoples who have embraced this faith are ethnically and culturally quite divergent (11). A variety of Central Asiatic tribes, the Chinese, Tibetans, Koreans, Japanese and South-east Asiatics, have all, in adopting it, contributed to alter the Indian version of Buddhism. The history of the Mahāyāna in these countries is bound up with the history and cultural development of their inhabitants (12). Most of the indigenous religions have influenced the 'Great Vehicle,' Hinduism especially. In many instances we are, as yet, not really well enough acquainted with some of these cults to assess adequately their impact upon the concepts and practices of the regionally differing 'denominations' of the Mahāyāna. The different forms of this faith within its Far Eastern constituency, that is, within the Chinese and especially the Japanese Samgha, add to the complexity of the picture. The study of the Mahāyāna denominations by Western students has only begun. Perhaps linguistic difficulties constitute the greatest single obstacle. Documents in at least four major languages—Sanskrit, Chinese, Tibetan and Japanese—are involved, of which only a fraction have so far been translated into Western languages (13). Mahāyāna Buddhist terminology is baffling even for those who have a knowledge of the idioms. Moreover, the sacred literature of the Great Vehicle, which is of central importance for any study of its beliefs and practices, is immense and, at least in part, so elusive and confusing that certain portions have been dismissed by Western students as plain 'nonsense.'

Yet the task is not quite as hopeless as these facts may suggest.

A great deal of work has been done, especially in the last decades, by the co-operative efforts of Western investigators in making available for the student of the history of religions a great deal of very useful material. Furthermore, some masterful though preliminary attempts by experts have been made to arrive at a working chronology of the historical development of Mahāyāna Buddhism, to interpret, not only to translate, some of its major texts, and to study its doctrine and philosophy. Following the great Burnouf, V. Vasiliev, Sylvain Lévi, and Louis de la Vallée-Poussin (14), Sir Charles Eliot, M. Walleser, Th. Stcherbatsky, O. Rosenberg, Winternitz, B. Keith, E. Lamotte, and E. Obermiller have worked in this field (15). Experienced travellers have reported on the conditions they found prevailing in the countries of Mahāyāna faith, its centres of culture and seats of learning. The impact of Western culture, science and technology upon the thought of Far Eastern Buddhists has interested some investigators, while others have specialized in inquiries into the influence of Christianity, its tenets and its techniques upon the adherents of the Buddha in the more progressive countries of the East. Moreover, comparative studies in Western and Mahāyāna Buddhist philosophies have been undertaken, though not as yet with really satisfactory results (16). In manuals and text-books, sketches of the Great Vehicle can now be found (17).

Meanwhile, Eastern scholars, partly Western-trained, have undertaken to study historically, critically and exegetically their own Mahāyāna Buddhist tradition. Max Müller's students, Bunyiu Nanjio, J. Takakusu, K. Watanabe, W. Wogihara, M. Anesaki, D. T. Suzuki and their students have written extensively. Unfortunately little of their work is as yet available in English translations (18).

We shall have to ignore here the numerous contributions made to the study of Mahāyāna Buddhist art (19). They are of great significance—the importance of imaginative expression in symbolic form surpasses the discursive, at least in some branches of this faith—but they need separate treatment, so that we shall have to limit ourselves in this context to the religious, philosophical and ethical aspects.

THE STUDY OF MAHĀYĀNA BUDDHISM

II

Mahāyāna Buddhism is a religion of salvation (20). Most Western students approach it from the *historical* angle, starting with an inquiry into the nature of early Buddhism—the life and teachings of the founder, the growth of the community—which, in turn, leads them to an examination of the way of the 'elders' and of Hīnayāna doctrine and practice. But it is difficult for anyone proceeding along these lines to do justice to the 'developments' which resulted in the full-grown Great Vehicle. The latter will appear to the student who does not eschew all evaluation, but limits himself strictly to 'facts,'as a degeneration, traceable, perhaps, to external influences which, he feels, have brought about the total corruption of the original teachings of the Enlightened One. Indeed, it seems a far cry from the rôle which Pāli Buddhism appears to allot to the figure of the founder, to the vision to which the great Mahāyāna Sūtras— the *Lotus of the True Law* or the *Descent into Ceylon*—testify, from the semi-agnostic attitude of the great teacher of the Middle Path as recorded in the *Longer* or the *Middle Collection of Discourses* to the subtleties of the treatise on *Transcendent Wisdom* or from the moral teachings of the *Path of the Law* (*Dhammapāda*) to the 'Imitatio' of the saintly Śāntideva. A very wide gap seems to separate 'worship' as it is practised in Ceylon, the centre of the Hīnayāna faith, from the cultus carried on in its 'heavenly counterpart' (21), as conceived in the *Lankāvatāra*, or from the ritual of the Shingon denomination in Japan.

Yet even from the purely historical point of view the balance need not be altogether in favour of the 'pure' Little Vehicle. A more realistic picture than that prevailing in the early twentieth century has emerged from studies in trends within Hīnayāna Buddhism (22). If the Buddha has never been regarded as 'merely a human teacher,' if the Nirvāna he preached was wrongly interpreted by a certain school of Western investigators as 'something purely negative,' if the concept of the Samgha as set forth in the early Pāli texts forbids its interpretation as a loose association of individualists, some of the 'accusations' levelled at the process of 'degeneration' in the

Great Vehicle will have to be dropped, or, at least to some degree, they will have to be made against the way of the Elders as well. It is of course possible to side altogether with the mystics and spiritualists, who tend to deprecate the process of historical growth which all religions exhibit, and who are inclined to be sceptical or critical of any kind of expression of religious experience. Such criticism would apply to the scholasticism of the Abhidhamma school as well as to that of Mahāyāna metaphysics.

However, the study of the historical development of Mahāyāna Buddhism (23) has to be supplemented by inquiries aiming at an understanding of the *religious experience* which manifests itself in the theology, devotional practice and worldview of the Great Vehicle. The fruitfulness of Rudolf Otto's categories (24) can be proved by analysing the expression of the experiences of the *numinous* to be found in the Mahāyāna Sūtras. In his introduction to the English translation of one of the major scriptures, the *Lotus of the True Law*, Soothill (25) has characterized the numinous atmosphere which surrounds the appearance of the heavenly Buddha, and Otto himself has illustrated this basic notion by reference to Mahāyāna theology and practice (26). The theology, the devotion, the ethics, and the metaphysics of the Great Vehicle have to be interpreted in the light of such analysis, that is, as the unfolding of a primary apprehension of the numinous quality of *ultimate reality*.

In each of the major divisions of Chinese (27) and Japanese (28) Mahāyāna Buddhism a special aspect of this apprehension is developed (29); we have the metaphysical approach of Tendai and Kegon, the symbolistic of Shingon, the experiential of Zen, the legalistic of Sanron, the pietistic of Jō and Shin, the symbolic-ecclesiastical of Nichiren (30). These *denominational* emphases correspond to some found in Christianity, especially in Protestantism (31), with the difference, however, that there is little positive reference to other interpretations in Anglican, Presbyterian, Lutheran, Methodist, Congregational or Quaker theology, whereas in most of the Mahāyāna denominations we find a definite theory of stages of revelation corresponding to the approaches of the various 'schools' (32). Thus Mahāyāna Buddhism possesses, in spite of its denominational and philo-

THE STUDY OF MAHĀYĀNA BUDDHISM

sophical differentiation, a consciousness of *solidarity*. This in turn rests upon the primary apprehension of *ultimate reality* referred to above. The teachers of the Great Vehicle (33), agreeing in this respect with Christian theologians, do not regard the so-called 'reality' of which we become aware through our sensual experience as ultimate; their point of departure is without exception a radical criticism of sensual experience (34). In this Hīnayāna and Mahāyāna teachings agree. There is, however, considerable difference between the various schools as to the nature of the 'dharma' (elements) which make up (support) existence (35), and as to the degree to which, in addition to negative or critical statements, *positive* assertions with regard to the nature of transcendent reality are admitted and essayed. 'From the point of view of ontology all Buddhists are realists,' says quite rightly one of the keenest students of their philosophy (36), and he goes on to say that what unites all Buddhists of different persuasions is 'idealism with regard to the inner and outer world, realism as far as the absolute is concerned' (37). The two most important philosophical schools of the Mahāyāna, the Mādhyamāka (38) and the Yogācāra or Vijñānavādin, disagree on just this point. Yet they agree in what may be called the use of the empirical method—at least in their negative 'critique.' The proponents of the former school (39), especially the great Nāgārjuna, insist upon the impossibility of going beyond the *epoché* (refraining from positive assertions) (40).

The dedication of Nāgārjuna's great treatise (*Mādhyamika-shāstra*) (41) may serve as illustration:

> The Perfect Buddha,
> The foremost of all the Teachers I salute.
> He has proclaimed
> The Principle of (Universal) Relativity.
> 'Tis blissful (Nirvāna),
> Quiescence of Plurality.
> There nothing disappears,
> Nor anything appears,
> Nothing has an end,
> Nor is there anything eternal.

Nothing is identical (with itself),
Nor is there anything differentiated,
Nothing moves,
Neither hither nor thither.

The exponents of the Yogācāra school try to develop a metaphysics in order to account for the relationship of the 'absolute' they postulate to the phenomenal world. Thus their speculation runs along lines familiar to the Western mind from the study of the Neoplatonists, or of Schelling and Hegel. The Mādhyamika supplement their theory of 'relativity' (Stcherbatsky) with practical postulates of a somewhat pietistic character. In order to do this, they conceive of a two-fold truth in the fashion of some Gnostics, of Averroes or—nearer home—of the Vedānta (Śaṅkara). Though the theoretical question as to the nature of Buddhahood is and must remain 'unanswerable,' the worshipper may and is even obliged to fulfil the religious ordinances. Nāgārjuna himself did so, and is regarded as a saint as well as a profound thinker (43). To the extent to which positive notions creep into an epistemology of the Mādhyamika variety (44), a rapprochement with the Yogācāra point of view is effected. We find indications of such an *intermediate position* more or less consistently developed in such texts as the *Mahāyāna-śraddha-utpāda* or the *Uttaratantra* (45). It is easily understandable that a considerable variety of approaches towards a 'realization' of ultimate reality, once admitted, could develop. Either *theologia negativa* or simple terms ('suchness,' *tathatā*) can be applied. Prof. Keith thus characterizes the Yogācāra thought: 'Suchness is the effulgence of great wisdom, the illumination of the Universe (*dharmadhātu*), true knowledge, the mind pure in its nature, eternal, calm, free, the womb of the Tathāgata (Buddha), where the essence of Tathāgataship dwells in the body of the law (*dharmakāya*)' (46). Inasmuch, however, as no distinction can be applied to 'suchness', this wisdom has no object, there is nothing to illumine. However, somehow it reaches into empirical reality. 'By some mysterious act of self-determination, no better defined than as spontaneous, the absolute self affirms itself in the form of the receptacle intelligence (*ālaya-vijñāna*). The origin of ignorance results in that which sees, that which represents, and that which constantly particularizes the entity which performs these functions being styled "mind" (*manas*) (47). There is the immediate or sudden apprehension to which the followers of the Zen masters aspire, there is the inward way through meditation indicated by texts such as the *Amitāyur-Dhyāna-Sūtra*, and there is the fideism of the Pure Land denominations.

To philosophical speculation concerned with ultimate reality corresponds the *theological* doctrine of the nature of Buddhahood—the theory of the Three Bodies—in the Great Vehicle (48). What the metaphysicians call the essence of suchness (*Bhūtatathātā*) is known to the theologians as the *Body of* ultimate *reality* (*dharmakāya*). It can be apprehended, given the necessary conditions, as the *Body of 'Enjoyment'* (*sambhogakāya*): manifestations of the Buddha(s) 'in the glory' are the 'heavenly apparitions' which delight the vision of the audiences mentioned in the great Mahāyāna texts. In the *Body of Transformation* the Absolute finally manifests itself as a human Buddha, adapting itself as it were (*upāya*) to the dimensions of this world. Sākyamuni, the historical Buddha, is of importance because he revealed the doctrine of salvation; however, it is not sufficient to see his bodily form (*rūpa*); his true body (*kāya*) is the Dharma, he is the Dharma incarnate.

The *Buddhology* of the Great Vehicle has been studied fairly thoroughly by a number of competent scholars, especially by L. de la Vallée-Poussin. Notwithstanding certain national and denominational preferences, the doctrine of a *plurality* of manifestations of Buddhahood is universally accepted in the Mahāyāna. While the notion of previous and future Buddhas remains somewhat academic in the Little Vehicle, the Chinese, Tibetan, and Japanese Buddhists extend genuine and frequently fervent devotion (49) to the great Buddhas (Amida, Amitābha, Vairocāna) and Bodhisattvas (Avalokiteśvara-Kwanyin-Kwannon, Maitreya, Mañjuśri, Samantabhadra).

Dogmatically, this pluralism is codified in the theory of Dhyāni-buddhas-bodhisattvas and Mānusibuddhas (50). Of greater consequence, however, has been the doctrine of the *'equipments,'* especially those of wisdom and compassion. The great illumination of the Buddhas (*samyaksambodhi*), in addition to the insight into the 'emptiness' of the notions of the ego, of existence and non-existence and of desire, consists of omniscience (universal knowledge), a prerogative which is due to their meditations and their merits (51). Through these they have acquired insight and power (52). 'Wisdom (*prajñā*) and compassion in the highest degree characterize the Buddha. The Mahāyāna stands primarily on two legs, *prajñā* and *karunā*, transcendental idealism and all-embracing affection for all living beings. . . . The former sees into the unity of things, the latter appreciates their diversity' (53). They are like the two wings of a bird (54). In the former notion theological and philosophical speculation are blended: transcendent *wisdom* (*prajñā-pāramitā*) (55), glorified in the sacred scripture of that title, is the attribute as well as the 'essence' of divinity and of perfection. 'The terms,' says one of the keenest students of the Great Vehicle (56), 'which designate the highest truth or reality—identity (*tathatā*), emptiness, perfection of wisdom, element Nirvāna, element Dharma, body of dharma, matrix of the Buddha's flesh on the borders of metaphysics, of mysticism and of devotion.' Boundless *compassion* (karunā) is epitomized in the 'vows' (cf. especially those of the Bodhisattvas Samantabhadra (57) and Avalokiteśvara (58)) which express the ideal of bodhisattvahood; here dogmatic and moral theology coalesce. As far as the notion of merit is concerned, it is closely tied up with the idea of grace which is constitutive for the religion of the Great Vehicle (59). Here it is possible to speak of the 'fatherhood of the Buddhas and the brotherhood of all creatures' (60).

III

Mahāyāna Buddhism is a doctrine of salvation. Philosophically speaking, salvation is achieved by and in the realization ('transcendental wisdom') of the impermanence of the phenomenal world (voidness, *śūnyatā*); theologically speaking, it consists in the achievement of the ideal of the *imitatio*: to be perfect, as the great embodiments of truth, the Buddhas and

Bodhisattvas, are perfect. To acquire the double 'equipment'
(*sambhāva*) of wisdom and merit is indispensable for one who is
embarking on the career of imitation of the Buddhas (61).
'Pour être delivré, il faut devenir Bouddha' (to be saved one
must become a Buddha) (62). Abstract knowledge, however
profound, of truth without growth in charity does not destroy
false beliefs. Wisdom must be sustained by energy and nourished
by meditation to illuminate and guide merit (63). The transcendental virtues (*pāramitās*) (64) (morality, charity, energy,
patience, meditation, and wisdom) have to be practised, even
if to fulfil them is beyond the power of an aspirant (*bodhisattva*) (65). Even the initial step of this career, worship of
the manifestations of divine (cosmic) truth, requires grace. The
aspirant thus becomes established in the path (66).

It is the great merit of Sylvain Lévi and Louis de la Vallée-
Poussin to have made accessible in translation the sources of our
knowledge of the *ethical* ideas and ideal of Mahāyāna Buddhism
(67). The preliminary resolve, the 'conception of thought of
bodhi' (enlightenment), marks the starting-point of the career
of bodhisattvahood, being its 'primary cause and basis.'

Three 'supports' (*ādhāra*) are necessary, which the
Bodhisattvabhūmi (68) enumerates: first, the 'breeding' (*gotra*)
which is either innate, acquired in a previous existence or per-
fected in the present birth, and which is in either the 'seed' or
the 'fruit' state; secondly, the first production of the enlightened
thought by virtue of which the Perfections are practised; and
thirdly, principles conducive to bodhi, which will assure its
full attainment (69). According to the 'Compendium of Doctrine' (*Śikshāsamuccaya*), however, *bodhicitta* (enlightenment-
thought) can be valuable in itself apart from conduct (*caryā*)
(70).

The preliminaries to entering upon the career, according to
Vallée-Poussin, are the practice of good from selfish motives
(for the sake of temporal reward or of Nirvāna) and desire
for the good of others for their sake. Whereas the former is the
Hīnayāna ideal, the latter is definitely the Mahāyāna notion.
The thought of becoming Buddha for the salvation of creatures
(*bodhi-citta*) is, as we saw, motivated by compassion (71) and
the realization of impermanence (especially of the Ego). It

consists in reflection on the advantages of such a vow, pious works, and the actual undertaking of the vow. It not only marks the entry upon the path of holiness, but also serves as a daily ritual to initiate the triple duty (to be performed thrice a day), that is: confession of sins, rejoicing in good, and prayer for the preaching of the law and delay of the entrance of the saints into Nirvāna (72). Thus the thought must be preserved and strengthened; to the vow practice (*carya*) must be added. Vigilance and watchfulness are needed. Only then can the great virtues (*pāramitās*) be practised. They are called 'natural' (*laukika*) as long as they are not illuminated by knowledge, and 'supernatural' (*lokottara*) if guided by transcendent wisdom (*prajñā*). The practice of any of these virtues benefits the future Bodhisattva only to the extent that through it other beings are 'matured' (73).

The Bodhisattva career proper is divided into *stages* (*bhūmi*, region, station) (74). The term and the idea occurs already in the Little Vehicle and apparently was developed further by the Mahāsamghika school which marks the transition from Hīna- to Mahāyāna. The difference, according to Vallée-Poussin, does not consist in the notion of successive stages but in the implication of its universal applicability—everyone is to become a Bodhisattva—and in the conception of the nature of him who dwells in the bhūmi. One of the great texts, the *Daśa-bhūmika Sūtra* (75), enumerates the following stages (76):

A *preparatory period*, wrongly called 'bhūmi,' precedes the first seven stations (77). It is divided into two sub-periods: that in which the right disposition is developed (*gotra-bhūmi*), and where certain positive properties ('kindnesses') are already acquired and certain negative ones (moral sins, heresies) are abandoned, and a second period in which, on the basis of these dispositions, aspirations grow which contain—in germ—the bodhi-thought (*adhimukticaryā-bhūmi*). These dispositions and aspirations may be attained by incentives such as the invitation of a preacher, the hearing of praise of the Buddha, compassion, etc. Yet there is still much imperfection (78). While the *first seven stages* constitute the 'active' career of a Bodhisattva, the last three make him more similar to a Tathāgata (Buddha). In one of the texts (79) the following somewhat scholastic characterizations of the first seven (80) *bhūmis* and their 'Achievements' are found (81). The *first* stage, the 'Joyful' (*pramuditā*), permits limited insight (82). Here the disciple is no longer an 'ordinary man but a saint; his thought is no longer in flux but fixed.' Joy prevails because of his spiritual birth in the 'family' of the Buddhas and the vanishing of the 'five terrors'. The great resolve is constantly strengthened and purified, the incipient Bodhisattva worships, listens to and preaches the Law, and begins to 'ripen' other creatures. Great spiritual and magical powers accrue to him (83). At the *second* stage, the 'Immaculate' (*vimalā*), he practises morality (*sīla*), and his actions are still more pure, that is, purged of notions of an Ego. The *third* stage, the 'Shining One' (*prabhākarī*), is marked by the display of infinite patience, which is challenged only by anger, to which even the Bodhisattva may be liable. Higher meditative insight and powers are acquired. At the *fourth*, the 'Radiant' stage (*archismatī*), the virtue of energy (*vīrya*) dominates, by which application, both intellectual and moral, is rendered effective; while the *fifth*, called the 'Invincible' (*sudurjayā*), is characterized by the depth of meditation (*dhyāna, samādhī*) conducive to distinguishing relative and abstract truths. The Bodhisattva, orientated towards wisdom (*prajñā*) at the *sixth* stage ('Turned Towards Knowledge') (*abhimukhī*), understands and teaches the true meaning of 'dependent origination,' that is, 'vacuity.' At the *seventh*, the 'Far-going' (*dūrangamā*), the great skilfulness in the use of the right approach (*upāyakauśalya*), glorified in the *Lotus of the True Law* (84), is acquired, by means of which the aim of salvation can be achieved. At the last-named stage the Bodhisattva, though no longer 'bound', is not yet completely free, as he is still desirous of the knowledge of a Buddha, and his intention of universal salvation is not yet fulfilled (85). At the *eighth* stage, the 'Immovable', all duality (self, non-self, etc.), has vanished. The Buddhas have to intervene at this stage to prevent the Bodhisattva from entering Nirvāna, and they do this by virtue of their great vows. Though master of 'indifferentiation,' the Bodhisattva does not, however, as yet possess certain powers which would make him a Buddha. No longer bound to his body, but capable of multiplying it infinitely, 'he knows and surveys the Universe' (86). With the *ninth* stage, the 'Good One,' the Bodhisattva achieves still greater knowledge of the law, resulting in further ripening of his fellow creatures; and with the *tenth*, 'Cloud of the Law,' he is in complete possession of the contemplations (*samādhis*) and formulas (*dhāranīs*). He is consecrated by all the Buddhas to supreme Buddhahood, having achieved the absolutely pure illumination (*bodhi*) (87). He receives the excellent rain of the True Law, and having himself become a 'Cloud of the Law,' he sends down on creatures the good rain which 'lays the dust of passions and causes the growth of the harvest of merits' (88).

According to the *Bodhisattva-Bhūmi* (89) the Bodhisattva is superior to the states envisaged in Hīnayāna Buddhism by (*a*) faculties, (*b*) perfections (*siddhi*) (90), (*c*) skills (*kauśala*) and (*d*) results (*phala*). He is, however, liable to fall a prey to the four depravities; that is, negligence, bad companionship, want of independence, and anxiety for the necessities of life; and on these grounds may be reborn in the state of perdition (*apāya*)(91). In spite of having 'breeding,' he may be prevented from attaining to his goal (illumination) by four circumstances, namely, failure to find the good friend or teacher (Buddha), perverted understanding of the teaching, slackness in carrying it out, or want of maturity in the faculties or completeness of equipment (92). Our text discusses, moreover, the problem of altruism and egotism, rejecting the extremes with regard to both, such as preaching morality for heavenly rewards or preaching to others by one who is wanting in morality or practice (93). The liberality and the patience of the Bodhisattva spring from compassion and aim at enlightenment. The pleasures accompanying altruistic and egotistical actions *svaparārthah*, etc.), causes and results are analysed (94). Merit and knowledge, besides ripening (*vijāka*), are the cause-results.

Scholastic systematization envisages a correspondence between the ten productions of the thought of becoming a Bodhisattva, the ten perfections (*pāramitās*) and the ten stages (*bhūmis*) (95).

IV

After having reviewed briefly the main difficulties with which the study of Mahāyāna Buddhism has to contend and the basic teachings of the Great Vehicle, we should like to add some suggestions as to how a *course* in this subject may be organized (96). Acquaintance with the sacred writings of the faith is indispensable. No one text is universally regarded as normative by all Mahāyāna Buddhists. A survey of the 'canonical' texts, however, is not feasible because of their number. So a choice has to be made with the view of making a selection which is representative of various emphases in the teachings and practices of the denominational groups of the Great Vehicle (97). The *study of the selected texts* in translations (98) will be preceded by a brief introductory presentation of the history of Buddhism, covering its origins, early development, classical and post-canonical Hīnayāna Buddhism (canonical writings, teachings, and practices). This would be followed by a summary of the characteristic features of Mahāyāna Buddhism: an exposition of its theology (Buddhology), of its theory and practice of devotion, and its philosophy; finally, brief sketches of the lives and work of some of its outstanding teachers, especially the Indian. Reports on the major texts would be arranged in the following order. First, a '*biography*' of the Buddha should be studied which would illustrate the transition from Hīnayāna notions to Mahāyāna Buddhology (99). Unfortunately, neither of the two great biographies (*Mahāvastu*, *Lalitavistara*) is available in translation (100). But a reading of Aśvagōsha's *Life of the Buddha* (*Buddhacārita*) is fitted to introduce the student into the hagiography of 'higher' Buddhism. This great poem is inspired by loving devotion (bhakti) to the Enlightened One, and thus prepares the way for the cult of the Great Vehicle as reflected in the Great Texts (*Mahāvaipulya-Sūtras*). (Cf. below.) It is interesting to compare it with the 'Account of the Beginnings' (*Nidānakathā*) of the extracanonical Pāli literature. Though the Sanskrit version is a torso, the Chinese and Tibetan cover the whole earthly career of the Buddha. The work is beautifully organized according to an architectural plan which contrasts favourably with the chaotic state of the 'Account of Great Things' (*Mahāvastu*).

Next, the *Lotus of the True Law* (*Saddharma-pundarīka-Sūtra*) (101) should be studied. This scripture is not only one of the most important of all, a religious classic of the world's literature and immensely popular among Eastern Buddhists, but it is also relatively easy for Western readers to understand and to appreciate. It is a work of medium size and, inasmuch as the content of most chapters (1–21, 25) is offered both in prose and in verse, its extent is further cut down if only one version of each chapter is taken into consideration. Great visionary power and creative imagination are revealed in the *Lotus*. Its beautiful parables, several of which parallel parables of the New Testament, are of special interest to the Christian student (102). There is a minimum of the epistemological distinctions and metaphysical speculations which are so prominent in other texts of the Great Vehicle. Its central theme is the attainment of Enlightenment by the way of Faith, its basic presupposition the notion of the universality of Buddhahood.

While Sākyamuni is the paramount eternal omnipresent Buddha in the *Lotus*, a great number of other Buddhas and Bodhisattvas appear and converse (Maitreya, Mañjuśrī, etc.) (103). The 'skilfulness' of the Buddha in his preaching which he adapts to the capacities of his hearers is emphasized (104). The meritoriousness of devotion to the Enlightened Ones, to their preaching and to the Lotus itself, which becomes a symbol of the Dharma (Universal Truth), is made much of throughout the text (105). Great rewards await the believer (106).

As a second selection we would suggest three shorter texts which Professors Max Müller and Takakusu translated for Max Müller's series *The Sacred Books of the East* (107), namely the longer and the shorter treatise *The Land of Bliss* and the so-called *Meditation Sūtra*. These books furnish an excellent introduction to the fideist and the devotional aspects of the Great Vehicle. The great popularity of these treatises among East Asiatic Buddhists justifies their study by the Western student. They do not present too great difficulties. Faith in the saving power of the Buddha Amida or Amitāyus and a detailed vision of the heavenly abode which awaits the faithful as a reward are the main themes of the *Land of Bliss* texts. The *Meditation* text (108) is not, as the title may lead one to believe, primarily concerned with the techniques of meditation, but rather with cosmology and theology. It stresses the saving power of adoration offered to the Buddha Amitāyus. The three treatises acquaint the Western reader with the eschatology of Mahāyāna Buddhism as well as with its notions of personal devotion and faith and of the good life (*pāramitās*). The descriptions of the Land of Bliss itself are vivid and highly poetic. They were to be the inspiration of innumerable artists in their visions of the state of the blessed. The historian of religion will not resist the temptation to compare the Hebrew, Judaic, Iranian, Manichaean, Moslem, and Hindu with the Mahāyāna concepts of *paradise*, even if the tantalizing question as to the exact relation between this last and some of the others is, as yet, unanswerable.

The third selection of texts of the Great Vehicle would include an analysis of the contents of the *Introduction to the Career of the Bodhisattva (Bodhicaryāvatāra)* (109). From this source the reader will derive an insight into the ethical thought of Mahāyāna Buddhism and into the implications of the Bodhisattva ideal for individual conduct. This magnificent poem, credited to Śāntideva, is to be regarded as another of the great religious classics of the world's literature. 'En lisant Cāntideva,' says the translator of his great work, which has been compared to the 'Imitation of Christ,' 'nous apprenons à connaitre le Bouddhisme du Grand Véhicule et la vie spirituelle qui l'enseigne' (110). Śāntideva mixes descriptive analysis with homiletic exhortation. Of special interest are the chapter on confession, which includes detailed prescriptions for the cult of the Buddhas (offerings of self, of gifts, of praise, adoration) and for the confession of sins (of body, word or thought) (112), and that on *morality*, in which the principles of the spiritual life (hierarchy of virtues, self-mastery, prayer, watchfulness) and rules of conduct (friendliness, modesty, silence, energy), are enunciated (113). One chapter treats of the *patience* which is necessary in order to persist in the search for enlightenment: anger as the gravest of sins, resulting from discontent; suffering as conducive to spiritual growth; injustice, really the result of (our own) previous actions; becoming free from anger towards our 'enemies', who really are our benefactors. These are some of the topics treated here by Śāntideva (114). Patience is the presupposition of the heroic virtue of *energy* or force (*vīrya*) (115) which a Bodhisattva has to display in order to 'gain all wisdom and magic power and to save all beings' (116). Its enemies are sluggishness and attachment to pleasure, to be countered by meditation on death and suffering; discouragement and self-contempt, to be vanquished by self-confidence and its tributaries: desire for the good, and joy in good works. No difference should be made between oneself and others. One chapter in Śāntideva's work is devoted to *meditation*, its conditions and its fruits (*dhyāna*) (117), that is the merit (*punya*) which it earns by strengthening and purifying charity, morality, patience and force. The understanding of the non-reality of the Ego is facilitated by the practice of recollection. Ego and non-ego will no longer be distinguished (*parātmasamatā*), my neighbour will be substituted for me (*parātmaparivartana*), I shall treat myself as I used to treat him and vice versa (118). Finally, *wisdom* is discussed, the crowning 'virtue' for which all the others form the preparation (119). 'Whosoever desires deliverance from suffering, will produce in himself this wisdom' (120). It consists in insight surpassing all sensual and intellectual experiences. From this point of view the fatal consequences of all positive notions concerning empirical reality are demonstrated. The Mādhyamika position is defended against Brahmanists, Hīnayānists and Yogācāras.

While the texts mentioned so far do not require too intimate a knowledge of the response and development of the epistemological and metaphysical thought of the Great Vehicle, the next treatise to which the student should be invited to direct his attention is more exacting.

There is a considerable similarity in the description of the Bodhisattva career in the text last named and in the *Awakening of Faith* (*Mahāyāna-Śraddhotpāda Sūtra*) (121). This famous treatise is not easy to understand. Though its basic teachings correspond to those of other Mahāyāna Sūtras, the exposition of epistemological and metaphysical topics which fills the first and major portion of this book is quite compact. Fundamental to it is the theory of the double aspect of what, speaking philosophically, may be called the Absolute, or theologically, the Dharmakāya. It is the essence of Buddhahood, eternal, permanent, and immutable (*bhūtatathatā*), deprived of all attributes, if seen in its true being (*svabhāva*); it is the 'womb' (*tathāgatagarbha*) of all that constitutes the pheno- menal world (*saṃsāra*) when viewed under the aspect of particularization (122). Only for the 'disturbed mind' does multiplicity exist; it disappears for the 'quiet mind' (123). Hence it can be said, paradoxically, that nirvāna (*bhūtathā*) and samsāra coincide, or that the terms śunyā and aśunyā (void and not void) are interchangeable. When the Absolute assumes relative appearance, it becomes all-conserving mind (*ālaya-vijñāna*). The 'defilements' which obscure the true essence (*bhūtatathatā*) are both affective and intellectual hin- drances in the mind. Thus flux of appearances has its ground in enlightenment (*avidyā*), its conditions in the external world, produced by subjectivity (124). Now, if all beings are in posses- sion of true essence (125), why then are they not all Buddhas or Bodhisattvas? Because, answers Aśvagosha, the *degree* of ignor- ance varies (126). Only by 'seeing' the Buddhas and by practising wisdom can sentient beings be freed. The Buddhas who in truth (*paramārtha-satya*) *are* the Dharmakāya, 'responding to the requirements of the occasion, transform themselves and assume the actual forms of personality' (127). They become parents, wives, servants, friends or enemies, thus enabling all beings to see and recollect them, thereby acquiring spiritual benefit (128). The doctrines of the three bodies, of the Bodhisattva career, of skilfulness in means (*upāya-kauśalya*) and of the six virtues (*pāramitās*) are all integrated into the teaching of the Awakening Sūtra. This treatise places great emphasis upon the notions of faith and of spiritual discipline (129). Intuition alone does not suffice. By four means: contem- plation of truth, obedience, repentance, reverence and vows, the defiling impurities can be removed. Of the virtues meditation (*samādhi*) especially is discussed in greater detail (130).

That part of the Mahāyāna texts which presents the greatest difficulties for the understanding of the Western reader is the group of works known as the *Perfect Wisdom* (*Prajñā-Pāramitā*) *Literature* (131). This term is used in three different senses, namely, as indicating supreme Wisdom personified in the

Buddha in his Cosmical Body (*dharmakāya*), as referring to the
path leading to the attainment of this Wisdom, and, finally,
as meaning the texts (*sūtras*) in which the teaching concerning
the two former are found (132). It is the term Perfect Wisdom
in the third sense with which we are concerned here. There are
a large number of treatises in this family, from among which
one has to be chosen as representative for our study. Because
the English translation is readily available, the *Larger Perfect
Wisdom Heart* (*Prajñā-pāramitā-hridāya*) Sūtra (133) is selected,
though the *Diamond-cutter* (*Vajracchedikā*) (134) would
be an equally interesting specimen of this type of
literature (135). The former treatise is centred on the notion
of '*relativity*' (Stcherbatsky) (*sunyatā*)*; that is: the earlier
understanding that the Ego etc. is impermanent, not 'real,' is
extended into a *universal principle*. All that is not ultimate
reality is '*devoid*.' The Perfect Wisdom Texts represent the
foundations upon which the teaching of the Mādhyamika
philosopher Nāgārjuna rests. He has systematized their arguments, which the Sūtras present in dialogue form (136). Because there is, unfortunately, no complete English translation of
his great systematic work (*Madhyamika-śastra*) or of Candrakīrti's
famous introduction to the Mahāyāna from the Mādhyamika
point of view (137), these works cannot be included in an introductory reading on Mahāyāna Buddhism. But we are, owing to
recent work done on Tibetan sources, now in the position to take
into consideration a highly important text which at the same
time summarizes the teachings of the Perfect Wisdom Sūtras
and develops the theory of the path to the attainment of
Nirvāna (cf. above on the three meanings of Prajñā) (138). Its
lengthy title is *Abhisamayālamkāra-nāma Prajñā-pāramitā-upadeśa-
śāstra* (139). It can be regarded as 'a catechism, a text to be
learned, and recited by heart.' A report on the contents of this
work, on which, according to tradition, twenty-one commentaries were written in India alone (140), should concentrate on a
discussion of the five stages of the threefold path (accumulating
merit, training, illumination, contemplation, further training)
by which the double aim of quiescence of the mind (*śamatha*)
and transcendental analysis (*vipaśyanā*) is achieved (141).
Obermiller, to whom we owe the first analysis of the contents of

the Sūtra, has shown that, philosophically, it is neither a pure Mādhyamika nor a Yogācāra tract, but that it reveals a middle position (Yogācāra-Mādhyamika-Svātantrika school) (142). It treats of eight major subjects. These are, first, the three kinds of omniscience of the Buddha (ultimate direct knowledge of all aspects of existence, knowledge of the Path, and, finally, in regard to the objects of the empirical world); second, the four methods of realization (concerning the process of illumination); and, thirdly, the cosmical Body of the Buddha. In addition, seventy single topics are discussed which need not for our purposes be included in the summary of the contents of the text.

The *Abhisamayālamkāra* belongs to a group of works known as the five treatises of Maitreya (143). While there exists a Sanskrit version of this text, another significant work of this group, the Sublime Text (*Uttaratantra*) is extant only in Tibetan as a part of the *Tangyur*, the Tibetan Canon (144). Obermiller has made the *Uttaratantra*, with Asanga's commentary, available in English. It is highly important because of the light it sheds upon basic theological, metaphysical, and devotional aspects of the Great Vehicle. Central in this treatise is the theory of the essence of Buddhahood (*tathāgata-garbha*), the fundamental element of the Absolute, also called the element of the Lineage (*gotra*). This topic is mentioned only briefly in the *Abhisamayālamkāra;* here, however, it dominates, and all other subjects are treated only as causes and results of its development (145). It is not surprising that this view was attacked by the great Tibetan reformer Tsong-kha-pa as Brahmanistic (146). According to this doctrine the essence of the Buddha in a living being represents an 'eternal immutable element identical with the Absolute' (147). It is unique and undifferentiated in everything that lives (148). 'The whole process of the liberation of the Absolute Essence from the worldly element which ends with the attainment of Buddhahood . . . is to be viewed as an uninterrupted practice of mind-concentration upon the non-substantiality of the elements' (149). Two aspects are distinguished with regard to the absolute element of the Lineage: a primordial one (immutable as gold) and a developed one, its reflection in the phenomenal world (a seed bearing fruit) (150). The purification from all defilement means the attainment of Buddhahood. 'The Buddha has a double outlook facing both the Absolute and the Empirical Reality and has for his chief aim the salvation of other living beings' (151). The *Uttaratantra* therefore sets forth the meaning of (*a*) the three jewels (Buddha, doctrine, congregation), (*b*) the Buddha-essence, (*c*) enlightenment, (*d*) the properties of the fully illuminated Buddha, (*e*) the acts of the Buddha promoting the welfare of all living beings (152). Because the characteristic Yogācāra doctrine of the "store-consciousness" is absent from the *Uttaratantra*, it cannot be regarded as belonging to this school; the introduction of the defilement theory, however, indicates that it does not reflect a pure Mādhyamika view either. The Tibetan theologians classify it as a Mādhyamika-Prāsangika work (153). This treatise is one of the most compact and lucid introductions to the thought-world of Mahāyāna Buddhism, and hence should be read and studied by everyone who desires to familiarize himself therewith.

Because of its high authority in Mahāyāna Buddhism, because the Yogācāra viewpoint is here represented, and, finally, because a translation and introduction are available, the *Descent into Ceylon* (*Lankāvatāra-Sūtra*) (154) must be included in our list of writings. Professor Suzuki, the well-known Zen acholar, has translated this text and given us a detailed analysis of its contents, and of its key concepts (155). He has rightly stressed the interest in the psychological or meta-psychological aspect of the Path of Salvation which characterizes it (156). Central to it is the 'turning-back' or transformation (*parāvrtti*) by which the 'all-conserving mind' (*ālaya-vijñā*) which undergirds the individual consciousness is purified from all defilement (*āsrava*) and ultimate reality is attained (157). A detailed analysis extends to the various states of consciousness (*vijñānas*) and the relations between them (158). The accessibility of the supreme insight and love of the Buddha is guaranteed by the notion of the Germ (*tathāgata-garbha*) (159), the universal essence which is the metaphysical aspect of the all-conserving mind (160). 'If the garbha or the ālaya while absolutely neutral and colourless in itself did not harbour a certain irrationality, no sentient being would ever become a Buddha' (161). All knowledge of the realm of the defiled mind in which the vijñānas are active is 'discrimination' (*vikalpa*) (162)—distinction between Me and Not-me; birth and death, saṃsāra and nirvāna (163), while that of the absolute is transcendental wisdom (*prajñā*), which, seeing things as they are (*yathābhūtam*) in their true being or suchness, is realization of voidness, nirvāna, enlightenment (164). This wisdom, different from abstract speculation (*tarka*), thus has an eminently *practical* significance (165). 'Not only seeing but living the truth' is the message of the Ceylon Sūtra, according to Suzuki (166). With the *Diamond-cutter* (Vajrācchedikā) the *Ceylon Sūtra* has been a favourite of the Chan or dhyāna (Zen) denomination ever since the Chinese patriarch Bodhidharma recommended it to his disciples as the great guide to self-realization (*svasiddhānta*) (167). All its great teachers found that it extols 'the state of consciousness in which the inmost truth is directly presented to one's mind' (*pratyātmāryajñānagocāra*). Not only wisdom but also compassion (*mahākarunā*) and skilfulness in means (*upāya*) are stressed in this Sūtra as in the other texts concerned with the Bodhisattva career (168). 'Though from a meta-physical point of view the other beings have no self-substance', yet, in Suzuki's words, 'the pitying heart that transcends the cold and severe contemplation of the reasoning philosopher has no inclination to ignore the reality of particularization' (169), it 'moves spontaneously and universally like the sun that shines on the righteous and unrighteous' (170). Effortless, its possessor preaches the law and practises the virtues (*pāra-mitās*).

V

Finally, we will consider briefly what benefit the Christian theologian may derive from a study of Mahāyāna Buddhism. He finds a religion which has developed in a part of the world far removed from the birthplace of Christianity, yet he realizes that there are reasons to believe that *contacts* have existed between the two great religions of redemption (171). Christianity in its Eastern forms penetrated at an early date into Western and Central Asia, and there have been connections as yet not fully explored between the Iranian religions, Gnosticism and Manichaeism on the one hand and Mahāyāna Buddhism on the other (172). A great deal of work will have to be done before definite 'influences' can be established and proved. The Christian theologian, meanwhile, cannot but be impressed by striking parallels between his own faith and that of the followers of the Great Vehicle (173). These are of a threefold nature. First, there are resemblances in the *theoretical* expressions of the two religions: namely, in the nature of faith, in the belief in an ultimate reality of numinous character, in the belief in the love, mercy, and grace of divine manifestations, in the hope for redemption, in the emphasis upon the relation of faith and morality, and finally, in the concept of virtues, especially compassion and knowledge. As far as parallels in the *practical* expression of the two faiths are concerned, devotion is stressed, prayer, oblations, charity, personal sacrifice are found in both. In both the notion of 'imitatio' of the perfect example is central.

With regard to the *sociological* expression, there are affinities between the Christian and the Mahāyāna concepts of 'brotherhood' in the transcendence of 'natural' ties, in the notion of authority and the differentiation along denominational lines, and in the tension between congregational and hierarchical orders. Monasticism and celibacy are found in both, as are 'reformed' groups which reject them. Sacred writings are possessed by both Christians and followers of the Great Vehicle, and their interpretation is of the utmost concern to theologians in both religions. In addition to these parallels in the structure of the two cults there are certain similarities in the dynamics of their *historical* developments. The life of the founder and his teachings mark in both the beginning of a process of 'crystallization'; they become paradigmatic (normative) in both. In both a 'cult' of the founder originates, and leads to theological discussions which show similarities (cf. Docetism). Both religious communities expand beyond ethnic, national and cultural frontiers. Both experience influences from the cultural environment into which they enter: in the case of Christianity the Greco-Roman world, in the case of Mahāyāna Buddhism the Indian, South-east

THE STUDY OF MAHĀYĀNA BUDDHISM

Asiatic, Chinese, Tibetan, Mongolian, Japanese, etc., environ-
ments. In both cases the theological articulation of the heritage
of faith is supported by philosophical argument, the categories
of which are in part taken over, here from Greek thinking,
there from Brahmanic-Hinduistic. In both, in the history of the
Church and of the Samgha, reactions ('fideism') and reformations occur. Both can boast of outstanding individuals, among
the early disciples of the founders as well as later in a series of
prominent saints, teachers, thinkers, reformers, and ascetics.
Both experienced the consequences of the clash between
religious (and ecclesiastical) and political and national institutions. Branches of both underwent 'nationalization.' In both,
breaks in the unity of the religious fellowship occurred. To the
division into Oriental Eastern Orthodoxy and Western
Catholicism and Protestantism corresponds the division into the
Lesser and Larger Vehicle. The Great Reformation in the West
is paralleled by the Japanese and Tibetan 'reformations' of the
thirteenth and fifteenth centuries respectively. For both faiths
the development of science in the West after the Renaissance
was to constitute a serious challenge, which, however, became
effective in the East only in the last seventy-five years.

To these parallels and resemblances we have to add features,
mostly of a practical character, which Mahāyāna Buddhism
has borrowed from Christianity. The influence of Nestorian
Christianity in the earlier centuries is difficult to assess in detail,
but there can be no doubt that the missions of the Mendicant
Orders in the Middle Ages made an impact in the countries of
the Great Vehicle (Tibet). Yet the effect of the Jesuit activities
in the Far East in the seventeenth century was all but wiped out
by the reaction which followed them, and it is rather from the
last third of the nineteenth century onwards that we can trace
the definite influence of Christian activities upon the practices
of the followers of the Great Vehicle in some countries of this
faith.

When it comes to pointing out the decisive *differences* which
exist between Christianity and the Mahāyāna, we have to
remind ourselves again of the complexity and variety of emphases within the latter religion. As against all superficial
comparisons, the contrasts have to be brought out by a thorough

127

examination of the characteristic teachings and practices on both sides. Few Christian apologists have taken the trouble to study the great Eastern faiths thoroughly enough to be competent to do this. Most liberal Protestant theologians are unaware of the full meaning of the central Christian tenets and hence too ready to identify statements in the two faiths, while many of the conservative or 'neo-orthodox' theologians lack intimate acquaintance with the various forms of the religion of salvation in the Far East. The task which Rudolf Otto and Schomerus have performed for Hinduism and Christianity needs to be tackled with regard to the Great Vehicle.

First of all, a distinction has to be made between the *formal* elements (approach, categories) and the *content* of thought in each faith. It is the difference between the How and the What in the articulation of both concerns. Problems such as the determination of the relation of faith and knowledge, or the rôle of the historical in the religious 'ideology', or the use of metaphysical speculation in both religions would fall under form, while the respective notions of ultimate reality, of the means of grace, or of the nature of redemption, would belong to the second group of topics for a comparative study.

Determination of the nature of sources of authority constitutes a first basic difference between the two religions. For the Christian the sources for his religious orientation—differently as different groups will evaluate each of them and their relations—are Christ, the Scriptures, tradition, the Church, and individual experience (rational or mystical), while the Mahāyāna Buddhist (with the same qualification) sees in the Buddha, the scripture, the law (*dharma*), tradition, the Samgha and individual experience the sources for his faith. Only in a very formal way does the notion of the *redeemer* in the two faiths correspond: Jesus Christ and Sākyamuni the Buddha are different not only in the sense in which any two individuals are different, but the concept of their humanity as well as of their divinity and of the relation of these characters is very far from being identical. The fundamental difference lies, of course, in the notions of *ultimate reality* in each case. The *scriptures* constitute for both religious communities the record of a normative past, but there is no

analogy in Mahāyāna Buddhism to the Christian concept of
the canonical. We lack as yet a comparative study of the
idea of inspiration in both religions. It would have to proceed
from the unique notion of the 'Word' in Christian theological
thought and include an analysis of the role of prophecy in the
Christian scriptures. As far as the Buddhist hypostasis of the
Law is concerned, we should search in vain for a Christian
equivalent. While in our religion the cosmic and moral law is
interpreted as an expression of God's divine will and power,
Mahāyāna theology tends to regard it as an aspect of ultimate
reality without reference to a revealed God. While the analogies with regard to the understanding and evaluation of tradition in the two religions are quite marked, the basic concepts of
the *communion*—here of the Church, there of the Samgha—are
very dissimilar. (It cannot be said that Buddhology is to the same
extent fundamental for the understanding of the nature of the
Samgha as Christology is for that of the Church.) Maximalist
and minimist ecclesiologies are found within both communities. The differences in the notions of the nature, function, and
value of *individual experience* within Christianity are probably
profounder than those within the Great Vehicle. Except for
Methodism and certain modern philosophical interpretations
in Western theology, however, the emphasis placed on individual
experience seems greater in Mahāyāna Buddhism than in
Christianity. The tremendous preoccupation with psychological and epistemological questions in the former witnesses to
this.

When we turn now, still concerned with the formal aspect, to
the *structure* and *order* in which articulated theological thought
has organized the main tenets of the Christian and Mahāyāna
Buddhist faiths, we find that, at least until the beginning of the
nineteenth century, the locus *de Deo* preceded in Christian
theology the locus *de homine*. Though the primacy of the anthropological topic which characterizes Hīnayāna Buddhism is
challenged in the Great Vehicle by the dominance of cosmological speculation, the Christian order: God—World—Man is
not paralleled in the Mahāyāna order: Cosmos—Man. It has
often been stated that to the extent that the Old Testament
concept of God has determined Christian theology—and it must

be one of its vital ingredients—the *doctrine of God* in both religions must differ. But the God of the New Testament, the God of Jesus Christ, is also very different from all Mahāyāna notions of ultimate reality. There are historical and logical reasons for this difference, as we have seen. The theological and devotional pluralism of the Great Vehicle is alien to Christianity. We have touched already upon the uniqueness of the *Christological* idea. The passion of Jesus Christ, his death and resurrection—there is not and cannot possibly be anything 'comparable' to this in Mahāyāna Buddhism. The cross is a stumbling-block not only to the Greeks and Jews but to the Buddhists as well. The expressed similarity between the figure of Jesus as interpreted in modern liberalistic Protestantism and the Buddha of the Hīnayāna as interpreted by Western scholars from the background of liberalistic Protestantism (H. Oldenberg), vanishes if Hīnayāna Buddhism is seen integrally. In order to see it thus, it is important to remember the common heritage of both schools, the Lesser and the Greater Vehicle. There is perhaps, with the exception of the Christological, no more exclusively Christian doctrine than that of the *Holy Spirit*. No equivalent exists in Mahāyāna Buddhism. Together with the notions of Divine Providence and of God's creative and redemptive purpose, it illuminates the Christian concept of *history* which is altogether alien to Buddhist thinking. In the latter there can be, consequently, no room for the *eschatological* expectations of Christendom, notwithstanding the fact that faith, charity and hope do play a significant part in the Great Vehicle. In comparing the Christian and the (Mahāyāna) Buddhist doctrines of *Man* we are struck by profound divergences which can be explained only historically (Greek-Hebrew versus Hindu heritage). There is no 'analogy' to the concept of the Christian *personality* (character) as there is none to the Buddhist notion of Karma. Moral responsibility, recognized by both great faiths, is justified on quite different grounds in Christian and in Mahāyāna theology. The ideals of the perfect Christian and of the perfect Buddhist are less alike than the list of 'virtues' in both religions would suggest. For both, the concept of *sin* transcends the moral, but the metaphysical explanation of this phenomenon is divergent in the two communities.

Though there are teachings on *grace* in them both—the necessity of divine help being one of the major tenets of Mahāyāna Buddhism—the notions of the *means* by which it is conferred do not coincide. It might be asked if the term *sacrament* could be used with respect to the *pratimokṣah* and the admission into the order. There are no analogies to baptism or the Lord's Supper. Adoration may be said to be the central act of both Christian and Mahāyāna worship, but while in the former *prayer* looms largest, *meditation* plays the dominant rôle in the latter. While *sacrifice* has a long and important history in the Christian religion, it is less emphasized in Buddhism.

The study of Mahāyāna Buddhism cannot and ought not to be shunned by the Christian theologian. It was the father of modern comparative studies in religion, Max Müller, who wrote: "I believe the final struggle between Buddhism and Christianity, whenever that comes to pass, will be a hard one, and will end in a compromise—there is a prophecy." The first half of this prophecy is not less likely of fulfilment because the second is open to grave doubt.

[C]
HISTORY OF THE CHRISTIAN RELIGION

CHAPTER SEVEN

CASPAR SCHWENCKFELD: A PUPIL AND A TEACHER IN THE SCHOOL OF CHRIST

I

THERE can be no doubt that Caspar Schwenckfeld von Ossig is one of the worthiest and most attractive figures in the era of the Reformation—nay, in the history of Christianity—and that the attention which has been given to his person and his work is in reverse proportion to their importance (1). With a few exceptions, only those have made the Silesian reformer and his thought an object of their study who have belonged to the wider or narrower group of sympathizers with the 'fourth reformation'—a confirmation of Wilhelm Pauck's statement that it is 'a noteworthy and regrettable fact that Luther research has been undertaken primarily by Lutherans, that the rise of Anglicanism has been the object of the study of Anglicans, that the study of the Anabaptists has been long neglected partly on account of denominational prejudices on the part of historians, and so on' (2). This leaves Schwenckfeld to the Schwenckfeldians, and it must be said that their labour has yielded fruits for which every student of the Reformation and of the history of Christianity is indeed indebted to them. The voluminous *Corpus Schwenckfeldianorum*, of which the greater part has now been published (3), will really 'prove to be a mine of future research' (4). But it is ardently to be hoped that the work of interpretation and evaluation will be carried on by many, that its results will be taken into consideration by all who are aware of the breadth and depth of Christian experience, and have a genuine interest in an understanding between the various official and unofficial groups into which the followers of Jesus Christ are divided. Such work will be

135

appreciated by those willing to acknowledge greatness of character, profundity of thought, sincerity, and true missionary zeal for Christ and his cause wherever they meet it.

For various reasons the time seems to be particularly ripe for an estimate of the intuition and the message of Caspar Schwenckfeld, truer and more just than that so far accorded to him in his homeland or elsewhere. The New World to which his followers flocked after harsh persecution had driven them from their home soil, having provided the means for so dignified and substantial a monument to the teacher of the 'middle way' as the *Corpus* represents, is now well equipped and prepared to do justice to the irenic prophet and thinker who worked for the very ideals to which not one group alone but actually all American Christians are pledged. The strongly Lutheran 'bias' with which Schwenckfeld has been judged in his native land through the ages until very recently (5) does not prevail among Protestant scholars in America, where, among church historians especially, a widening and promising interest in non-official Christianity of both past and present can be observed (6). This latter fact, moreover, augurs well for Schwenckfeldian studies. The whole complex of the 'fifth reformation'—the Lutheran being the first, the Zwinglian the second, the Anglican the third, and the Calvinist the fourth—has recently come under new and very fruitful scrutiny. There is universal agreement that much still has to be done before satisfactory general conclusions can be drawn from the multiple facts which far-flung and assiduous monographic work has yielded; yet, together with individual studies of leading figures and regional movements, a series of promising attempts has been made to develop categories for the understanding of basic trends, types, and schools among those who worked for reform and reformation in the sixteenth century (7).

I am not convinced that the Silesian theologian has found his niche as yet, though he figures in practically every one of the classifications of types of Christian faith and experience which have been put forward. But how could we expect a satisfactory solution as long as the basis for arriving at conclusions on Schwenckfeld's work is as slender as it has been up to now? (Quotations from the *Corpus* are usually limited to Vols. I-VI.)

The editors of the writings and correspondence of the teacher from Ossig have made the beginning of an analysis of his thought, for which all future students will be indebted to them. It has rightly been said that we should be fortunate indeed if we were in the same position with respect to other leaders of sixteenth-century movements. Though one monograph on Caspar Schwenckfeld exists —in German (8)—a comprehensive English study of his work is as yet lacking. Perhaps the finest exposition of Schwenckfeld's thought in the English language is Rufus Jones's chapter in his *Spiritual Reformers of the Sixteenth and Seventeenth Centuries* (9). Yet thirty years ago the publication of the *Corpus* had barely begun. In short: There is a task to be performed and the stage for it is set.

II

There are some important issues in the rich and complex world of Schwenckfeld's thought (10) which have attracted the attention of scholars throughout the ages (11). They are mostly those controversial topics which loomed large in the theological discussion and struggle of his own days: his Christology, his concept of the means of grace, his ideas on liberty and toleration, his views on the church. But more light is needed on other essential topics of Schwenckfeld's theology: his use of the Scriptures and the Fathers; his hermeneutics, as well as his exegesis; his idea of God; his view of man; his concept of the 'world'; the doctrine of the Holy Spirit, so central in his teaching, and that of the Last Things; his teaching on regeneration; his views on 'discipline'; his criticism of Catholicism and of the 'Anabaptists.' Yet, important as it is to investigate thoroughly the views which the Silesian reformer held on the central problems of the Christian faith, we should ever be mindful that Schwenckfeld was not a theologian.

It is indispensable for everyone who wishes to do justice to the personality and work of Caspar Schwenckfeld to understand his primary purpose, to which his whole life and his every effort in thinking, writing, and teaching were dedicated—the service of Christ (12). I do not think that it would be wrong to designate his theology as 'christocentric,' if we bear in mind that this theology is only one expression of his paramount concern to promote the cause of Christ in and through his life and work. In other words, it is not possible—as can be done in studying the theology of many a modern author—to abstract Schwenckfeld's theological statements from his personal religious life as it manifests itself in his prayer and his meditation; in his reactions to privation, illness, and suffering; and in his untiring efforts to bring encouragement and comfort to others. Only if we omitted all this would we be able to agree with those of his critics who deny originality—or, what is really the same thing, vitality—in the expression of his thought. Yet there is a great deal of freshness, immediacy, and profundity to be found in it, once we consider Schwenckfeld's work as the product of 'experimental' theology, grown out of an ever-active and spontaneous religious experience. He belongs with Luther, not with Flacius; with Newman, not with Ritschl; with Kierkegaard, not with Schleiermacher. Any Christian thinker and theologian can be rightly understood and evaluated only if he is seen in the context of the tradition to which he belongs. It is certainly interesting to attempt to enumerate and classify the Catholic and Protestant, Lutheran or non-Lutheran, elements in the piety and theology of the Silesian reformer; but it is more important to understand which great Christian personalities really influenced him. It is significant that, in contrast to other early Protestants, Schwenckfeld insists upon a sharp distinction between the world of the Old Testament and the world of the New, turning, as did many reformers before and after him, to the latter as the canon or ideal for the restoration of Christianity. Furthermore, it is characteristic of him that, again in distinction from other contemporary reformers, he is most anxious to substantiate his teachings with exhaustive references to the Fathers of the Church and, though less frequently, to the scholastics (13). There is no doubt that if ever a history of 'Christianity in earnest' is written, Caspar Schwenckfeld will have to figure in it; but most attempts, so far, to classify him and to trace his 'lineage' have not been satisfactory. He belongs indeed to the history of the Christian church and of Christian theology, but evidently not to that of the Roman Catholic church. Lutheranism, as we saw above, is very reluctant to reserve for him his rightful place (14), and the historiography of the 'left-wing reformation' is likely to lump him together with spirits with whom he himself declined to be associated or identified. There are, it is true, two other historically recognized traditions: mysticism and spiritualism. Schwenckfeld is not a mystic (15), at any rate in the narrower sense of that much-abused term. Is he a 'spiritualist'? Perhaps, if care is taken not to use this word, as is often done, with a purely negative connotation, i.e., to reserve it for those who protest against or abstract from some or all traditional or historical or symbolical forms of expression of religious experience. Not only does Schwenckfeld object to certain concrete doctrines, rites, and forms of organization (16) in the Christendom of his day—Roman, Lutheran, Zwinglian, Calvinist, 'Anabaptist'—but he insists upon a perpetual protest against any objectification of religious experience which is not genuine, adequate, and legitimate. (His criteria for drawing this distinction in principle and empirically will be discussed later.) Yet this negative criterion (17) alone should not be regarded as the essential feature in his 'spiritualism.' As the term indicates, it is the positive role attributed to the *Spirit* which is central in all truly spiritualist teaching. Now there is nothing unusual, unheard of, 'sectarian' (in the negative sense of the word) in the concept of the Holy Spirit and in attempts to put its nature and operation into the right relief. Catholic (Orthodox and Roman) and Protestant theology reserve a central place for teaching on the 'operation of the Holy Spirit.' Histories of this concept have been written, tracing its development through the earliest and some later phases of Christian thought and life. Yet it seems characteristic that one of the greatest weaknesses of modern theology, especially in Protestantism, is the lack of productivity and originality in its thought on the Holy Ghost. As usual in such cases, sectarianism (in the narrower sense of the term) has thriven on this omission and has known how to make the most of it. In the crucial period of the Reformation, Schwenckfeld was aware of this embarrassment, as were Edward Irving and many others in later Protestantism, and his theology is an attempt to unfold the basic conception of the work of the Holy Spirit (18), a conception which plays a determining rôle even in his earliest writings (19).

III

Some day a Life of Caspar Schwenckfeld will be written. It will be an absorbing picture of a great Christian, a great Bible student, a true theologian, a courageous fighter, a penetrating thinker, a strong yet mellow character, a cultured yet simple personality, a man with a genius for winning and leading souls, a friend and helper of many. Until that time it must suffice to single out a few aspects under which to view the life of this great pilgrim, truly a *viator indefessus*. Unfortunately, there is no documentary evidence which enables us to write a sketch of the early life and development of Caspar Schwenck-feld. Such evidence does not go back beyond the beginning of his active interest and participation in the reform of the church of his day. The references to his youth in his later writings are sparse. However, the zeal of his early followers and biographers enables us to paint, at least in broad strokes, the background of his later life and activity (20).

Only six or seven years younger than Luther—he was born in 1489 or 1490—Schwenckfeld grew up on the estate which his family owned in Lower Silesia (Ossig, in the duchy of Liegnitz). His education, the foundation of which must have been good, was continued at the universities of Cologne (21), Frankfurt-on-the-Oder, and, possibly, Erfurt. He seems to have concentrated on the study of law. It is regrettable that we have no way of ascertaining which of his teachers may have made an impression on his youthful mind and what kind of reading he may have done in those years. The place for a young nobleman with his family connections and education was at the court of one of the princes, in his case successively with the dukes of Oels, Brieg, and Liegnitz (22). Silesia, that border province, has played an important part in the political, cultural, and religious history of the German Reich from the days of the Mongol invasion to the present. Depending upon the force with which the central imperial power made itself felt, the dynasts were more or less their own masters in their territories, and a change to greater assertion by the imperial government and a tightening of its influence upon the religious affairs of the border provinces during the early phase of Schwenckfeld's reforming activity was to have a decisive influence upon his personal destiny. During his service at court he frequently stayed on his estate, the administration of which later passed into the hands of his brother.

The connection between Luther's reforming activities and his own religious interests and theological studies cannot be accurately determined. We know that in 1519 Caspar read daily a portion (four chapters) of the Scriptures; and that the struggle against the abuse of indulgences in 1517–18 was followed with attention by him. In 1522 or 1523 he left the court. Again we are not sure what part his deficiency of hearing and what part his religious views played in this decision. Unfortunately, it is also impossible to trace the development of these latter up to the time of his correspondence with Hess and the writing of the *Christian Admonition*, addressed to the Bishop of Breslau. This prince had decided on a course of reform for his country in 1521. In 1524 the former courtier received a mandate to assist in this attempt. Schwenckfeld had visited Wittenberg in 1521–2 and on that occasion had met Melanchthon, Bugenhagen, Honas, and also Karlstadt, but not Luther. During his second visit, which occurred after the publication of his *Admonition* (1524), he conferred with the great reformer and his associates, and we are fortunate in being able to reconstruct the conversation on the basis of the Silesian visitor's diary (23). These relations with Luther deteriorated after Schwenckfeld's criticism of his eucharistic views and of the course of the Lutheran reformation. Meanwhile, Caspar must have had a decisive religious experience—'eine gnädige Heimsuchung' (24)— his references whereto were interpreted by the Wittenbergers as a claim to extraordinary personal revelations. One of the most important, though shorter, of Schwenckfeld's treatises—*De cursu verbi Dei*—was written in 1527 (25). This work and one on the Eucharist were published without the author's consent, though with friendly intention, by Oecolampadius and Zwingli respectively (26). A *rapprochement* is noticeable between the Silesian reformer and the Swiss after the controversies with Wittenberg. Schwenckfeld was invited by the Duke of Liegnitz to submit suggestions for changes in the church order in his territory (1528). Meanwhile, attacks on the lay reformer increased: he was accused of making common cause with the

Anabaptists and incurred especially the hostility of King Ferdinand of Bohemia. In order not to compromise his protector, Caspar Schwenckfeld decided—in 1529—to leave his native province. He was never to see it again.

The second half of his life he spent in exile (27). At first, he found hospitality in some of the free cities of south-western Germany, mainly in Strassburg, Augsburg, and Ulm. During this time Schwenckfeld carried on his work of writing and speaking for his cause. Though living quietly with the friends who offered him shelter, he participated in colloquies and discussions to which he was invited or in which he desired to take a share (28). He incurred the growing enmity of the official preachers, Lutheran and Reformed, of various persuasions, his most formidable adversaries being Martin Bucer, Ambrosius Blaurer, and Martin Frecht (29). The retirement at Ulm was marked by the start of a new controversy, this time on the Christological question (from 1538 onwards). After having been officially condemned by the conference of prominent theologians under the leadership of Melanchthon at Schmalkalden (1530), Schwenckfeld found himself involved in a sharp and prolonged dispute, first with the Swiss theologian, Joachim von Watt (Vadianus), and later with the Lutheran dogmatist, Mathias Flacius Illyricus (30). Proscribed by the assembly of Protestant authorities (*Stände*) at Naumburg (1554) and previously threatened by the stipulations of the Interim (1548), the lay reformer led an ever more precarious and hidden existence. Frequently changing his abode—country estates, burghers' homes, monasteries—he suffered from various physical ailments towards the close of his life (31). Yet as his character remained unchanged under all these hardships and persecutions, he never ceased to call as many as would hear him by word or letter to Christ and the gospel of the renewing and regenerating Spirit, to comfort the afflicted, and to help seekers after truth (32). It was at Ulm in the house of his friends, the Streichers, that Caspar Schwenckfeld died on December 10, 1561, in the presence of several of his followers; his passing and his burial were kept strictly secret (33). He never married, 'for reasons satisfactory to himself' (34).

IV

In an age in which epistolary communication was infinitely more developed than in our own, in which correspondence would, in addition to the conveying of personal news, always tend to blossom into the most elaborate and comprehensive statement of the writer's views on whatever subject was dear to his heart or mind and into a refutation of opposed ideas—even in such an age, Schwenckfeld's correspondence is exceptional (35). True, the—partly voluntary—lack of 'official' duties and responsibilities left the reformer the best part of his time to be devoted to conceiving and writing the innumerable larger and smaller epistles which form so important an addition to his formal treatises, pamphlets, and books (36). There is comfort in the idea that this wanderer for over thirty years, who had no permanent home after he had left his own, was yet the centre of a vivid and thoroughly productive exchange of letters, which secured to him an otherwise impossible participation in the religious, intellectual, and spiritual life of his times; in the welfare and actions of his friends; and in the struggle against all that was objectionable, repulsive, or odious to him. It is in this correspondence that we come to realize that this man who was involved in so many controversies and to whom so much injustice was done was singularly free from hatred. He condemns actions, practices, and views, but he does not condemn persons, not even his bitter adversaries. In this respect the tenor of Schwenckfeld's correspondence reminds one much more of the letters of the humanists than of those of some of the great reformers. 'Suaviter in modo, fortiter in re'—how well do these two go together in the expression which the Silesian nobleman gives to his mind! 'In charitate loquamur cum fratre' (37). It is this combination of courage, fortitude, and dignity on the one hand, and true humility and clemency on the other, which distinguishes Schwenckfeld from some 'Anabaptist' leaders, as well as from Luther, Zwingli, and Calvin (38). It is this attitude which gives a ring of truth to the frequent quotations from the Scriptures and references to primitive Christianity in Schwenckfeld's writings, because we know they are not used to cover up methods and procedures at variance with the spirit of the great Example, yet they do not flow from the pen of one who is altogether alien to the world, owing to temperament or lack of education in the knowledge of its ways.

The editors of the *Corpus Schwenckfeldianorum* have done well to call attention to the unique place which will have to be accorded to the Silesian reformer as a stylist. 'The Latinity,' they say of one of his earliest letters, 'is assuredly equal if not superior to any example of the literature of correspondence in his period. Neither the Ciceronians nor the Erasmians captured him; there is no imitative quality in it, it is as fresh and original as any bit of dead language can be' (39). 'Next to Luther there is no more eminent master and former of German style than Schwenckfeld' (40). In his mother-tongue he exhibits a mastery of expression which would in itself be a subject worthy of a monograph. Though some of his favourite ideas recur like leitmotivs through the hundreds of letters he wrote, he carefully fits their expression to the recipient's status, character, and relationship to him (41). Schwenckfeld is a master of the word. He presents his arguments forcefully, logically, and consistently—yet *ad personam*. His presentation reflects the vividness, imagination, and freshness of his thought. His erudition, though unmistakable, is never thrust upon the reader. The coarseness which mars the communications of so many of his contemporaries is entirely absent from his letters. Fine metaphors and analogies betray a culture not only of the mind but also of the heart and, in addition, a very keen observation. Though there is a great deal of repetition and redundancy in his larger works, this is due, at least in part, to the isolation in which they were written and the dispersal of the addressees, cut off from each other over great distances. The lack of attention and response from some of the leaders of thought of his day forced Schwenckfeld to repeated attempts to find an adequate, more detailed, or more concise formulation or summary of his views.

V

Schwenckfeld's correspondence can be studied under various aspects: first, according to the character of his missives and their content: short communications, lengthy personal letters, exhaustive treatises; second, according to the extent of the interchange: in some cases only a few letters, in others an exchange over a period of years or even decades; third, according to the sex, occupation, and position of the addressee and his relation to the writer (42). On the whole, the number of women among the recipients is greater than that of men, particularly as concerns more intimate correspondence (43). Theologians and laymen interested in theological problems stand out among the addressees. A great variety of occupations is reflected among them. High personages, princes, electors, and bishops, as well as persons of low estate (handicraftsmen, housewives), were written to by Schwenckfeld (44). As far as concerns their relation to him, they can be divided into three categories: followers, neutrals, adversaries, the second group being the smallest. The editors of the *Corpus* have gone to great pains to investigate as fully as possible the character, history, and environment of Schwenckfeld's correspondents. In some cases it is very difficult to arrive at definite conclusions, and in a number of these we may hesitate to agree with the identifications suggested by the editors. They have—and, we think, with every right—included among the documents published, certain letters and treatises of some of the reformer's faithful friends and followers. In some instances it has not been easy to gauge the exact amount of Schwenckfeld's direct co-operation in the writing of epistles, poems, or tracts. Many of his correspondents were known to him personally, but a large number of letters are directed to persons whom he had never met in the flesh. It is significant that the general tenor of practically every personal letter of Schwenckfeld is determined by the attitude which the addressee has exhibited towards him or, better perhaps, towards his message. The editors emphasize repeatedly that the reformer rarely wrote to persons who did not approach him first (45). That, however, is true only of his personal correspondence; it is not the case when we come to public discussion on theological or political matters.

As far as the content of Schwenckfeld's letters is concerned, it seems easy, at first glance, to distinguish personal from general matters dealt with. There are some documents exclusively of the former variety, and others exclusively of the second. But in a great many the writer changes over, often more than once, from one form or content to the other. Though political discussions have their place in his letters, they interest him, as do all other questions, almost exclusively in their religious implications. Religion is the one all-pervading issue in the life and literary productions of Caspar Schwenckfeld—religion, not theology. Though a match for the dogmatist when it comes to defining theological principles and the finer points of doctrine, faith, and practice (46), Schwenckfeld will necessarily be misjudged if he is taken primarily for a scholar or a theoretician. His emphasis is eminently practical, and this interest characterizes his whole activity, his thinking, writing, and teaching (47). Though never in charge of any locally defined congregation, Schwenckfeld's concern is always pastoral. Speculation as such has no interest for him, though we find him over periods of time absorbed in the discussion of vital theological problems and busy studying and sifting, examining and verifying, theological material for this purpose. Though it is true that the Silesian reformer is much more prone to react to the statements and challenges of other theologians than spontaneously to suggest and promote any theologumenon, it is not difficult to prove that this fact is not due—as some have thought (48)—to any lack of theological (or even religious) originality, but that it is only the consequence of this primary concern with the practical promotion of what was for him the cause of Christ. If it would not appear too far-fetched, it would be easy to draw a parallel with the great religious leader of Asia, Gautama Buddha, who expressed his intention of concentrating in his teaching solely on what pertains to salvation. Schwenckfeld, irenic by nature and conviction, was bent on the practical purpose and aim of edification—'only the truth that edifies is truth for me', he might have said with Søren Kierkegaard. It seems paradoxical that one of the greatest strategists of soul-winning between St. Francis and John Wesley should have indulged, with so much apparent gusto, in controversies (49) over the most intimate and subtle theological issues, as in the biblical, sacramental, Christological, and ecclesiological disputes he carried on with Roman, Lutheran, Zwinglian, and Anabaptist dogmatists. I think it is characteristic of Schwenckfeld that —though, as we should always remember, he was a layman—he studied the Greek as well as the Hebrew language, apparently with the double purpose of enabling himself to ascertain the exact meaning of a scriptural passage or a theological definition and to check and verify interpretations suggested by others. He has been accused of being quarrelsome and easily provoked, and the numerous controversies and many partings in his life are interpreted as instances of this disposition. Yet in comparing the style and tone in which these discussions were carried on by Schwenckfeld on the one hand and Luther, Melanchthon, Bucer, Vadianus, Frecht, and especially Flacius Illyricus, on the other (50), we cannot agree with this contention. The noble layman consistently refrains from using the vile and coarse language in which even theologians of that era were accustomed to express their disapproval and contempt of opinions and teachings other than their own; he goes, in each case, to great lengths to ascertain the intention and the meaning of the opinion of his adversaries, to whom he attributes good faith until given proof of the contrary (51). Caspar Schwenckfeld's letters are either hortatory or expository or a combination of both. He never tires of exhorting his correspondents to read, meditate, and pray. Study of the Scriptures and the writings of great Christians (52) must be combined with reflection upon one's own and the Master's experiences and with continued communion with the Divine.

Schwenckfeld considers meditation as a first and indispensable step in the search for truth (53). He practised it consistently and never tired of recommending it to his correspondents. Prayer and study he deems of central importance. We have, inserted in his larger works, wonderful specimens of prayer. Sometimes he interrupts the train of thought in his letters with prayers; many of them begin and end with one. In one of his most beautiful epistles ('On the Edification of Conscience') (54) he gives detailed advice as to how prayer should be said in the morning and at night. Schwenckfeld's theory of prayer (55), very much in accordance with that of his friend Crautwald, has found a marvellous expression in his meditation on the Lord's Prayer (56). Here he defines prayer in faith—no one can pray except a believer—as an intense and fervent lifting of the believing heart ('ein jnnige hertzliche und begirliche erhebung des gläubigen gemüts in gott') (57), as the devout and vivid conversation of man with God and Christ. It must be a prayer in the spirit and come most truly from the heart (58). Many words, frequently repeated, will not do. Though we indeed have to speak in words, they should never be formulated without inner contemplation. The lifting up of our eyes and the folding of our hands may, in case of great bodily weakness, take the place of the spoken word (59). To pray is to judge ourselves with a repentant heart, in tears and on our knees (60); to knock on God's door means to insist and persist in prayer and supplication, but never defiantly and petulantly (61). In a special 'Christian Missive on Prayer' (62) Caspar enumerates four types of prayer—confessional, supplicatory, intercessory and thanksgiving—and then proceeds to list twelve essential elements of true Christian prayer (63): (i) preparation, consisting in abstaining from all injustice, forgiveness, charity, and right disposition of the heart; (ii) understanding that God wants us to turn to him, realizing the example Christ and his apostles gave us; (iii) being mindful of God's promise to hear us and of his conditions for it, and, furthermore (iv), of the necessity of Christ's mediation; (v) knowing the difference between praying for temporal and praying for eternal blessings; (vi) and realising the indispensability of genuine faith; moreover, to be aware (vii) that it is to God, not to other powers, that we should pray, and (viii) that it should be done in humility, and (ix) persistently, and (x) with true comprehension by the mind. The eleventh element is identical with the fourth, and the twelfth concerns the right expectation and anticipation of God's answer to our prayer.

Of his habits of study we can form some notion on the basis of frequent scattered remarks in his letters: how he dictated and was read to by his amanuensis, how he used books and libraries (64). Every day Schwenckfeld read reflectively four chapters of his Bible. He coins the wise maxim that a little read daily with understanding is better than much with the lack of it, or without reflection and attentiveness.

VI

Though the direct influence of Plato is hardly traceable in Schwenckfeld's studies and work, Platonic and Neoplatonic thoughts and concepts, transmitted through patristic writings, had their effect upon the formation of his views. The 'realism' (in the medieval sense of the term) on which his whole philosophy is based is unmistakable. A *supranatural order* underlies this visible reality which it precedes ontologically and epistemologically. Not only is God the ultimate and consummate reality, but in and through his Son or Word—this identification is characteristic—he sustains and preserves this world, which becomes 'real' only to the extent that it reveals through the agency of his Spirit its true, i.e., divine, nature. 'Veritas semper praecedit, imago sequitur' (65). Schwenckfeld developed these thoughts in his early, very important treatise *On the Course of the Word of God* (66). 'Cursus verbi dei vivi liber est, non haeret in visibilibus . . . sed totus in invisibilibus quiescit, quanquam per visibilia nobis adumbratur' (67). Hence: 'Hoc qui in scripturis non observat et spiritalia spiritualibus non comparat neque spiritualiter dijudicat, sed spiritalia carnalibus confundit et permiscet, totus a scopo veritatis aberrat' (68). Clearly, Schwenckfeld distinguishes a twofold nature in man: the internal and the external—'. . . homo Christianus duplex homo est, ut ita loquar, Internus et Externus'—which, significantly enough, are for him the true and the imaginary ones (69). To this anthropology corresponds his epistemology: God acts with man also in a double way, with the inner man by the inner word, with the outer by signs or symbols both to be verified on the ground of their specific evidence; in other words *verbum naturale, spiritus veritatis, internum* should be distinguished from the *verbum prolativum, literale, imaginarium, externum* (70). Against Luther and his followers Schwenckfeld holds that faith

(71), by which we grow in the knowledge of the divine word, does not come in or by the outer word or sign ('fides ex auditu') but, being of the spiritual or inner order, it comes from God, is his work, and hence cannot have its origin in the external or material: 'Ergo fides non provenit ab externo sive per externum' (72) and 'non igitur est fides ab auditu externo sed ab inspiratione Dei' (73). Abraham, that great example, believed God, not the preached word, and it was counted to him for righteousness. If the word of God were preached a thousand times to unbelieving ears, they would hear only the physical sound. 'Deus solus dat incrementum' (74). God himself speaks the living word through the Holy Spirit in our hearts (75). Outward signs can be read and understood only by those who have faith (cf. below, Sect. VIII).

The word of the Spirit and the word of the Letter correspond to the difference between God and creature, between heaven and earth (76). Here Schwenckfeld follows St. Augustine, whose famous treatise (77) apparently made a profound impression upon him. Though Caspar firmly believes that 'Gott ist nu an eusserlichen dingen nicht gelegen' (78) he stresses that he himself does not intend to draw anybody away from any outward doctrine or order. He has no contempt for whatever is done or used according to the discipline of Christ or his gospel, but all outward signs should be taken for what they are: pointing to or depicting ('fürbildung,' 'abmalung') eternal divine truths. ('So doch die Creatur nur zum Schöpfer weiset, der Buchstaben zum Geiste und das Bild zur Wahrheit' (79).) Caspar insists that the whole Gospel of John testifies to this view (esp. chap. 6) (80), and the 'sursum corda,' as well as St. Stephen's vision, are interpreted by him according to this theory (81). In other words, he does not wish to force his views and practices on anybody: 'Solches will ich allein auf mich gedeutet haben,' and 'Ich lasse einen jeden seines sinnes walten' (82). The famous "suspension" (*Stillstand*) (83) is a personal and temporal practice.

His° concept of sacraments and sacramentalia is clearly stated even in Schwenckfeld's early writings (84). It is formulated as against two extreme positions, the views of those who reject them altogether and those who do not differentiate between the outer form and the inner content. The sacraments, says Schwenckfeld, are not sacraments because they are the things of which they are the sign or image, or because they have an independent power or efficaciousness. 'Sie deuten und zaigen, sie geben aber noch brengen nichts' (85). They remind, yet they do not point to themselves but to something else. This does not mean that they are without use or significance (86). But it is God alone who must touch man in the innermost being of his self without any 'mittel irgendtains Bilds, Ceremoni, Creatur oder Sacrament' (87). God's all-powerful eternal word proceeds without other means from God's mouth, not through Scripture, outer word, sacrament, or any creature in heaven or on earth. Caspar distinguishes between 'schriftgelehrte' and 'Gottesgelehrte,' the former deriving their knowledge ('erkannt-nus') from the Scriptures, which they interpret according to human understanding ('menschlichen synn'). The latter owe their wisdom to God, Christ, and the revelation through the Holy Spirit, in the light of which they judge and examine everything (88).

The Holy Scriptures (89) are, as Caspar maintains with Ezekiel (ii, 9, 10), a book that is sealed inwardly and outwardly. Only the Key of David, which means the Spirit of Christ (90), can open it. Though apparently contradictory, these writings are altogether consistent and of one spirit (91). To understand God's words and acts we must become other than what we are by nature, with 'different ears, eyes and hearts,' reborn of God the father, and of grace which Caspar calls the mother, of divine water and spirit, ever growing in the affection and knowledge of heavenly things and the mysteries of God (92). Spiritual judgement ('geistlich Urtheil') is necessary for the interpretation of his holy word (93). 'Denn Gottes Wort kan niemand wahrhafftig hören, er sey denn aus Gotte geboren' (94). Schwenckfeld insists that the interpreter should proceed according to order; he should not tear quotations out of their context but should compare passages in order to ascertain their correct meaning (95).

Schwenckfeld, though himself a humanist by education, does not concede the necessity of employing the hermeneutics of the classics: Christ's disciples, he says, need not use Quintilian and

Cicero to find the meaning of the Scriptures; they have another master who has his own (spiritual) grammar and rhetoric (96). The Silesian does not, as some have accused him, feel contempt for the letter and its exact study, but points with satisfaction to his own knowledge of the original languages (97), a possession not too common among the leaders of the left-wing Reformation. Yet he does not like to see the Holy Spirit and his work bound to the letter ('Ich werde aber den heiligen geist und sein werck nicht dran binden') (98). The gospel is something other and more than the letter: the living power of God capable of moving the believing heart, of regenerating and purifying, of befriending and guiding man's conscience. It is not law but life ('nit ein gesetz leer, sonder ein hertz leer') (99). The 'disciples of truth' will not cleave to the outward voice of the preacher, or to the word, writing, or letter concerning Christ, but they will be led by the Spirit (100); not following their own mind ('vernunfft') or fleshly judgment (101), they watch in service, reading and listening in their hearts for the sound of the living word of God and the Spirit's operation in teaching them ('innerlich'). It was in his controversy with Flacius Illyricus that Schwenckfeld elaborated his hermeneutics most clearly and comprehensively (102).

VII

In one of the earliest extant documents of his correspondence, his letter to the nuns of the Convent of Naumburg in Silesia (103), Caspar Schwenckfeld defines a true Christian life ('eyn recht Christlich leben und wesen') as consisting in unequivocal trust in God, through the experimental knowledge of Jesus Christ, which the Holy Spirit begins to bring forth in our hearts from the hearing of the Divine Word and the sedulous pursuit thereof (104). Thus the receiving of the Word of God in the receptive heart under the illumination of the Holy Spirit is the first step; the understanding and appropriation of the work of Christ the second; and implicit confidence in Divine Providence the third in the development of a Christian, all of which is not dependent on external conditions, time, space, persons, or any other medium (105). In another of his early and important writings, *On the Way of the Word of God (De cursu verbi Dei)*, the reformer repeats: 'Unus est magister noster Christus, lapis ipse angularis, super quod aedificium domus spiritualis struitur. Ille ut dominus praecepit ministerium servi quod etiam in domini iussu sequitur. Ille docet internum hominem non per externa sed per spiritum suum' (106). Divine action precedes human reaction: 'Consequitur ergo operationem divinam precedere' (107). Faith—this is one of Schwenckfeld's most basic tenets and, incidentally, one of his major deviations from Luther's teaching—does not depend upon the hearing of the outward word: 'non igitur est fides ab auditu externo sed ab inspiratione Dei' (108). He points to Jeremiah and John the Baptist, who were sanctified in their mothers' wombs before the outward word could reach them. The natural man does not have an organ for the understanding of the divine word (109). At all times we have to start from within the heart, to build out, not vice versa: 'Dass er je in allem auff den rechten grund des hertzens sehe, von innwendig heraussen, und nicht von ausswendig hinein bauete' (110).

From Schwenckfeld's edition of the *Catechism* of his friend Valentin Crautwald, we gather in what way he expects Christian education to proceed (111). Here are to be found fine hints and keen observations on Christian nurture in agreement with Gerson's statement: 'A pueris videtur incipienda ecclesiae reformatio' (112). The sound catechist will take the little boys and the little girls separately—'sie werden sonst ihre sachen nur mit schwätzen ausrichten'—and, like a father, adapt his teaching to their level of understanding; like a mother he will see 'dass man den jüngsten bapp, den mittelsten griess, den eltern brot, und den stärkeren fleisch gebe' 113). The master has to become a student again for the student's sake. 'Welcher Meister dem Schüler und Leerjünger zugut nit wider ein Leerjünger wird, der zeucht nicht gute Leute. . . .' (114). The author is, according to his own words, well aware that it is not enough to have good wares, one has to know how to sell them (115). He is aware that dogmatics are not much appreciated by the people in these days: 'Sie lauffen lieber umb, und folgen der narrheit, die alten und jungen wissen nit was jhnen gut ist.'

There is no use in taking a mouthful out of a book and passing it on. Various means have to be used to get it across: 'bald mit vermanen, jetzund mit drewen, darnach mit grossem nutz und thewrer fürlege und kurtz allen fleiss thun,' so as to build something, even if it be little. Example means much, and so the teacher will have to qualify (116). It is a fine observation that the 'glaubenslehrer' should watch not only the ears but also the eyes of those who learn. As a good psychologist the author knows that the youthful mind is impressionable. We do not have to worry about its easily retaining and imitating pranks and mischievous tricks ('denn buberey wirt von eim jeden alter bald begriffen . . .') (117), but to implant the seed of the good and salutary necessitates great pains and patience ('Aber das gut einzubilden, auch eusserlicher gestalt, will manichen fleiss, mühe und arbeit brauchen'). To make the young heart receptive to an understanding of God's creation, the teacher should point to heaven and earth, fields, corn, day, night, winter, summer, sun, moon, stars, thunder, lightning, rain, snow, dew, wind, green grass, trees, flowers, meadows, animals, and fowls of the air, on the ground, in forests, rivers, houses, and other places . . . . (118). He should point out the nature, habits, and peculiar beauty of animals and flowers and not omit to preach the gospel as revealed in these creatures, so as to lead to meditation and questioning, as the sculptor does, who first has to hew the trunk and then proceeds to carve out the head, the body, etc. The teacher should use documents also, pictures and letters which tell of God's works, of Christ and Christian teachings. They may at first appear dead to the young, but serve to aid the older ones to recollect and to refresh what they learned. A story of the Passion is especially suitable (119). Schwenckfeld himself published a *Passional* in 1539 in which some remarkably beautiful prayers are inserted in the form of a meditation on the Passion of Jesus Christ. The reformer, like the fathers of the Pietist and Methodist revivals later, is well aware of the value of song and recitation for Christian life and worship (120). They help to activate the congregation. The Magnificat, the Benedictus, and the Te Deum are especially mentioned in this connection (121). Useless prattling and unnecessary multiplication of words are to be eschewed as not tending to edification. Here is an example

of how the catechist is expected to proceed (122). He asks: 'My
son, dear child, what is your name?' Answer: 'Niclaus.' 'What
kind of name is that?' 'A Christian name.' 'Who is Christ?'
'He is the Lord of heaven and earth in the heavenly divine
essence (*Wesen*).' 'When shall we be Christians?' 'What does it
mean to be Christians?' Other questions and answers: 'So you
really live?' 'Yes.' 'By what do you live?' 'By the life of my
soul ("auss dem leben der Seelen").' 'Who has given you the
soul?' 'Christ created it and gave it to me.' Schwenckfeld expresses the belief that, once the way has been shown to the
messenger or the 'wanderer,' it will not be necessary to point
out to him each single step (123).

In a letter to Emeranus (124), Schwenckfeld discusses the beginning, growth, and perfection of the Christian life (125). He
emphasizes that we should not expect it to come to fruition all
of a sudden ('nach einem schlage'), nor everywhere by the
same means and methods. Though he himself would not
dare to suggest a 'system' of such ways and means, he knows
that the Lord does not deal with everyone in one and the same
fashion: to some he will give much at once, to others slowly,
some he elevates to great heights rapidly, others he keeps
waiting in lowly states. In other words, God is not bound to any
order of grades or estates ('aestates') (126). In his treatment of
the love of God in our heart, Schwenckfeld envisages some
as beginners in it, some who are advanced, and some who
are perfect. The first are 'children,' the second 'youths,' the
third 'men' in Christ. In the first, love is mixed with fear; in
the next stage a richer love becomes possible; and in the third,
the soul completely loves and trusts in God, abandoning itself
('Gelassenheit') (127). The sinner is to know Christ again. In
Christ we have all fullness; he will give us rebirth in his spirit,
increase his grace, and make us perfect. There is no standing
still in the Christian life; it must progress, because not going on
would mean regression (128). There are, however, various rooms
in Christ's great house, with different kinds of workmen, and
there are different grades of pupils in the school of Christ (129).

In a letter to Cecilia von Kirchen (130), Caspar outlines the
grades through which we are expected to progress and through
which Christ works in us. First the Lord calls and invites us to

his kingdom, then he leads us into the (bondage of the) desert: suffering under the cross ('da müssen wir mit den Kindern von Israel ein weil umbher ziehen biss wir ins gelobt land kimmen. . .'). By means of this cross the Lord teaches us to praise him and exult in his love until we enter the promised land where unheard-of riches will be ours (131). Who will not remember in this context Søren Kierkegaard's profound observation that each individual life has its own Genesis and its own Exodus, its Leviticus when it turns to the Divine, its Numbers when the years begin to be counted, its Deuteronomy (132); or Luther's statement that whoever has not tasted bitterness will not enjoy sweetness, and he who does not experience misfortune does not know what happiness is? (133).

There are few truths which Caspar Schwenckfeld more frequently insists upon, in his tracts and in innumerable letters, than the necessity and the value of suffering for the development of faith and the growth of the Christian life (134). As he himself experienced sickness, disappointment, and persecution, living in exile the greater part of his life, harassed by attacks from all sides, winning friends and followers only to lose them by separation, imprisonment, and death, Schwenckfeld's thoughts are not the result of abstract speculations on St. Paul's epistles or on the sayings of great Christians before him; nor are they easy and cheap words of consolation addressed to those in danger and distress (135). To him pain, misfortune, suffering, persecution, mean that the second stage of the road to Christian perfection has been reached. They must be borne and borne patiently, even if they should last 'until the night and again until the morning' (136). If they tend to increase his faith, man experiences an anticipation of that blessed state which is the reward of perseverance, even if he should die before attaining in his growth the state of perfection ('So ist er selig, ob er gleich also stürbe, ehe er im gewechss zum vollkommen Mann werde') (137). As these experiences imply alienation from the 'world' and isolation is characteristic of the desert, they are really the opportunity for learning to abandon the world for our Lord and Redeemer, for the right inner growth ('So werdet ihr am Innerlichen Menschen krefftig wachsen') (138). In his interpretation of Ps. 102 (cf. verses 6 ff.), Caspar has given a beautiful expression to this thought (139). He who embarks on the Christian life is compared to the owl that lives in unfrequented places and in an isolation which calls forth the hostility and attacks of other creatures. Those who confess Christ have no place with the children of the world, for they turn away from what the natural man desires and clings to. They emulate their Master, who, with respect to his birth, is likened to the pelican—a strange and ungainly creature; with respect to his sufferings, to the owl— shunned and persecuted; but with respect to his resurrection, to the phoenix.

In his *Book of Consolation* (140), of which three different versions exist, Schwenckfeld interprets sickness in this light. His aim is twofold: to encourage the afflicted (141) who have as yet little faith to avail themselves of the help of Christ for the betterment of their lives, and to suggest to those further advanced in truth and righteousness how to learn better the meaning of pain and death and to accept them gladly(142). Sin is at the root of it all—'wie sich wurmb aussem holtz gebiert unnd doch das holz frisst und verzehret, also gebiert sich trübsal, sterben und traurigkeit auss der sünden' (143)—only to vanish with a turning of the soul to Christ. Yet winter must precede summer so as to make us really long for summer; for only if we have had to walk in rain, wind, cold, and snow do we appreciate the warming rays of the sun (144). The true Christian responds, thus, not only to his bodily infirmities, despair, and poverty, but also to his inner sickness, hungering, and thirsting after the righteousness of Christ, trusting in the promises made to the bride by the bridegroom (145). Then even death is no longer feared: it is somewhat like the baby chick piercing through the shell of the confining egg or the mason making a hole for the captive through which he will crawl to liberty (146). Thus death opens the way for the 'guest' of the prison to be united with his redeemer. A true Christian—a new man—does not die; the husk which conceals him is merely broken so as to make him better fitted for the eternal indwelling of God in the divine being (147). Christ is likened to the good gardener 'der alle disteln . . . und dörner auss dem verwüsten Garten unsers ellenden gemüts und sündthafftigen Hertzen bald kan ausreuten und eitel Rossmarin eitel Cynamon und Nardenkraut dafür kan einpflanzen' (148).

Christ is also the good physician. In one of his most admirable and edifying writings (149), Schwenckfeld has elaborated this idea to a very fine point. His treatment of the problem of sickness again reminds us of Kierkegaard and his powerful analysis of the sickness unto death, especially of that sickness of which the sick man is not aware (150). As the editors are careful to point out, it has had a deep influence upon later generations, particularly the Pietists, contributing, for example, to the conversion of Christian Hoburg (151). The treatise deals in four sections with the sick, the sickness, the physician, and his medicine. The sick are all mortal men without exception; the sickness is nothing but sin engendering eternal death inherited from the first Adam (152). Christ Jesus is our one true physician and saviour, who reveals to us through the Holy Spirit the damaging and pernicious character of spiritual sickness and who is ever ready and untiringly prepared to heal those who long in their hearts for his help, approach him in faith, and make use of his medicine (153). This medicine, in turn, is the word of Christ and his blood which was shed for the forgiveness of our sins, for the healing of our affliction, and for our eternal restoration (154). The recipe called for his own death, his bloodshedding and martyrdom; and no other means, balm or pill, can or should be employed (155). The pharmacy from which we secure our medicine is divine grace. We obtain it at the heavenly throne and receive it through the Holy Spirit with the *sursum corda* in our heart. The hospital, where the sick man is laid up, is this world with all its sin and defects, from the squalor and odour of which we are led out into healthiness and fresh air and separated from those doomed to die by the healer and renewer of our heart—the healed forming the assembly without blemish which we call the 'Church of Christ' (156). The prophets and apostles have borne witness to the perseverance of the healed; they make a beginning in the cure of the great physician to whom the sole access is by the prayer of faith. What, then, can health and well-being mean except holiness, righteousness, wisdom, blessedness: a new life? The rôle of the physician is the conversion of the sinner by forgiveness, justification, and sanctification; the diet prescribed to the patient (*regimen salutis*) is obedience to the physician's orders in the practice of faith and love and in perseverance in the new life (157). Thus the 'knowledge of health' (*scientia salutis*) consists in the twofold knowledge of Christ the physician and of one's self (158). There are also three kinds of sick persons: those who immediately turn to the best physician as soon as they feel sick; those who delay and put off—'*cras cras*'—until the deterioration of their state forces them to call him in, and those who do not want him, even if he comes by himself or sends his advice through another, and who drive him off. It should be added that the great physician ('ertzartzt') asks for no fee, money, or reward (159). He also always begins his cure from within, in the heart, and then turns to the outer symptoms; his purgative drives all sickness out from the very centre ('Er muss das hertz zuvor reformieren, den bösen geist inn seinem nest daheimet suchen und ausstreiben. . .') (160). There is no substitute for him; the helpers who carry his vials, balms, syrup, etc., can only point to him, describing the remedy and cure and thus assisting him. He himself is free, bound to no service or servant, because God acts in Christ according to his liberty, without any law (161).

There are also, according to Caspar Schwenckfeld, three kinds of life (162)—the description of which again reminds us of Søren Kierkegaard's analysis of the three stages on the Way of Life: a carnal and ungodly; an intelligent and honourable; and finally, a holy Christian life. The first is an animal existence, given up to the lusts of the flesh: gluttony, avarice, usury, unchastity, wrath, revenge, and injustice, without care or responsibility, as if there were no judge or judgement (163). The intelligent or rational life follows the law of nature or the law of Moses, man existing by his own power and insight according to his creaturely gifts, following the letter of the Book, bent on doing right in his outward conduct with an eye to the reward, abstaining from all crude wrongdoing out of fear of the consequences ('eine äusserliche bürgerliche gerechtigkeit') (164). Such an honourable existence will be rewarded, yet only with temporal well-being. Good works without the faith and spirit of Christ are not rewarded by eternal life. Another new holy devotion ('ain newe heilige frumbkait') implanted in the heart of man, in his soul and conscience, by Jesus Christ, is necessary, a life which human efforts alone cannot obtain (165).

The beginning of the Christian life is made through Christ by the grace of God ('die uns zuvor kumpt') which is its ground and origin. Schwenckfeld described and analysed this process in one of his earlier writings, *On the Rebirth and Origin of the Christian Man* (166). A new heart and a new spirit reveal God as a re-creator ('Widerschöpffer') who acts through the Holy Ghost, blood and water symbolizing the purification of the old creature made possible by the work of Christ (167) ('Die Widergeburt zeuget Christene leut') (168). There are two, and only two, kinds of birth: an earthly, fleshly birth and a heavenly spiritual one. The first is altogether from the flesh, the second altogether from and in the Spirit ('Dass die leipliche geburt von der die aus Gott ist gesündert wird') (169). A prophetic vision of the new creation by the initiative of God ('Du wirst nit auffsteigen durch staffell, dz ist durch Menschen werckh') (170) is seen by the Silesian reformer in the book of the prophet Zechariah (chap. i), which he interprets (171) as a figure of the new building, the rebirth and regeneration of our heart, soul, and conscience (172). His friend and close associate, Valentin Crautwald, systematized this doctrine of the New Man in a treatise which Schwenckfeld edited, discussing 'naturam veteris et novi hominis, conceptum novi, cibum ejus' (173).

VIII

A Christian, according to Schwenckfeld, is 'one anointed of the Lord', a child of God and a new man, a man reborn, who resembles his father ('der nach seinem vatter artet') and serves him in love (174). Few of the Silesian reformer's tenets are as strongly emphasized by him as his conviction that the criterion of the new man and his life is love. John xiii, 35 is the *locus classicus*. No bodily signs are necessary but only this spiritual one ('dass man die Jünger Christi nicht nach den leiblichen Zeichen sonder vil mehr nach den geistlichen zeichen und furnehmlich nach der Liebe mus richten und erkennen lernen ob sie ihrem Meister Christo nach arten') (175).

In his adaptation of Johannes Staupitz's book on the love of God (176), Schwenckfeld shows how whosoever begins to love

God will become another, a new man (177). This love cannot be taught, it has to be learned by experience ('erkannt in einer empfindlichen experientz') (178), and proceeds through various stages. The love of Christ gives rise, as Caspar has shown in one of his most beautiful letters (to Margaret Engelmann), to a veritable song of songs (179), spiritual liberty; it drives out fear and makes for joy. Moreover, Christ, the life of the loving soul ('das leben der liebhabenden seele'), is also a giver of love: 'die liebe Christi gebiert liebe in unser seelen' (180). The two commandments, to love God and one's neighbour, refer really to *one* love; we always love for God's sake. Only he who loves Christ can truly love himself and others ('Wer Christum liebet, der liebet wahrhafftig seine seele') (181). The heavenly Jerusalem, filled with divine love, despises itself; the hellish Babylon, in loving itself, will despise you. To love the world and creatures instead of God brings fear and sorrow; he who accepts this love is deceived. The inordinate love of creatures is a snare of the soul, prevents true friendship with God, turns a man's mind into a woman's. The love of riches likewise is not conducive to happiness (182). All natural love must yield to the love of Christ; all other kinds of love fade away; the love of Christ alone endures (183).

Schwenckfeld enumerates three kinds of good works in the Christian life: those towards God, those towards our neighbour, and those towards ourselves (184). Adoration and praise of our Lord and Redeemer in prayer and with patience in affliction constitute the first kind; works of love and of charity, of exhortation and encouragement extending not only to our brethren in the faith but to all who are suffering and needy, fulfil the second requirement; sincere repentance, mortification, and conformity to Christ, the breaking of every self-seeking will and self-discipline (Mark viii, 34, 35) (temperance, fasting, vigils, prayer) are good works of the third kind (185).

One of the most serious shortcomings of the Lutheran Reformation which Schwenckfeld criticized from its earliest days was its lack of discipline. He agrees with the Anabaptists, from whom otherwise important differences divide him, in emphasizing the necessity of the separation of the children of God from the children of the world (186). Schwenckfeld reiterates this demand throughout the years of his activity as a reformer. He could not envisage a Christian life without such limitations. It is necessary, he insists, even to avoid every wrong appearance, making clear at the same time that he is thinking of what is evil not in the world's sight but in God's. What fellowship has 'righteousness with unrighteousness, Christ with Belial?' (187).

Because the Silesian reformer agreed with Luther that the condition of the Roman church made an 'Absonderung' necessary, he holds it against him that his own followers did not really improve their lives (188). Schwenckfeld goes so far as to say that after discovering this he would sooner remain with the Papists if he could follow his conscience (189). He suggests following the 'middle, royal way' and not swerving to the right or to the left (190). The Papists he sees trusting in good works, the Lutherans in saving faith, one side 'going on stilts,' the other 'trying to walk on their heads.' Already in his early correspondence he justifies himself for not joining either of them (cf. letter of October 1527, to the Bishop of Breslau) (191). Later on, he reaffirms this principle (192).

He refrains from participating in the celebration of the Eucharist for himself, and recommends 'Stillstand' to his followers (cf. esp. Vol. III, Doc. LXXVIII, 'Some Reasons for Suspending the Observance of Communion'). His reasons are the lack of seriousness, of love, of discipline ('Ich syhe da kain ware andacht, kainen rechten ernst, kain besser ordnung, khain ware liebe, kain frucht des hl. gaists, kain bruederliche straff . . .') (193).

In a very revealing interpretation of Christ's parables (194), the Silesian reformer reaches the conclusion that, as long as a man is just a mediocre Christian, he can yet remain a member of the church, but he will be weeded out by the Lord of the harvest on the judgement day. Those, however, who openly live a scandalous life, Schwenckfeld desires to see excluded by the servants of God, referring to 1 Cor. v, 7 and 2 Cor. vi, 14. Though the 'foul fish,' the unbelieving and the Pharisee, intrude into the church, they are not of it. The right spirit will illuminate us as to the right judgement (195).

From the beginning of his literary activity, Schwenckfeld insisted that the Christian life is built on, inspired by, and centred in right faith (196). In his early 'Ermanung des Misbrauchs' he reminds us that as natural men we are 'children of wrath', but that by faith in Christ Jesus we become children of God and heirs of his patrimony (197). In other words, a new life must be begun before we can reach the highest peak of a living faith. This establishes in the heart of man the Kingdom of Christ and with it the joy of spiritual peace. The indication of a growth of faith can be found in a keen concern over one's shortcomings and sins (198). Moreover, such faith not only engenders in the heart of the believer sympathy for others but prompts him to ready and active deeds in their behalf. As against the extreme 'solfidians,' Schwenckfeld points out that faith will necessarily bring forth fruits ('Sintemal sie ertichtenn einen blossen glauben ane gutte werck welchs wir nicht eynen glauben sunder opinion ader wan heissen') (199).

True faith, according to Schwenckfeld (200), is not an illusion or persuasion that the Scriptures and their content are true, but a grasp of the eternal and divine truth itself ('ein ergreifung der ewigen, göttlichen Wahrheit selbst'),to which the Scriptures testify within the heart ('mit dem herzen glaubt man zur Gerechtigkeit'(Rom. x, 10)). It is a gift of God, yes; but, more than that, it indicates a participation in essence with the giver. Here the exact wording of the German text is important: 'er (der glaube) ist ein wesen im grunde mit deme der jhn schenekt' (201) ('Faith is the enjoyment of him who works it all, a drop from the divine fountain, a little ray of the eternal sun, a spark of the divine fire which is God himself'). This statement is, we may say in passing, the closest approximation to a mystical concept in Schwenckfeld's theology. Paraphrasing Heb. xi, 1, Schwenckfeld defines faith as a 'true hypothesis,' a 'conviction' ('überweisung'), through persuasion 'earum rerum quae non videntur.' These things are seen in the heart as clearly as external objects are perceived. To have faith means, persuaded by God, to be as certain in the thinking or feeling of our heart of the presence of spiritual truths as if we could see them with our eyes or possess them. The reformer refers to the Pauline concept of the 'plerophoria fidei,' which he calls 'gewissenschaft,' a newly-coined word ('Gewissen' = 'conscience,' 'Wissen-(schaft)' = 'knowledge') (202).

Schwenckfeld deplores that the nature of justifying faith is taught and contemplated rightly by so few (203). He has developed his own thought on this important locus in criticism of the theologies of Mathias Flacius Illyricus and Andreas Osiander. According to Schwenckfeld, Jesus Christ the God-Man, with his merit, grace, love, and work, is our Christian righteousness—to be believed not historically but inwardly, so that he lives, through faith, in our hearts, regenerating and ruling us. This means that God not only reputes us righteous ('für gerecht achtet') but that he makes us righteous ('gerecht macht') by his mercy and grace (204). Justification, the merciful action of God with man for the purpose of his salvation—a process by which the sinner is converted, reborn, made just, holy, and blessed—is not man's doing but the work of Christ, which he effects in man through the Holy Spirit by converting, forgiving, and imparting in his rebirth to man his own righteousness, his piety, and the fellowship ('Gemeinschaft') of his nature and being (205).

As to the origin of justifying faith, Schwenckfeld believes that it comes from above, a gift of the Holy Spirit, and that it is of divine nature and essence, transforming man, purifying the heart, uniting us with God, and causing us to act effectively by love. Hence he opposes the view that it results from ('outward' hearing of) the Scriptures or from human reasoning or per- suasion or from preaching. Such faith consists of human wisdom and does not come from the power of God; it lacks experience and feeling ('ist on erfarung und one geistliche entpfindlichkeit des hertzens'), and leaves the old Adam unchanged (206).

Schwenckfeld agrees with Osiander that we should believe not only in 'imputativam justitiam extra nos,' an external righteousness imputed to us on the basis of Christ's obedience, but 'in veram et essentialem Dei justitiam,' that is, that we need to have God's essential righteousness in us if we desire eternal life (207). He also rightly warns us against the assump- tion that we shall please God by merely having faith in Christ, yet never advancing in devotion or sanctification. The 'fruits' or their absence will tell. Opposing Osiander's limitation of Christ's redeeming and justifying work to his divinity, Schwenck- feld emphasizes his humanity (208). Moreover, he holds, as

against that theologian, that justifying faith is not conditioned by time and space; for the redeeming work takes place
outside these limitations ('das das Lamp von anfang der Wellt
sey gedöttet (nemlich dem glauben)') (209), not as a historical
event but as ever present to us in faith.

As against the Lutherans' doctrine (Justus Jonas) which
denies that God dwells *essentialiter* ('wesentlich') in the believing
heart and which assumes that he is there only *effective* (by the
power and energy of the Holy Spirit), Caspar insists that he is
present *substantialiter* (210). He also objects to their doubt (Nik.
Amsdorff) whether man here on earth will ever be just and
holy, pretending as they do that God will declare them, sinners
and unjust as they are, righteous on the basis of Christ's suffering and death. Finally, a third opinion which he rejects is
Flacius Illyricus' identification of righteousness with obedience
to a new version of the Mosaic law expressed in the suggestion,
blasphemous according to Schwenckfeld, that Christ, after
fulfilling the Pharisaic righteousness, would give it free
('schenken') to those who believe in him (211). The Silesian
vigorously denies the idea that to justify means to declare a
'crook' ('bub in der hawt') righteous (212). Regeneration is
regarded as a consequence of, and not a contributing factor to,
justification by faith. But justification means the change of the
old into a new man.

In a short but important treatise Caspar refutes the thesis of
Melanchthon that justification means forgiveness of sin (213).
'Christus in nobis habitans per fidem est justitia nostra,' says
St. Paul (Eph. iii, 17). We are reborn and have to accept in
faith the Holy Ghost conveyed to us by the Passion of our Lord,
which will renew us so that we live in the fear of the Lord (214).
No-one can be justified who has not become a new man through
Christ. Hence we have to examine ourselves daily as to our progress ('wieviel wir durch ihn frommer werden'). After Melanchthon had issued at Nürnberg his *Scriptum de justificatione*,
which criticized Schwenckfeld's teachings on this point, the
latter wrote a Second Apology (1555) (215) re-emphasizing
that to justify means to declare righteous, to renew, to give a
new heart and spirit, and reiterating his protest against a purely
historical faith in the work of a Christus 'extra nos' and the

limitation of his redemption to his divine nature. Finally, Schwenckfeld in a discussion with Johann Agricola (216) insists that it is the love of God—'activa enim est et energetica caritas Dei'—which justifies through faith, causing in turn our love for him, a love which is a fruit of the justifying love of God (217). His opponent, however, holds that love is not the 'causa efficiens' but the 'sequens fructus' of justification, thus failing to distinguish between the love of God and our response ('a nostra vicissitudinaria caritate').

Scripture, as well as experience, tells man that he is not absolutely free to do good (218). Even if he should be willing to rid himself of his shortcomings and sins, he cannot by himself turn his heart to God ('es ist nichts weniger in unserer gewalt denn das hertze') (219). God will give this at will through his spirit. Schwenckfeld, great teacher and good psychologist as he is, realizes, however, that we should take heed in imparting this knowledge to the beginner in the Christian life lest he be discouraged at the start (220). Freedom, once possessed by man, was lost when Adam fell; yet Christ regained it. His spirit frees us ('Wo nu der geist ist, ist auch die freyheit') (221), our self-will is broken; we can surrender ('gelassenheit') and will the good. This freedom is also a true indication that we have the right faith. Yet Schwenckfeld sees it abused and misinterpreted as man's own achievement by some 'Schwärmer'; he confesses that to such an understanding he prefers complete denial of any freedom of the will. In this world ('yomertal') freedom can only have a beginning, until eventually the flesh and death are vanquished (222). In his later years Schwenckfeld criticized Luther for the determinism implied in his wholesale dismissal of free will, pointing to St. Paul, who states (Phil. vi, 13): 'I can do all things,' but 'through Christ who strengtheneth me' (223). The new man is, by *gratia preveniens*, capable of knowing and doing good (224).

We saw that Schwenckfeld is vitally interested in the effect which the assumption of an unlimited freedom on the one hand, and its denial on the other, must have particularly on the incipient Christian. Antinomianism and legalism are the result of the former extreme view; what is the danger of the latter? (His thought, though already present in germinal form in his earlier writings, was fully developed in answering the theologumena of Luther, Zwingli, and Calvin.) To the natural man the idea that his destiny is known and foreordained in God's providence and predestination is abhorrent, while it means comfort and hope to the advanced ('den vollkommnen Christen'), to the 'grown-up' children of God (225). The former will hold, as the followers of Epicurus did, that man is not in a position to do anything because, should he be predestined to salvation, nothing he could do would prevent it, whereas if he is not, nothing whatever would change it. So they will advocate a carefree existence, one of mere waiting, or at least they will be inclined to consider faith and confidence in their maker sufficient, without feeling obliged to strive through repentance to better their lives (226). The latter, trusting in the work of Christ and his spirit and far from dismay or despair on account of teaching on the decree of God, aware of his mercy and love, fully trust and submit to his will and his providence, thus growing in patience and understanding ('Caro sciat predestinationem ut terreatur, humilietur et ad Christum fugiat. Filii dei ut consolentur, letentur et in timore dei vivant') (227).

There is another corollary to the views on predestination which Schwenckfeld rejects: the Zwinglian thesis 'quod justus non potest excidere' (228): because providence has willed a man to faith and he is justified without works, he will not be able to lapse. The Silesian points to the false fleshly sense of security and arrogance which might arise from such a conviction, particularly if the reference of the elect were to the ecclesiastical party in question (229). But one gift of grace does not make a Christian—'eben so wenig ain heller tag den sommer macht'— nay, even a just and faithful man may lapse. There are 'abortive' fruits that fall before the final ripening; growth in Christian life is a slow and painful process. Salvation is dependent not only on providence but on constancy and perseverance ('ausstheilung mit empfintlichkeit') in our hearts, in and through Christ in whom we are re-created to good works. This 'perseverantia et obsignatio' by the Holy Spirit alone is the sign that nothing can separate us from the love of God (230). And Schwenckfeld quotes Augustine: 'Si non es predestinatus, fac ut predestineris.' Again the old and the new man must be dis-

167

tinguished: in so far as we are born anew from God, we do not and cannot sin; in so far as we are still fleshly, we shall still sin frequently. And the Lord who gives faith, righteousness, grace, and the spirit can take them away, and has frequently done so, as Schwenckfeld proves by a number of scriptural quotations (231). It is essential to distinguish two aspects of this great article of our faith: the eternal *predestinatio* before God, hidden in his inscrutable will, and the revealed will of God calling us in the redemptive work of Christ through his Holy Spirit to his Kingdom ('occulta et revelata voluntas Dei'). God's knowledge and our knowledge ought not to be confounded (232). Is it God himself, as some—Schwenckfeld singles out Peter Martyr Vermigli (233)—seem to infer, who works sin in man ('quod Deus etiam ad peccatum concurrat')? (234). Not he who has numbered the hairs of each head and keeps all and everyone in his care and watchfulness ('duplex presentia Dei potentia et gratia'), but the devil, is the cause and the father of evil (235). Confusion has arisen because *malum* may mean not only 'sin' or 'wickedness' but also 'misery,' 'misfortune,' 'hunger,' and 'war' (236)—forms of God's punishment for the sin of man.

When it comes to describing the final aim and goal of a Christian life (237), Caspar Schwenckfeld, pointing to the Johannine concept (1 John iii, 2), is not entirely averse to calling it 'deification' (*Gottwerdung*), provided we are ever mindful that Christ takes precedence in all perfection and that it is from him as head that this glory reaches us: 'per caput in membra corporis sui.' He anticipates strong objections from all those who abhor the pagan idea of apotheosis and hold that it is impossible for us ever to become like God ('er sey unmöglich das ,Gott werden'). Schwenckfeld agrees in condemning the proponents of apotheosis who leave out Christ. With them, he asserts, Christ is forgotten ('so entfallt ihnen Christus gantz und gar') and so is the testimony of the Scriptures that we should become conformed to Christ. He cautions a friend, therefore, because of this danger, to confine the term 'apotheosis' to Christ, we ourselves not being Christ, but only 'filii adoptionis' while he is 'filius naturalis' (238). In this context we should remember Schwenckfeld's warning that it is just a drop ('ein tröpfflin') out of the divine fountain, not the whole fountain—

just a ray of the sun's nature and essence, not the divine fire
itself—which is ours (239). God is not identical with his gifts,
as Schwenckfeld insists against Flacius. But the Holy Spirit and
its effects also cannot be separated from their source, just as we
cannot separate the carpenter from the house he builds. There
is no identification of creator and creature so far as the Silesian
reformer is concerned. Schwenckfeld is not a pantheist.

IX

To sum up: the memory of Caspar Schwenckfeld will live cn
in the Christian church as that of a true pupil and teacher in the
school of Christ. Others have surpassed him as thinkers and
theologians and not a few as leaders and organizers of Christian
group-life, but not many in saintliness of character, in love
for Jesus Christ, and in zeal for the cause of the gospel. More of
the rich heritage of the past lived on in Schwenckfeld's thought
and attitude than he himself was aware. Of paramount importance in his life and thought was his experience of the living
Christ. Though deeply influenced by the Pauline interpretation
of Christ, he belongs to the Johannine type of Christian
piety. He learned more from St. Augustine than from any other
of the Fathers. In reading Schwenckfeld's treatises and letters,
we are reminded of the great masters of devotion of the Middle
Ages: Bernard, Hugo of St. Victor, Bonaventura, whom he
resembles in temperament and in the character of his spirituality.
The Silesian knight turned reformer, but he was of the humanist
not the radical party. He belongs with the leaders of the Christian
Renaissance—Groote, his beloved à Kempis, Gerson. The
development of his theological thought was, of course, profoundly influenced by Luther, though in its result it resembles
rather the Zwinglian interpretation. In many respects Schwenckfeld, the most 'Catholic' among the Continental reformers of
the sixteenth century, might be called a Protestant Francis de
Sales. There are also resemblances to Jeremy Taylor, the great
Anglican divine. As we learn more of the real origin of pietism,
we shall be better prepared to assess the contribution of this
Silesian advocate of the middle way. The ecumenical move-

ment will remember him as the uncompromising critic of the church of his day, the antagonist of a barren orthodoxy of the Flacian type, and the opponent of Anabaptist radicalism; as one ever mindful of the ideal of one Holy Christian Church, an ideal for which he sacrificed even the thought of founding a new Christian community. The first Epistle of John is the text which the life and work of Caspar Schwenckfeld von Ossig—teacher, preacher, martyr—interprets to us.

CHAPTER EIGHT

THE RÔLE OF RELIGION IN THE SOCIAL PHILOSOPHY OF ALEXIS DE TOCQUEVILLE (1)

The first of the duties which are at this time imposed upon those who direct our affairs, is to educate the democracy; to renovate, if possible, its religious belief.—Democracy in America.

THAT the writings of Alexis de Tocqueville (2) should be much better and much more widely known than they are to-day is the prevailing opinion among those who are acquainted with his work. Some excellent contributions have recently been added to the literature on one of the most acute and stimulating thinkers of the last century, a man whom no less a historian than Wilhelm Dilthey mentioned in one breath with Aristotle and Machiavelli. Yet these studies have dealt almost exclusively with his political philosophy. They have evaluated his inquiries into the structure and working of the two great democracies in which he was interested—France and the United States—and they have tried to familiarize us with the fascinating personality of the man and his career (3). But there are many aspects of de Tocqueville's life and thought which still lack adequate treatment; the role of friendships in his life and the ideas on religion in his writings are two of them.

It is characteristic of the man that his theoretical views and his practical attitude towards any important subject will be rightly understood and appreciated only by those who include his correspondence in their study of his thought. And not until his letters have been published in their entirety—a day unfortunately far off—will any biographer be able to portray this great man satisfactorily (4).

Let there be no mistake: de Tocqueville's personality and work are not, as some may think, of purely historical or antiquarian interest. True, his historical and analytical studies may have been superseded by more modern and more detailed research. Yet it is not only the cold classical quality of the 'standard work' which should induce the modern student—or any educated person—to familiarize himself with de Tocqueville. If he approaches his author with this expectation, the reader will find to his great surprise that there is much more to be gained than acquaintance with a masterpiece of the past. Inasmuch as two great talents, often mutually exclusive, were combined in the person of this French *grand seigneur*, those of the thinker and of the scholar, the talent for observing and the talent for systematic and abstract thought, his writings—now nearly a hundred years old—are still both informing and stimulating. Granted that far-reaching historical, cultural, social and economic developments have taken place since he died, on both the continents he knew, the student of contemporary France is yet apt to find as much food for thought in him as is the observer of things American. We know that although many changes occur in the lives of nations, certain attitudes and characteristics remain; and an examination of de Tocqueville's observations offers startling proof of this contention.

The 'modern Montesquieu,' however, was not only interested in informing his reader; he wanted to instruct and enlighten him. De Tocqueville was conscious and proud of the 'principles' which he knew underlay his philosophy of life and society. The ability to formulate them marks him off from his great fellow-historians to whom narration was the historian's whole task. In this he resembles Leopold von Ranke and Jacob Burckhardt. Yet there is a profound difference between these fathers of historical study and the great analyst of the French revolution. The comparison with Burckhardt's *Meditations on History* offers a particularly interesting illustration of the wide gap separating the sceptical pessimism of the Swiss and the Frenchman's indestructible faith.

Then again his insistence on 'principles' seems to place de Tocqueville nearer to those liberal historians of the middle of the century whose ethical impulse and zeal at times rivalled their endeavour to study and portray the past and link it to the present. But here again the difference cannot be overlooked. It is not his 'aristocratic' background and his emotional attachment to times and things he knew to be irrevocably gone which set de Tocqueville apart from the group of French, English and German 'liberal historians.' No, there is something more fundamental. The latter were, as we have said, dominated by moral considerations. Most of them were not inclined to base these on religious premises. As a matter of fact, they were cool, even antagonistic, to religion. De Tocqueville's outlook on life, on the other hand, was—as he himself repeatedly insisted— most decidedly and firmly rooted in religious conviction and religious faith. 'Liberty cannot be established without morality and morality without faith' (5). And the context makes it plain that only a religious faith can serve that purpose.

Here we have a problem, one which would not only baffle the superficial modern newspaper reader to whom religious convictions and a 'liberal' attitude seem to be irreconcilable alternatives, but one which intrigued de Tocqueville himself. In a letter (July 24, 1836), written to one of his friends, he says: 'What has always most struck me in my country, especially of late years, has been to see ranged on one side the men who value morality, religion and order, and on the other those who love liberty and legal equality. To me this is as extraordinary as it is deplorable; for I am convinced that all things which we thus separate are indissolubly united in the eyes of God. They are all *sacred*, if I may use the expression; men can only be great and happy when they are combined' (6). This combination was the great Frenchman's ideal all through his life. He gave it much thought and was anxious to defend it against all dissent among friends and foes.

He frequently took issue with those who objected to the inclusion of traditional religious concepts in the reconstruction of society and against those who stood more or less unreservedly for the restitution of the *status quo ante* of society in social, economic and religious respects.

De Tocqueville's biographers could not help casting some light on his religious development. Here again we hope more insight will come from a more generous publication of docu-

ments. We do not agree with a recent writer (7) who quotes
statements from his early correspondence to show that in his
youth the great scholar had lost faith in the Catholic religion in
which he was reared in accordance with the traditions of his
family, and had embraced scepticism. There is every indication
that he never did lose faith, that he could not conceive of a life
worth the name without the integrating power of religion or of
a society that could function well without it. Christianity was
for him not only the inherited but also the most adequate form
of religion, and Catholicism the most adequate form of
Christianity. This identification, however, never kept de Tocqueville from a willingness to study other expressions of the
Christian religion. The author of *L'ancien régime* and *Democracy in America* died as he had lived, a practising Roman
Catholic.

In his *chef-d'œuvre* on the most momentous event in the
modern history of his country, de Tocqueville asks why it was
that the French revolution seemed hostile to religion, and
whether all revolution and progress would necessarily be so.
The analysis of the pre-revolutionary history of France, in
which he attempts to answer this question, showed that the
French revolution differed from all other 'partial' ones in
being 'total,' as we would say.

The author examines the anti-religious attitudes of the
'*beaux esprits*' who prepared the way for things to come, but is at
pains to point out that the revolution which he sees as a 'kind
of religion' itself is not hostile to religion, but only to the political
power of the church. The French revolution is, in the words of
its great historian, a social and political revolution, and not a
religious one. Because the pre-revolutionary church was based
on tradition, authority, and hierarchical order, and because it
was opposed to '*la pensée libre*,' it was attacked—an attack of
which de Tocqueville does not approve.

He enumerates in detail the measures which the Restoration
in France took to make good the harm done to the church in
the revolutionary days (8). Yet he saw clearly that increased
respect for religion does not necessarily mean an increase in
religious life. It was painful to de Tocqueville to think that in
his country men who value morality, religion and order should

be ranged on one side, and those who love liberty and legal equality on the other (9). The example of America convinced him that it does not have to be so. Only through unfortunate circumstances, writes de Tocqueville, has religion been for a time entangled with institutions assailed by democracy, and forced to reject the equality which it loves and to curse as foe that cause of liberty whose efforts it might 'hallow' by its alliance (10).

He is interested in the comparison of the nature of religious and political emotions. Both are universal and 'aim at a certain perfection of the human race.' Political freedom, he thinks, is on the whole apt to increase religious feeling (11). They both help each other. If political liberty has at times had a beneficent and at others a damaging influence upon religion, it is because of the condition or state in which religion happened to find itself at the time. 'If religious excitement be in its decline, and political excitement just beginning, the latter passion will extinguish the former' (12).

It is interesting to note that Jacob Burckhardt in his meditations on history (conceived at approximately the same time) tries to formulate some general rules as to the relation of religion and socio-political forces. The Frenchman is certain that no one form of government is necessarily, as such, hostile to religion; democracy can definitely be an advantageous environment (13). With his deep-rooted conviction that contemporary society is in process of transformation and that the transition is from an aristocratic to a democratic world, de Tocqueville realizes that a tremendous task lies ahead for those who feel that the latter will have to rest on definite principles. According to his own words, it is his dream to 'reconcile modern society to the Church' (14).

Should religion change? De Tocqueville, who was hoping for the 'new liberality,' did not like the idea of 'progressive Catholicism.' He found it and its doctrines 'detestable' (15). In a revealing passage in one of his letters he states his opinion: 'A religion must be absolutely true or false. How can it make progress?' But he conceded that there may be progress in its application, if not in its dogma. A recent commentator, Schapiro, rightly reminds us of the fact that there existed in

France a third attitude besides traditional Catholicism and Voltairianism, Jansenism, which he interprets as a Puritan attitude, creating a pattern of liberalism different from that of 'philosophy' and revolutionary inspiration. However, I should not like to characterize de Tocqueville's religious attitude, as Schapiro does unreservedly, as 'Jansenist,' because it is the application and not the dogma which he sees change with the times. And I further disagree with the statement that de Tocqueville's reverence for religion was really reverence for the moral nature of man (16). His explicit words contradict such an identification.

The best insight into the views of the author of *L'ancien régime* is to be gleaned from his unusually revealing correspondence with Comte de Gobineau, the well-known propounder of the race theory. To re-read these letters, written nearly a century ago, in the light of contemporary events is immensely rewarding. The keen analyst of society was well aware of the dangerous implications and consequences of his friend's views. And he does not hesitate to risk breaking his friendship rather than accede to opinions which were diametrically opposed to his principles. 'Il y a un monde intellectuel entre votre doctrine et la mienne' (17). *Magnus amicus Plato, magis amica veritas.* De Tocqueville understood that there existed between him and his diplomatist friend not only a difference of opinion as to the best form of constitution and government, and in their evaluation of the primary moving forces in history, but that their views on the nature of man and his destiny were definitely irreconcilable. It would be superficial to say that the issue was an ethical one, or that a difference of temperament might be held responsible for the optimism of the one and the pessimism of the other.

In his letters, which resemble rather a systematic treatise than a private expression of opinion, de Tocqueville bases his argument on broad historical considerations. He is not satisfied with summarizing the different moral codes of the Christian and pre-Christian world. He follows in detail the development of Christian ethics and its influence upon public and private morality, in order to show that to dispense with their achievements and their inspiration would mean a return to the anarchy, violence and tyranny which, though not abolished, were at least checked by Christian ideology. 'The conditions of men are more equal in Christian countries at the present day than they have been at any previous time, or in any part of the world,' he states in the Introduction to his great work on Democracy in the New World (18).

De Tocqueville recognizes the idea of the equality of races, or in Christian terminology of the brotherhood of man, in all its importance, and insists that Gobineau's twofold assumption of the static character and inequality of races is both wrong and dangerous. He shows insight when he suggests that his friend would do well to defend himself against the charge of materialism, to which his theory of the determining nature of blood lays him open (19). De Tocqueville would not deny that the different racial groups comprising mankind show characteristic tendencies and aptitudes, but he protests vigorously against considering them unalterable. Not only do these groups undergo profound changes owing to the initiative of great leaders, ideas and movements, but they transform themselves by mixing with others. De Tocqueville readily admits diversities of race, as he makes clear in his comments on Flourens' book on Buffon (20), but he believes with these two authors that man is originally of one species and that variations are due to three factors, climate, nourishment, and mode of life (21). The friend of democracy knew that he had to defend liberty and man's freedom of choice and self-determination against the determinism, materialism and pessimism he sensed in the work of his correspondent. His verdict on this work—and it is Gobineau's *magnum opus* he has in mind—is that it tries to prove that man simply follows his temperament, and has almost no power to shape it by his will, as an opiate given to a sick person automatically stops his blood flow. De Tocqueville feels very strongly on this point; he does not hesitate to confess that Gobineau's ideas are actually repulsive to him. He sees a deep gap separating their views. No mediation seems of any avail here.

Apparently his frank and straightforward criticism hurt Gobineau so much that his friend had to comfort him and to exonerate him explicitly from the accusation of hypocrisy which Gobineau read in de Tocqueville's letters. Could Gobineau call himself a Christian? That was the question. The difficulty of reconciling his theories of deterministic materialism with the letter or even the spirit of Christianity could not, according to de Tocqueville, have escaped his friend. The letter of the Mosaic account testifies to the unity of mankind, and the spirit of Christianity extends it beyond the particularistic interpretation of Judaism (22). The Christian religion has tried, he says, to make all men brothers and equals. It is impossible to reconcile with this ideal a view according to which victor and vanquished, master and slave, are born as such of a common, distant Father in Heaven. Significantly enough de Tocqueville invokes the consensus of Christian teachers against those who concur with Gobineau's interpretation, the preachers in the South of the United States (23). He will take the word of his friend when the latter claims the title of an 'absolutely convinced' Christian. But he confesses to preferring those who are pagans of clean conduct, of a clean soul and pure hands, to the little minds capable of all kinds of low actions and violence while talking devoutly of their saintly religion (24).

Religious attitudes and decisions always imply political orientation and decision. De Tocqueville does not hesitate to point out this connection in a beautifully concise and poignant letter to Gobineau, which must be read in the light of the events in France when it was written (25). The dictatorship of Louis Napoleon had been established. The admirer of force and compulsion approved of it; it seemed to him in harmony with his ideas on predestined inequality. De Tocqueville is saddened at seeing his friend, by temperament essentially a '*frondeur*,' now 'satisfied with men and things.' The liberty of the preceding era gone, Gobineau prefers to have none; fear of the despotism of the party line-up, where de Tocqueville still sees a chance of defending personal dignity and independence by the spoken and printed word, induces him to approve of oppression of *one* kind by one individual at a time (26). '*De gustibus*,' says de Tocqueville, '*non est disputandum.*'

But it is not merely a question of taste to him. We belong to diametrically opposed worlds, he writes to Gobineau. There is no hope of the one convincing the other (27). The difference between the two men in their ideas of God and man, in their theology and anthropology, is too profound. Whereas the one

178

would regard his contemporaries as very degenerate and badly educated children for whom spectacles, noise, and uniforms are good enough, the other is inclined to regard this very lack of education as the first cause of their misery and weakness. He is convinced that a better education would correct the short-comings produced by the bad one. An adroit appeal to their natural honesty and to their common sense, he feels, could still have an effect. Therefore he wants to treat them as men (28). 'J'aime les hommes,' says de Tocqueville (29). If he cannot admire some of them, as it happens, he loves to pick out the good sentiments which are mixed in with the average and the bad, watching out for some small white points in the otherwise black picture.

Here is all the difference between the two *Weltanschauungen*. Gobineau, in the words of his friend, has a profound contempt for the human species, which he deems not only fallen, but incapable of ever rising again (30). De Tocqueville suggests that this attitude may be due to his nature, or might be a result of the painful struggles of his youth. At any rate, he sees the political consequences of such an attitude clearly and distinctly, irreconcilable for him with Christian principles; only a regimen of the sword fits the situation. De Tocqueville protests against this view; human societies, like individuals, he retorts, have no significance except as they use their freedom (31). Admitting that freedom is more difficult to establish and keep in demo-cracies than it had been in the preceding aristocratic societies, he feels inclined to pray to the Deity that he might never be tempted to despair of the possibility of preserving this freedom (32). Gobineau could not object to his having more confidence in divine goodness and justice than in his friend. With caustic humour de Tocqueville speaks of himself as an invalid whose doctor diagnoses a mortal illness, and adds that because it is due to the patient's constitution, there is absolutely no hope of recovery. He feels that in such a case, though tempted to beat the merciless fellow up, he could do nothing but sit back await-ing the end, or indulge as much as possible before the end comes. Yet unfortunately doctors may be wrong at times, and not a few patients have been unnecessarily frightened and discouraged by such a prediction (33).

The dominating role of the idea of liberty in the political and social thinking of Alexis de Tocqueville has been generally recognized and adequately emphasized in older and more recent studies of his views. The reason that comparatively slight attention has been paid to the religious foundation of this idea in his thought, is very possibly the concern of some of his modern followers lest a set of ideas they consider a remnant of a past era, *une partie honteuse*, should deter the 'modern' mind from accepting him as a teacher of our age. Yet it may prove that because he felt the need of anchoring his central political conception on ultimate principles of a religious character, de Tocqueville has been more than a century ahead of contemporary advocates of liberty. Far from deducing these fundamentals from any preconceived or inherited dogma, the Frenchman, rightly famous for his keen observation and desire for information, arrived by the empirical method, by the study of a number of contemporary societies—French, American, English, German, and Italian—at the conclusion this paper has tried to analyse.

Because of the influence de Tocqueville's study of conditions in American democracy had upon the formation of his systematic views, a word must be added concerning its significance in an examination of the role of religion in his thought. Not only the *chef-d'œuvre* in which he summarized his research and deliberations on life in the United States, but also the material on which it is based and which acute scholarship has recently made available, gives us most valuable information. Among the aspects of American culture on which the young de Tocqueville was eager to gather information were religious conditions. Frequent conversations on this topic are recorded. In a most interesting and exquisitely formulated essay-letter we find a summary of his observations on religion in America (34). The religious state of the people of the United States is, he says, the 'most curious thing to examine there.' The young visitor was impressed by the part religion played in the New World. His critical mind drew parallels. 'Up to the present I don't see a trace of what we generally consider faiths, such as customs, ancient traditions, and the power of memories' (35).

He soon realized the importance of a plurality of religions.

Catholics and Protestants differ. American Catholicism interested de Tocqueville because it was his own, and also his
country's predominating faith; and besides, with the principles
for which it stands, it was the touchstone for the working of
democracy. He is aware of the prodigious growth of the
Catholics. 'New England, the basin of the Mississippi, begin to
be filled with them' (36).

With regard to Catholicism and its effect upon the conditions
and life in the United States, he offers two significant observations. Negatively, he emphatically denies the thesis of the incom-
patibility of Catholicism and democracy; and positively, he
asserts that among the various Christian denominations Catholicism is one of the most favourable to equality of conditions
(37). He points out that its religious community consists of only
two strata, priests and laymen. All the latter are equal as
regards doctrine: wise and ignorant, man of genius and vulgar
crowd; as regards worship: rich and needy; as regards authorities: strong and weak. Catholicism resolves all distinctions of
society at the foot of the same altar, as they are resolved in the
sight of God (38). This statement is concerned with principles;
the second is an empirical observation. The amalgamation of
ecclesiastical and political power which had occurred in the
Catholic countries of the Old World frequently led to an
alliance between Catholicism and aristocracy (39). Yet with the
separation between church and state, as in the United States,
one would find 'no class of men more naturally disposed than
the Catholics to transfer the doctrine of the equality of conditions into the political world' (40). In other words, it is his
conviction that the American Catholics, if not 'forcibly led' by
the nature of their religion, are at least favourably inclined to
adopt republican and democratic principles (41). Their clergy
are not opposed to this trend, dividing the intellectual world
into two parts, that of doctrine, which they adhere to without
discussion, and that of politics, which 'the Deity has left open
to free inquiry' (42).

The Catholic people of the United States are 'poor but full of
zeal,' and their priests, de Tocqueville finds, are more thoroughly
devoted to their religious duties than the Protestant ministers,
whom he calls 'business men of religion' (43). On the other

hand, he mercilessly points to the danger he sees in the paradoxical situation of an authoritarian establishment in a democratic community. Because of their significance we quote his
observations on this point in full. 'Above them'—the Protestants, forming the basis of the population in the States—'are a
handful of Catholics, taking advantage of the tolerance of their
former adversaries, but still at bottom as intolerant as they have
ever been, as intolerant in a word as people who believe. For
them, there is no truth except in a single point, a line on this or
that side of the point, eternal damnation. They live in the midst
of civil society, but they forbid themselves all relations with the
religious societies which surround them. I even suspect that their
dogma on the liberty of conscience is about the same as in
Europe, and I am not sure that they would not persecute if they
found themselves the strongest' (44). In other words: If they
were rich and in a majority, they might adopt another attitude
than they do now.

Protestantism, the prevailing form of Christianity in the
United States, the French visitor views with even more detachment than his own church. He studied it in New England as
well as in the Middle West, in the South, in Pennsylvania, and
in the State of New York. He is baffled by its traditionalism,
by its latitudinarianism, and by its sectarianism. The first he
criticizes severely: he misses the vitality of religious faith with
which he credits the fathers and founders of the republic. He
suspects obedience to law and custom of being stronger than
personal religious convictions. Thus he interprets church
attendance, which at first tends to impress the observer so
favourably (45); he imagines that a great depth of doubt and
indifference 'must be hidden' under the external forms. Faith
is evidently inert.

With these observations he touches upon the second point.
De Tocqueville misses the 'abstractions of dogma, the discussions especially appropriate to a religious doctrine' which
according to him is what the human spirit loves to 'plunge in'
when a belief has seized it strongly (46). What he found in
listening to Protestant sermons was morality, 'of dogma not a
word' (47). He clearly discerns that this latitudinarianism is
most pronounced in Unitarian Protestantism. Evidently he

made a point of studying Unitarianism at its sources. He himself has recorded an interesting conversation with Channing on the principles of Protestantism, especially Unitarianism, and Catholicism. His criticism is very trenchant. The sect is Christian only in name. He explains the favour it finds with so many people by the statement that the 'argumentative classes' among the Protestants, whose minds are 'cold and logical,' tend to embrace an 'entirely philosophic faith' which allows them to make almost public profession of pure Deism. Their services, according to de Tocqueville, culminate in the reading of moralistic discourses and verses on the existence of God and the immortality of the soul by Dryden or other poets. He admits, however, the otherwise dignified nature of Unitarian worship (48).

The visitor sees how Protestantism, which he calls a mixture of authority and reason, will, in the long run, be faced with a twofold attack from those two extremes. He asks himself if Deism will ever be able to satisfy the religious needs and desires of all classes of society, or whether it is not by its nature limited to the educated; 'with them it might live on, provided that the belief in the two or three great truths it teaches is sound and some sort of external cult is added, to unite men visibly in the public profession of those truths' (49). As the alternative he envisages—a strangely prophetic anticipation of pragmatism— a 'headlong thrust into the single doctrine of interest.'

It is a painful dilemma which presents itself to the searching mind of the young student of American religion, prepared to estimate the impact of Catholicism and Protestantism on the life of the people in the United States. 'The one religion has a great influence on the desires, it dominates the imagination, it inspires real and profound beliefs; but it divides the human race into blessed and damned, creates divisions on earth which should exist only in the other life, breeds intolerance and fanaticism. The other religion preaches tolerance, appeals to reason, makes its symbols of it; yet it gains no power, is an inert thing, without influence and almost without life' (50).

One aspect of American Protestantism fascinated de Tocqueville: its tolerant attitude despite its denominational divisions (51). Laudable as the absence of hatred and persecution may seem to the student of the French revolution, he is inclined to interpret 'this pretended tolerance' as nothing but 'good, round indifference' (52). The reason why Anglicans, Lutherans, Calvinists, Presbyterians, Anabaptists, Quakers and 'a hundred other Christian sects,' according to his enumeration, can get along so well is to the French observer the sad fact that religion here 'does not profoundly stir the soul' (53). Doubt must increase with the plurality of competing sects. De Tocqueville does not anticipate a long life for this type of Christianity. The foreign observer will be forgiven for marvelling at the coexistence of an apparently boundless tolerance and a 'considerable zeal' of each individual for his own religion (54). How can one have equal respect for religions whose dogmas differ? (55) How can a lively and sincere faith get on with such perfect tolerance? He wonders if there is more breadth than depth in the manifestations of religious spirit. De Tocqueville could not help feeling that there was more doubt in the mind of believers than they would be willing to voice, because of the pressure of public opinion. He suspects that the 'enlightened classes' in particular would harbour these doubts, but refrain from letting them become vocal because they consider a positive religion a moral and political institution important to preserve (56). The problem of majority control, which was to occupy so important a place in de Tocqueville's thought, thus poses itself in the religious field too.

Another question in which the visitor showed an interest from the beginning of his tour was the relation of church or churches and state. He, as well as his friend Beaumont, became convinced of the soundness of the American solution of the problem (57). Through conversations with many Americans and Canadians and through his own observations, de Tocqueville was eager to gather material for a comparative study of the relation of religious and political doctrines. He realizes the danger of generalization. Indicative is the programme of the preface to *Democracy in America*: 'Let us look to America, not in order to make a servile copy of the institutions which she has established, but to gain a clearer view of the policy which will be best for us; let us look less to find examples than instruction; let us borrow from her the principles, rather than the details, of her laws.' What is true in the New World need not necessarily work in the Old; conditions are different in Canada and in the United States. So the conclusion is reached that 'in each religious doctrine there is a political one by affinity joined to it' (58). This connection will, however, manifest itself clearly only where other factors do not intervene. More often than not, economic considerations will enter. Material interests, according to de Tocqueville's observation, have in all countries of the world worked to deflect the religious tendencies. In this respect he appears as a forerunner of Max Weber, Ernst Troeltsch, and H. R. Niebuhr, who have investigated this interrelation with so much care and success. He concedes to his American friends and hosts that Protestantism has substantially contributed and still continues to supply strength to republicanism, yet he would hesitate to state that the latter is determined by the former, for the same reason that would prevent him from concluding that because the Catholics of Canada are ardent supporters of democracy, Catholicism leads to the democratic spirit, just as it is wrong to say that it is *per se* hostile to democracy (59). These Canadian Catholics are poor and come from countries where the aristocracy is Protestant.

The ripest and most concise expression of de Tocqueville's views on religion and its function in American society is to be found in his *magnum opus* on democracy in the United States. In the historical parts he stresses the importance of the contribution of religion to the building of the early colonies, particularly in New England. He does not picture the early settlers who left the Old World because of their religious convictions as wholly absorbed by their religion; he knows that they were seeking 'with nearly equal zeal for material wealth and moral good' (60). Yet de Tocqueville would have sided with modern research, which has rediscovered the role of religion in early New England Puritanism and repudiates an exclusively political or economic explanation. In a characteristic sentence he summarizes the meaning of this great experiment of combining loyalty to religion and to liberty. 'Religion perceives that civil liberty affords a nobler exercise to the faculties of man, and that the political world is a field prepared by the Creator for the efforts of mind. Free and powerful in its own sphere, satisfied with the place reserved for it, religion never more surely establishes its empire than when it reigns in the hearts of men unsupported by aught beside its native strength. Liberty regards religion as its companion in all its battles and triumphs as the cradle of its infancy, and the divine source of its claims. It considers religion as the safeguard of morality, and morality as the best security of law, and the surest pledge of the duration of freedom' (61).

But, according to de Tocqueville, religion has not only worked at the establishment of the new republic; the alliance between politics and religion has never really been dissolved (62). The analyst of New World society traces the indirect influences which religion continues to exert upon the 'manners' and intelligence of the Americans in several concisely and circumspectly worded paragraphs, scattered through the two volumes of his book (63). Although he sees that religion is not taking a direct part in the government of society (64), it is to be regarded as 'the first of their political institutions' (65). Since it facilitates the use of freedom, it appears to all Americans 'indispensable to the maintenance of republican institutions' (66). And there is good reason for this, because 'despotism may govern without religion, but liberty cannot' (67). In other words, democracies, where the political tie is relaxed, need their moral ties strengthened. What can be done with a people, asks de Tocqueville, who are their own masters, if they be not submissive to the Deity? (68).

CHAPTER NINE

CHURCH, DENOMINATION AND SECT (1)

I

A NEW and lively interest has arisen to-day in the discussion of the nature and interrelationship of church, denomination, and sect. Why should this be? Let us consider some of the factors which cause this renewed interest. There is first the historical research of, shall we say, the last decade or even century, which has unearthed and placed at our disposal a great deal of material concerning leading personalities, movements, schools, divisions and groups in the Christian and non-Christian worlds. We know infinitely more about the teachings, forms of worship and patterns of organization of all these groups, the very existence of which was not or could not be known to previous generations of scholars. The second factor which may call for a renewed examination of this problem is a trend that has assumed growing importance since the turn of the century in the minds of the clergy and laity alike. The ecumenical movement has gained strength in a great number of non-catholic and even in some catholic bodies, and a vivid discussion in their ranks has resulted regarding the basis upon which a closer co-operation, or even some form of union, can be contemplated and achieved. The basic concept of the nature of the Christian fellowship and the institutions which represent it has been subjected to a thorough inquiry. Furthermore, and this is the third motive, the renaissance of interest in systematic or constructive theology which can be traced back to the end of the First World War, and which is not limited to any one of the Christian bodies, has very naturally led to a concentration upon the doctrine of the Church, its historical and its doctrinal implications. Inasmuch as this ecumenical movement has provided opportunities for an exchange of views and a certain amount of co-operation in joint meetings of

HISTORY OF THE CHRISTIAN RELIGION

leaders and representatives of different faiths, both trends have tended to blend and interact (2).

On different grounds from those upon which the above-mentioned developments have taken place, another line of studies has been followed during the last century, and more particularly the last half-century. The remarkable growth of social studies, especially of the discipline called *sociology*, was the result of the deep and far-reaching process of the transformation of Western society as a consequence of industrialization and urbanization. Social conditions, institutions and trends have been subjected to searching analyses by the sociologists and social philosophers of England, France, Germany and the United States. Interestingly enough, religion did not receive, until lately, the share of attention it could claim. The reasons for this I have tried to deal with in my book on the *Sociology of Religion* which appeared some years ago, and in a recently published essay on the same theme in the *Symposium on Twentieth-century Sociology* (3). More recently sociologists of religion have shown a livelier interest in the study of church, denomination and sect, and their mutual interrelationship. Yet considerable differences exist between the approach of the sociologist and that of the theologian, though it is to be hoped that, in time, they will come to know each other better and to learn from each other.

It may be expected that a historian of religion would present, in his analysis of this as of all subjects in which he is interested, a broad treatment of the non-Christian as well as Christian religious groups. If that is not done here, it may be assumed that the limitations of this essay, and not necessarily any theological considerations, prevent such a procedure. We shall concentrate our attention upon Christianity, though denominationalism and sectarianism are found in non-Christian religions as well.

II

The problem of diversity of opinion and practice is as old as Christianity, and its records go back to 1 Corinthians. Dissent occurs in all three fields of expression of religious experience, in doctrine, cult, and organization. Quite early a distinction was made between 'heresy' (αἵρεσις) and 'schism' (σχίσμα), terms originally used interchangeably, as in St. Augustine's definition: 'haeretici falsa credunt . . . schismaticos non fides diversa (facit) sed communionis disrupta societas' (*Quaest. in Matt.* xi) (4).

Cyprian, as is generally known, is the first to define more clearly the relation of the Church to schism in his fight against Novatian, Montanus and Donatus in the tract *De Unitate Ecclesiae:* 'Deus unus est, et Christus unus, et una ecclesia eius, et fides una, et spes una in solidam corporis unitatem concordiae glutino copulata. Quidquid a matrice discesserit, seorsum vivere et spirare non poterit.' The theological judgment is tinged with a moral colouring in St. Augustine's sentence against Donatus: 'Securus iudicat orbis terrarum, bonos non esse qui se dicident ab orbe terrarum. Habere autem caput Christum nemo poterit, nisi qui in eius corpore fuerit.' This unity is guaranteed by the sacraments, especially the Eucharist, the 'sacramentum unitatis,' as well as by the episcopate, as Ignatius had already indicated. With the designation of the bishop of Rome as *the* bishop the development toward a supreme episcopate was indicated which St. Thomas was later to crystallize in his definition: 'Et ideo schismatici dicuntur qui proprie sponte et intuitione se ab unitate ecclesiae separant; caput ecclesiae est ipse Christus cujus vicem in ecclesia gerit summus pontifex. Et ideo schismatici dicuntur, qui subesse renuunt summo pontifici' (II, II, 39). So we see that in the mediaeval view only three possibilities existed: the community of faithful Christians (united under Christ and his Vicar in the Church), the heretics who within it hold views at variance with the accepted standards of faith, and the schismatics who have placed themselves outside it by thought as well as act (secession). It is well known that all through the Middle Ages, especially after the eleventh century, protests were voiced against not only the 'practice' but also the basic theology (ideology) of the Church as expressed in its doctrine, forms of worship and hierarchical order. In his brilliant essay, *Ecclesia Spiritualis*, Ernst Benz has traced the history of these movements within and outside the twelfth- and thirteenth-century Church (5). The connecting link between the individual and organized dissent of the High Middle Ages and that of the Reformation is the Flemish movement known as the Christian Renaissance, to which Dr. Hyma has devoted some excellent studies (6). The Brethren of the Common Life represent this movement, which was to influence Luther as well as Calvin, and Erasmus as well as Loyola. Individual protests and group movements of this kind paved the way for the Reformers. The Great Schism followed. In the official terminology and theology of what since Trent is known as the Roman Catholic Church, no term is applied to the groups of 'schismatics' into which the 'heresies' of the sixteenth century, the followers of Zwingli, Luther, Calvin, the Anglicans, the Independents and the various so-called Anabaptist leaders and separatists had become organized. It is significant, however, that a recent Roman Catholic theologian (Otto Karrer), whose outlook is more 'ecumenical' than that of some of his brethren, was able to quote St. Augustine, Cusanus, de Lugo, and Newman as authorities for the view which Baron von Hügel formulated, that the Catholic Church is not religious mankind but 'that religious mankind is the Catholic Church.' Karrer points to the rejection by Pope Clement XI (1713) of Quesnel's opinion that grace is not to be had outside the visible Church, and quotes Pribilla's opinion according to which the invisible Church of God and his grace transcends the visible organization (7). Had not St. Augustine already envisaged 'fides conversioque cordis' as constituting the former?—God alone knows who really belongs to the true church, if not 're' then 'voto.'

Yet the Council of Trent decided that pagans and non-Catholics cannot either be saved or participate in eternal life, and Pius IX reiterated in 1854 that those who do not in some way belong to the Catholic Church cannot be saved.

We have arrived at an important juncture in our survey. The frame of reference, to use a modern phrase favoured by sociologists, the traditional trichotomous division, was no longer acknowledged by the schismatics who, though their theologies and forms of organization differed greatly, were still regarded as essentially one group. On two points these 'protestants' agree: on the criticism of and objection to the practice of the old Church, and to the more or less complete identification by Rome of the ecclesia with the visible institutional body.

Disregarding for a moment the self-interpretation and theological ideologies of the groups which in the struggle with Rome and with one another now began to crystallize into new religious communities, and viewing them from a sociological point of view, we can distinguish several types of organization. We shall enumerate three. First: *ecclesiastical bodies* such as the Lutherans, Zwinglians, Calvinists, Anglicans, which, though at variance on points of doctrine, of habits of worship and of polity, all appeal, as it were, from the empirical, i.e., corrupted, Church to the ideal of the true ecclesia, which they conceive as invisible. The reformers and their successors differ in the way in which they regard the nature of the visible body and its relation to the invisible ecclesia. The Lutheran Church has experienced considerable difficulties from the days of the founder's struggle with Carlstadt to the controversies of our own day in the German church. As Walter Köhler has convincingly shown, in his recent *Dogmengeschichte*, a dualism exists between Luther's idea of the invisible church: 'omnis structura ecclesiae est intus, coram Dei, invisibilis . . . abscondita est ecclesia, latent sancti' and the visible body organized in accordance with the exigencies of the world (8). The further paradox that the ecclesia is both visible to the eye of faith and invisible to the eyes of the unbeliever is, as we now know, not only the result of his double struggle against Roman hierarchalism and Anabaptist spiritualism, but is also rooted in the Reformers' basically paradoxical view of the Deity: at once 'Deus absconditus' *and* 'Deus revelatus.' The external ecclesia is the 'larva' within which is hidden the true congregation which can be identified by the eye of faith, and by it alone, according to the two 'notae ecclesiae' of pure teaching of the word and right administration of the sacraments (*Augustana*, VII) (9), to which were later added by some Lutheran theologians the further notae of love or charity and, significantly, that of the institution (*Anstalts-Charakter*). A crucial step in the development is indicated by the definition in the eighth chapter of the *Augustana* which acknowledges the *opus operatum* principle and in which some have seen an accommodation to Catholic institutionalism, resulting from the necessity of safeguarding the Lutheran ecclesiastical body against individualistic and spiritualistic claims. Only if this tension in the Lutheran concept of *ecclesia* is remembered can we understand the later development in the Lutheran Church which Erich Seeberg has outlined so brilliantly in his study of Gottfried Arnold (10). This development can be characterized as a continual struggle with latent spiritualism which tended, as with Pietism for example, to abandon the traditional religious and moral condemnation of the heretic and schismatic. In other words there is a radical rejection of the idea of a visible church on the one hand, and an institutionalism on the other, which identifies, in the Roman manner, with the help of the notae, the empirical institutional body with the true ecclesia.

Of all the great reformers Calvin has given the most concise expression to his interpretation of the ecclesia. In the second chapter of the fourth part of his *Institutes* (11), he contrasts the 'True' and the 'False' Church, identifying the latter with the Roman. His statement in the preceding chapter of his great book is quite definite: 'God deposited his treasure, the preaching of the gospel, with the Church in whose bosom it is God's will that His children should be collected, not only to be nourished by Her assistance and ministry but also be governed by Her maternal care.' Quite logically he continues: 'It follows that all who reject the spiritual food for their souls which is extended to them by the hands of the Church deserve to perish with hunger and want.' And, 'since they do all in their power to dissolve and break asunder the bond of unity, no one of them escapes the just punishment of this impious breach, but they all involve themselves in pestilent errors and pernicious reveries.' The double aspect of the ecclesia, invisible and visible, is Calvin's too: 'It is,' he says, '[necessary] therefore to believe of that Church which is invisible to us and known to God alone, so of this Church which is visible to us, that we are commanded to honour and to maintain communion with it'—a confession of faith, exemplary life and participation in the sacraments being the notae of the Calvinist body (12).

Though varying in their respective conceptions of the nature of the Church, these groups constitute themselves as *ecclesiastical bodies* with the claim of exclusiveness, authoritatively defined doctrines, sacraments and distinct orders. This implies, at least in the earlier phases of their history, sharply drawn distinctions, corresponding to the middle position in which these groups find themselves between the Church of Rome and the left wing of the Reformation, distinctions between (a) one's own church, including individual or collective holders of heretical views, (b) false churches, including the Roman and those regarded by Rome as schismatic bodies, (c) bands of 'heretics,' dissenters, and independents, including those of a different type of fellowship.

The Anglican Church with its insistence upon apostolic succession, a concept which owes much to the famous sermon of Richard Bancroft (1582), appears to have sensed and posited more clearly than the other reformed ecclesiastical bodies the continuity upon which this distinction could alone be logically and successfully based (13). Richard Hooker has expounded his views on the nature of the Church in the third book of his *Ecclesiastical Polity* (1593) (14), defending it against the Roman, the Presbyterian and the Anabaptist concepts. Luther, according to this eminent divine, does not mark a break in a continuous tradition: 'We hope therefore that to reform ourselves, if at any time we have done amiss, is not to sever ourselves from the Church we were before. In the Church we were and we are still.' Even heretics form a maimed part of the visible Church of God (III, No. 9). Not assemblies (in the denominational sense) but societies would he call the communities which belong to the visible body, as the societies of Rome, Corinth, or England. Of the notae 'one of the chiefest' is the ecclesiastical polity. Hooker considers it rightful that, 'touching this polity, what scripture and nature tell us should be supplemented by the discretion of the Church' (IV), not too much and not too little (V). 'It follows that sundry things may be lawfully done in the Church, so as they be not done against the Scripture, although no Scripture do command them but the Church only following the light of reason judge them to be in discretion meet' (VII, 2). (On reason: III, VIII, 4–18). 'This reason being guided by the general law of nature and the moral of Scriptures, the Church has in matters of polity, if not in doctrine, authority to make canons, laws and decrees, even as we read that in the Apostolic times it did.' (X, 7) He sums up his views: 'so far forth as the Church is the mystical body of Christ and His invisible spouse, it needeth no external polity. But as the Church is a visible society and body politic, laws of polity it cannot want.'It is interesting to note that the report of the Archbishops' Commission on Doctrine in the Church of England insists that the Christian body is not to be regarded as consisting of a single true Church or group of churches with a number of schismatic churches gathered about it, but as a whole which is in a state of division or schism (15). 'If any are in schism all are in schism' (16).

A second type of organization of Christian fellowship resulting from the Reformation can be discerned in the 'Independent' bodies in England, on the Continent, and later in the United States. Different as were their ideas on the constitution of their fellowship, nevertheless the congregational principle is one form which appears more or less recognizably in the various groups (cf. the Brownists, the Baptists and the Quakers). They agree in the triple opposition to the practice of the Roman Church and of the Reformed ecclesiastical bodies, to the identification of the ecclesia with any of these institutions, and to the notion of fellowship of the 'extremists', however closely the constitution of these groups might resemble their own. Their insistence upon their own concept of the Christian religious community as the true one is buttressed by the evidence of a purged conception of tradition, more radical than that of any of the reformed ecclesiastical bodies (that is, the early Church) but apparently less exclusive, owing to a less institutional and more spiritual notion of Christian fellowship (17). Every association of Christians was in immediate contact with Christ to receive its instruction directly from his life. 'But,' as the historian of English Nonconformity (18) has aptly remarked, 'these men, asserting that organization must be the product of life, nevertheless made organization to be the product of life only at one remove: they interposed between the spiritual relation and its working out in organization with a dogmatic assertion of what the product was to be: the resulting organization, in consequence, even taking it at its best, came to be such as would obtain *if* the inner life had made it, without being actually the inner life's own making; and witness to the Nonconformist spirit, therefore, though true as far as it went, was not actually borne.'

The Baptists and the Congregationalists did not share in the opposition to the identification of the ecclesia with any of the historic institutions and their practices (19). But they share an insistence upon the independence of the local congregation, with correspondingly less emphasis upon unity and universality (an emphasis common to the Catholic *and* Reformed bodies), basing their community, as we have seen, upon the central Calvinistic idea of the covenant. That concept afforded the possibility of a new development into an ecclesiastical body, as we find it in the so-called New England Puritan establishment, where because of the Calvinist interpretation of the ecclesia it could assume the aspect of a theocracy, such as Morrison, Perry Miller and others have vividly described in the Back Bay Colony. We find here condemnation and persecution of heretics and schismatics, both as individuals and as groups (Roger Williams, Ann Hutchison, Baptists, Quakers *et alii*). It was thought at one time by W. W. Sweet and others that this development was caused by the exigencies of the conditions under which New England Puritanism established itself.

The theology of the covenant was only one element in Congregationalism, the others being local independence and the active rôle of the laity, and the choice and appointment of ministers. It is the merit of a recent thesis of the Dutchman, de Jong, on 'The Denomination as the American Church form' (20) to have demonstrated the part which this factor making for democracy has played in the formation of modern American denominationalism. This denominationalism can be described as a blending of the Congregationalist and Rationalist concepts, the latter illustrated by Locke's famous definition of the Church as 'a voluntary society of men joining themselves together of their own accord in order to the public worship of God in such a manner as they judge acceptable to him and effectual to the salvation of their souls.' We owe to R. B. Perry an analysis of the philosophical and political implications of this marriage between Puritanism and Democracy (21).

Thus the Congregational establishment represents a special version of the ecclesiastical body. But this version is not characteristic of the denomination, which de Jong rightly regards as typical of the American scene (22). (Not exclusively so, of course, as so-called nonconformist grouping along denominational lines in England, Holland and to a lesser extent Scandinavia and Germany shows.) The reserve towards and criticism of the State which the denomination shares with the sect, and to which Calvinism tends only where its theocratic ideal is not deemed realizable, has ever remained one of the basic tenets of the Baptist denomination. Anabaptism, at least in its right wing, is committed to it most fervently. To this problem we shall return. The terms *heretic* and *schismatic* have lost some of their validity in this context. This does not mean that there was or is no exclusiveness or discrimination practised in these groups, but that where it does occur it is inspired by theological as well as by political and personal motives (alliance with the State as in Massachusetts, and the ambition of individual leaders).

Finally, history has supplied us with examples of a third type of organization of Christian fellowship, which is characterized by a threefold protest directed (*a*) against the practice of the ecclesiastical bodies, Roman as well as Reformed, and of independent communities of the denominational type, (*b*) against the identification of the ecclesia with either of the former in any fashion, and (*c*) against all individual and collective hostility or indifference anywhere towards the principles upon which its own fellowship is based. In other words, these groups are characterized by a rigid exclusiveness which distinguishes them from the Independent type, an exclusiveness which differs from that of the ecclesiastical bodies in that it is qualitative not quantitative. That is to say, this fellowship is based not only upon the sharing of a tradition of definite norms of faith, of ritual and of order, but upon criteria (discipline) in which loyalty to this principle and conduct in accordance with it is supervised and hence discipline is ensured. A definite form and order of Christian fellowship is envisaged (and its legitimacy proved by tracing it to the primitive Church) which may be more or less negatively or positively conceived, yet definitely affords the possibility of recognizing and classifying 'heretics' and 'schismatics.' We call such bodies 'sectarian', and to them alone should the term be applied.

American sectarianism offers a fruitful field for study. Though the sociologist is right in calling attention to the environmental conditions which favour this type of association, it should not be forgotten that for nearly every important type we can point out antecedents in the earlier history of Christianity. E. T. Clark, in his studies of small sects in America (23), divides the multitude of them into eschatological, charismatic, holiness, and communal groups. It is easy enough to illustrate each type with examples taken from early Christianity, the Middle Ages or the Reformation period. We find in sectarianism all kinds of constitution, varying from the rigidly hierarchical to the maximally egalitarian, and autocratic rule by a spiritual head is as frequent as thorough disapproval of all ministry in favour of spiritual 'democracy.' To the extent to which exclusive claims give way to a more relativistic recognition and tolerance of other views, practices and fellowship (though they may appear inferior in sectarian eyes), the sect assumes denominational features (Quakers, Disciples, Brethren, Christian Scientists, Swedenborgians). The condemnation of outsiders (to the 'heretic' of the ecclesiastical body corresponds the 'unbeliever' of the sect) may be based on intellectual or moral criteria (incapacity or unwillingness to see or acknowledge the truth, 'worldliness,' etc.). It expresses itself in more or less definite rules, avoidances and taboos. To these may correspond *notae gratiae*, such as glossolalia in the charismatic, 'perfect' conduct (the 'second blessing') or healing powers in the holiness sects, as well as peculiar practices of a sacramental or semi-sacramental character (kiss of peace, washing of the feet, etc.).

The foregoing analysis indicates that it is possible to distinguish three types of organization of Christian fellowship: the ecclesiastical body, the independent group or denomination, and finally, the sect. (All these notions are used purely in a descriptive sense. We have avoided the term *church* as much as possible in this classification because it implies a theological (normative) decision which at this point we are not ready to suggest.) The sociologist realizes that in reality, that is, in history including the present moment, these types are not always found in unadulterated purity. He is aware of the deep and far-reaching

developments and transformations which religious groups as
well as others undergo in the course of any length of time. Not
only are there changes from one type to another, exhausting
practically every conceivable transmutation, but there are also
types not unmixed: semi-ecclesiastical bodies, independent
bodies with ecclesiastical (Brethren) and sectarian (Disciples)
features. We submit, too, that numerical strength is not
a decisive criterion in our classification: there are large and
small ecclesiastical bodies, large and small denominations, and
large and small sects. It is our contention that this typology is
not merely a convenient system of classifying Christian bodies
which originated in the Reformation era. In other words, it is not
our purpose to describe historical developments, but rather to
define types occurring again and again in different historical
contexts.

We shall now consider the movements of the seventeenth and
eighteenth centuries in and through which new grouping
occurred, and judge whether that grouping can be said to conform to our categories. The reaction to the 'orthodoxy' of the
established bodies on the Continent, in England and the United
States (which is known as the Pietist and Methodist movement)
produced the Moravian community, an ecclesiastical body with
sectarian features, and a number of Methodist communities
which exhibit the ecclesiastical as well as the sectarian type. The
Moravians in successive transformations tended to assume
denominational aspects. The process repeats itself in the
secession of groups from the Methodist family, as in
the so-called Holiness communities among which an
extreme form of sectarianism is represented. A number
of more recent developments in the history of Christianity furnish us with new material and suggest some interesting problems. The so-called Irvingites, who seceded from the
Anglican Church in the nineteenth century, can be defined as an
ecclesiastical body with sectarian features, the same being true
of the community of the Latter Day Saints in the United States.
It will be interesting to observe if the last-named will in the
future develop into the denominational type, possibly with new
sectarian reactions, or if it will develop its sectarian traits further.

Among the denominations which are most radically opposed

to the more or less pronounced exclusiveness characteristic of the ecclesiastical and sectarian bodies, the American Unitarians (24) and Universalists, who significantly are constituted as societies, are faced with the alternative of strengthening their theological foundation or dissolving into philosophical associations or secular fellowships (25).

With the help of our categories it should not be difficult to decide how we shall classify one of the more recent American movements, Christian Science. It is neither an ecclesiastical body nor a sect, but seems to have the characteristics of a denomination. Now there may indeed be a question with regard to several of the last-mentioned groups. Ought they, one wonders, to be considered Christian? Who shall decide where the limits must be drawn? What shall be the criterion? All that the sociologist or historian can contribute is the questions: (a) How are these questions answered by the self-interpretation—or, to use the modern term, ideology—of the groups themselves? Do they affirm, however indefinitely, a sense of orientation toward the message of Christ? (b) To what extent does this norm actually regulate and determine the life and order of the group?

It was a definite step forward in the study of the structure of types of Christian fellowship when recently, in an article in *Church History* (26), Robert Friedman, reviewing the theories of Troeltsch, Johannes Kühn, and H. R. Niebuhr, suggested as an important criterion the attitude towards the Scriptures and the special emphasis placed upon any one part thereof.

Christian groups vary first as to the rôle which they assign to the Bible as the more or less exclusive norm of faith, and here again we find a division crossing the lines: ecclesiastical bodies and some sects in one group, and certain denominations and some sects in the opposing group. It would be misleading to say that, while the interpretation of the Scriptures is safeguarded by tradition in the Catholic churches, the Protestant groups can be characterized by their rejection of tradition. We have here to qualify our statements. In most ecclesiastical bodies a hermeneutic and exegetical tradition has developed, Luther's insistence upon the 'perspicuitas' of the Scriptures notwithstanding (27). According to this tradition individual exegesis, to which the denomination accords a measure of freedom, is limited. In sectarianism we find, in accordance with the leadership principle, a standardization of interpretation, in harmony with the practice of the founder. Friedman has shown in a tabulation of groups of the Reformation period that certain preferences within the Scriptures exist in ecclesiastical bodies, denominations and sects. The Synoptic gospels, with the Fourth as well, were favoured by Luther and Zwingli; the Fourth enjoys a special popularity in the Eastern Orthodox Church; while the Evangelical Anabaptists and the rationalistic bodies leaned on the first three gospels; the mystical and spiritualist congregations on the Fourth; the sects, especially the eschatologically oriented ones, concentrate on the Book of Revelation, for which Luther held no brief and which is but little used by the denominations. The rôle assigned to the Scriptures of the Old Testament varies considerably, and an investigation of their use in sectarianism would prove very fruitful (28).

III

We have, so far, examined the three types of Christian fellowship: ecclesiastical body, denomination, and sect, *in abstracto*, so to speak, taking into account merely the immanent dialectic of the development of their constitutional principles. But this development has, of course, been definitely influenced by other factors: political, cultural, economic and intellectual. Moreover, personal elements have entered: ideas and tendencies, aspirations and ambitions of leading personalities, as well as the psychological reactions of individuals and groups, parties and congregations. Let us consider the former factors first. Any religious group, once the old identity of tribal and sacred organization has disappeared, as in the case of most founded and of all world religions, finds itself in a political environment. The religious community may be narrower or wider than the State in which it finds itself in its entirety or in part. Now, our point is that the character of the relationship between the body and the State will, in its structural nature as well as in its spirit, differ according to the constitution of the group. Typologically, we submit, the orientation of an ecclesiastical body, of a denomination or of a sect will differ irrespective of historical circumstances. Actually the attitude towards the State of different Christian communities of similar type exhibits parallels. The violent struggle which exists between some ecclesiastical bodies and sects and the State has no counterpart in denominational history, not necessarily owing to a greater amount of toleration on the part of these groups, but because their principle of organization does not afford the basis for a clash between two totalitarianisms. All three types of Christian communities have suffered at the hands of the State and have sustained defeat, but they have also moulded and conquered it. While the sect is at a disadvantge in any open conflict with the State, owing to its limited size, the smallness of numbers being accidental or intentional, the ecclesiastical body will be the most prone to identify itself with the State or to carry on warfare with it with a chance of success. It is the sect which will be most radical in the criticism of civil authority, owing to its rigid or even extravagant standards.

We can trace, inversely, the influence of the body politic, State or community, upon the form in which Christian fellowship is organized. Sociologists and political theorists have a wide field for their studies here. It may suffice in this connection to refer again to de Jong's interesting attempt to characterize the denomination as the American church form, though even he admits that the danger of oversimplification has to be avoided. Characteristically, the Episcopal body hardly figures in his account.

Closely related to the first factor, the political, is the second, the ethnic. Except for the few great universal faiths, most religions in the world have been of a tribal character. The glorious beginning made with the emancipation of Christianity from Judaism came to its full fruition in the ideal of the universal ecclesia of the early concept of the *una sancta* only after certain Oriental minorities had already established themselves on a national basis (Eastern dissident churches), a procedure which was to be often repeated in the period of the Reformation (29). But this cannot stand without qualification. Thus the Anglican body holds, to quote the *Report of the*

Archbishops' Commitee on Doctrine in the Church of England, that 'the Church is supra-national, and links in fellowship the citizens of every rank in every nation, though, in its mission to each, it may rightly admit a certain recognition of distinctive national characteristics' (30). The powerful influence of the rising national consciousness in the fifteenth and sixteenth centuries is reflected in the national character of the reformed ecclesiastical bodies (Anglican, German, Scandinavian, Scottish, Dutch, etc.), to a much less extent in the denominations, and less still in sectarianism. In the United States the differentiation of ecclesiastical bodies along ethnic lines is greater than that of the denominations or even that of sects, except for certain German and Russian sects, as for example the Dunkers, the Dukhobors. Negroes are found in all three types of Christian groups and have in addition brought forth some new and exclusive sectarian groups of their own, to which Jones, St. Clair Drake, Faucet and others have devoted very illuminating studies (31).

After the official historians of Christianity had for a long time neglected to consider developments in the Christian Church in their relation to economic conditions, a reaction set in during the second half of the nineteenth century. Under the influence of Marxist teachings the relation of economics to religion was conceived in many quarters in a spirit of rigid determinism, a one-sided emphasis which scholars have only of late begun to overcome. Max Weber, Werner Sombart and Ernst Troeltsch in Germany, R. Tawney in England, W. W. Sweet and S. Kincheloe, Samuel Morrison, and Percy Miller, and now the Niebuhrs in the U.S.A., have shown that religious concepts and institutions, in turn, profoundly influence social and economic conditions by their theological concepts and ethical standards (32). Again it is needful in our examination of this interrelation to qualify these judgements with regard to the three different types of fellowship herein considered. One super-denominational movement, that of the Social Gospel, originated from social concern and sought to bring the impact of the Christian message to bear upon the social and economic order of our society.

All men, those of low as well as of high estate, were members of the sociologically static all-inclusive Church of the Middle

Ages. The protest movements in the Reformation era, though led by theologians, scholars and intellectuals, and joined by court and military aristocrats, were popular movements, burghers and peasants forming the majority of their followers both on the Continent and in England. Though not limited to the economically and socially depressed, certain types of sects draw their followers most successfully from the dispossessed. H. R. Niebuhr and E. T. Clark have demonstrated that, with the ever-increasing mobility of modern times, the religious organizations of the dispossessed, once their constituency has achieved a greater amount of economic and social security, tend to transform themselves into bodies of greater social 'respectability,' and that this transformation frequently occasions changes from the sectarian to the denominational and ecclesiastical types (cf. formerly Baptists, Methodists, Quakers, now the Nazarenes) and a loss of their appeal to the 'disinherited', who are obliged to find or to create new communities which will respond to their need. Liston Pope has studied this process in a modern community of the Southern U.S.A. (Gastonia) (33), and Walter G. Muelder has traced it for some groups (Nazarene and Pentecostal) in California. I should like to call attention also to the most recent study of the effects of mobility in the wake of the war upon Southern and Central Western Sectarianism in H. P. Douglas' article 'Cultural Differences and Recent Religious Divisions' (34).

It seems necessary in this connection to address a warning to those sociologists who have taken a special interest in sectarianism. They should not overlook the fact that religious bodies are not, certainly not primarily, associations for the fostering of any material or even ideal purpose, though such notions do of course, play a part, but that they desire to be worshipping groups and should be understood and interpreted with this intention so long as it is not disproved. There must be some reason why many people of the very low income groups are legitimate members of ecclesiastical bodies (the Roman Church, for example), without 'joining', as according to certain over-simplifying sociological theories they should, the next best sect, and why persons of considerable means are to be found in denominations and sects alike. Individual psychology (desire to be different, etc.) may play a part in the latter case, but not to the exclusion of other motives. In his analysis of West Coast sectarianism in America, Walter Mueldern has shown that the Nazarenes, for example, though their original constituency came from among the poor, cannot simply be regarded as a group of economically disinherited persons, but that 'personality factors, religious incentive and doctrinal issues are equally important along with the social situation' (35).

Next to the political and economic factors, the intellectual has to be considered. The so-called intellectual as a sociological type appears in the history of the West and of western Christianity only in modern times, though it has its forerunners in earlier periods (Gnostics, medieval 'philosophers' and publicists). The nineteenth century can be considered as the heyday of the intelligentsia, as Max Weber, Groethuysen, Sombart and others have shown (36). Its fortunes have declined constantly during the interval between the two World wars. It appears that neither the ecclesiastical body nor the sect appeals to the intellectual as long as he remains such and no more. He flourishes in the 'liberal' atmosphere of the denomination, his 'free' spirit shrinking from the rigid organization of the 'body' and the rigid moral demands of the sect. Those sects which appeal to the intellectual by their mystical, philosophical or metaphysical teachings, assume usually a denominational aspect.

Finally, let us consider the problem of leadership as it presents itself with regard to the three types of organization of Christian fellowship. Seen historically, the often studied process of the gradual substitution of official for pneumatic (spiritual) charismata which the development of the early Church of the first two centuries represents, repeats itself in the history of practically all Christian groups. The semi-canonical authority of the founder in the early Lutheran Church was based not on the prestige of the office but rather on a personal charisma. But in all reformed ecclesiastical bodies spiritual authority is vested in an order of offices supposed to reflect the actual organization of the Primitive Church (episcopal, presbyterian, etc.). Pneumatic spontaneity ('prophecy') has, if it has not been eliminated, receded into the background, though the Catholic Church of the

West has seen revivals of it in periodic movements (Montanism, Spiritualism of the twelfth and again of the fifteenth centuries). The Eastern ecclesiastical bodies, less institutionalized and centralized, have tried to maintain a balance which favoured pneumatic authority more than could have been done in the Western Church (Hesychast movement, the Russian Startstvo). In the Anglican Church ecclesiastical leadership has remained practically unchallenged, owing probably to two factors: the Anglo-Saxon temper, which seems more or less indisposed to emotional outbursts of spirituality, and the carefully guarded tradition of its order of church government. Only certain marginal phenomena of the evangelical movement of the eighteenth century (preceding and accompanying the secession of the Methodists) and the Irvingite schism can be mentioned as exceptions. Buchmanism and its leadership are not over-popular in the Anglican community.

The denominations, less committed to a rigidly stratified order of offices than are the ecclesiastical bodies, leave, in theory, a wider field to the exercise of different forms of authority. Genuine prophecy and enthusiastic spiritual charismata, however, are not frequent in denominational history, except occasionally at the beginning. The teaching and pastoral charisma outweighs the prophetic in importance. Leadership in denominations is little centralized and stratified, if it be not egalitarian. The distinction between clergy and laity, characteristic of the ecclesiastical body even in its reformed variants, is replaced by a concept of the ministry which tends to take seriously the ideal of the priesthood of all believers (Quakers).

Much as sectarianism differs as to temperament and basic attitudes, teachings and practices, it affords without exception an important rôle to charismatic leadership. As in the incipient stage, so all through the history of sects, the leader dominates. It has been said: 'the leader *is* the sect' (37). Personal charisma either of a spiritualistic or didactic or administrative character, most frequently a combination of all these elements, charac-terizes sectarian leadership. It may or may not be organized in an order, usually conceived in literal imitation of the primitive Church. It tends to be 'totalitarian' to the extent that the sect represents a 'closed' community not only of faith but of life as well. Though excesses and caricatures of leadership are by no means absent from ecclesiastical history, it is in sectarianism that they abound ('King David,' 'Bishop Grace,' 'Father Divine' etc.). Says Hooker: 'Those, therefore, who are most daring in promoting a separation from the Church, and act, as it were, as standard-bearers in the revolt, have in general no other motive than to make an ostentatious display of their own superior sanctity rather than true holiness and a real concern for its interests' (*Laws*, I, 4, 16).

A final consideration suggests itself. The historian of the Church will tell us how ecclesiastical bodies, denominations and sects have come into being, what their histories have been; he will explain their relation to one another, he will trace antagonism and co-operation, report transformations and mergers. But in addition to the question: How did these typologically different groups come into being? there is another which is more difficult to answer. Some will feel that the psychologist should be called upon to answer it. We saw that the character of leading personalities played a considerable role in the emergence and development of the various Christian groups, ecclesiastical, denominational and sectarian, especially in the last, in which the counterweight of a more or less official tradition can make itself less distinctly felt than in the others. Are there, generally speaking, types of personality roughly corresponding to the sociological types of fellowship which we have outlined? R. Faris, Gillin, E. T. Clark, Howard Becker and R. P. Casey, to name a few investigators (38), have tried to characterize the typical sectarian with his peculiar motivation (desire to be different from others, attraction to extreme forms of thought and practice, inclination to 'radicalism' and possibly eccentric behaviour and thinking). Do 'Catholicism' and 'Protestantism' correspond to 'eternal' types of religiosity, as Frick and Tillich have intimated? Many sociologists have repeated E. Troeltsch's distinction between religious groups into which an individual is born and those he freely chooses, but that is not a very helpful criterion, because it is much more important to know why he chooses a certain fellowship, which to-day will be just as often an ecclesiastical body as a denomination or a sect. Though the psychologist, or the sociologist disguised as such, will be ready with a theory of the weak character looking for authority and of the strong as a lover of liberty, reality does not seem to corroborate such simplification. Weakness and strength, the desire for authority and for freedom, the wish to conform and the urge to dissent, a will to believe and an inclination to doubt, are found in each of us. As with so many problems which appear more modern than they actually are, so it is with this. It is actually a theological question, involving a theological decision. If I have a good brain, I may like to speculate along either rationalist or spiritualist lines; if my aesthetic sense is strong, I may be interested in richly elaborated liturgical forms; if my moral consciousness is highly developed, I may look for satisfaction of its claim; and if I feel keenly about justice, I may look for ways to ensure that it is done. In all these cases it may be felt that here is a legitimate concern which could and should be fruitfully developed in the Christian fellowship. We are still in the realm of psychology when discussing desires and urges; we enter into that of theology when we think in terms of catholicity, of tradition and of obedience to the one master who is the Lord of his congregation. 'Ubi Christus, ibi Ecclesia' (39).

The student of the forms of organization of the Christian fellowship will have to guard himself against two extreme views which suggest themselves. The first is a radically exclusive position which sees all truth and all goodness and beauty in one community, usually his own, treating the rest unqualifiedly with contempt or neglect. The other is an equally radical relativism, for which all the historical and sociological formations of Christianity are equally good or equally bad, and which, in consequence, is too timid or sceptical to commit itself to any one form or ideal. As it is the task of the historian and the sociologist to study the genesis, development and structure of all these groups, so it is the function of the theologian who is religiously committed constantly to examine and revise the theological presuppositions upon which the basic concept of the ecclesia of his own community rests, in the light of an ever-continued study of and meditation upon the teaching of Christ, the master of us all, trusting in his solemn promise that where two or three are gathered in his name, he will be present, and

207

that his holy spirit will ever be a comforter to his people. It is difficult to see how a Christian theologian, especially if he be a sociologist and an historian to boot, could find rest in any but an ecumenically orientated theology. He is aware of the fact that in the rich heritage of which the Christian fellowships are stewards, important concerns may easily become lost and hence have to be rediscovered in renewed emphasis, one-sided as such an emphasis will appear to anyone who is conscious of the whole of Christian tradition, trusting not to his own limited vision, but entrusting judgement to God, reminiscent of St. Augustine's phrase: 'Multi qui foris videntur, intus sunt, et multi qui intus videntur, foris sunt' (*de Baptismo* V, 38).

CHAPTER TEN

RUDOLF OTTO AND THE
IDEA OF THE HOLY

Two theological books profoundly impressed the generation of students which populated the German universities after the First World War: the *Commentary on the Epistle to the Romans* by Karl Barth and *The Idea of the Holy* by Rudolf Otto. It is not without significance that these were both books which made considerable demands on their readers. The effect of the work of Barth might be called sensational. This, however, did not prevent it from being not only a widespread but also a profound one, as the last three decades have demonstrated. While there was, even shortly after its publication, much talk of 'Barthians', and a Barthian 'Orthodoxy' began to develop, not always necessarily with the blessing of the master, there were never really any 'Ottonians.' But laymen and theologians, theologians of very different schools and denominations throughout the last thirty years, have read *The Idea of the Holy*, and have confessed to having been deeply stirred and influenced by that work. Both thinkers have found echoes far beyond the borders of Germany, especially in the Anglo-Saxon countries.

Why did a school of Barth begin to assemble so rapidly, while the permeation of theology with the thought of Otto did not result in producing such a 'school'? Different answers might be given to this question. There is, first, a notable difference in the 'concern' of both scholars, as well as in the goal towards which they worked and in the means which they employed to achieve it, but there is also, and more important, the difference in their personalities.

While innumerable books, articles and reviews have been devoted to Karl Barth and his theology, very few monographs or studies have been dedicated to Rudolf Otto and his teachings. The first full-length American treatment was published only in 1947 (1).

It is difficult to convey to those who did not know him personally a picture of the unusual personality of the author of *The Idea of the Holy*. Rudolf Otto was possessed of an imposing appearance. He held himself straight and upright. His movements were measured. The sharply-cut countenance kept a grave expression which did not change much even when jesting. The colour of his skin was yellowish-white and betrayed past illness. Otto had contracted a tropical sickness in India which forced him ever after to husband his strength strictly. His hair was white and clipped, except in his last years, when it formed a crowning mane over his high forehead. A small white moustache covered his upper lip. His most fascinating features were his steel-blue eyes. There was a rigidity in his glance, and one would have the impression that he was 'seeing' something, as he spoke, to which his interlocutor had no access. I can remember him, stretched in his chaise-longue, on which he had to rest as much as possible, his shoulders covered with a shawl because he easily took cold, with a tom-cat perched on him which he admonished occasionally when it grew restless, without interrupting the serious conversation. No other background for him could be imagined than the many books heaped up in his study all around him. But I also recollect Rudolf Otto in a different environment which fitted him no less than his quiet study. I see him, wrapped in his cape, as we strolled in the neighbourhood of Marburg, his eyes fixed on the hilly scene, a *viator indefessus*. Nobody who knew him will expect that a biography of the author of *The Idea of the Holy* will ever be written, least of all one which would aim at bringing its hero 'close to the people.' An air of genuine mystery surrounded Otto. Familiarity was the last thing which a visitor would have expected of the great scholar or which he himself would have encouraged. The students who followed his lectures tensely and with awe called him the Saint ('Der Heilige,' an allusion to the title of his *magnum opus*).

In the sense in which he himself used this term, not in its modern sentimentalized or moralizing meaning, this designation was singularly appropriate. Neither before nor since my meeting Otto have I known a person who impressed one more genuinely as a true mystic. There was something about him of the solitude into which an intimate communion with the Divine has frequently led those who were favoured in this way. In the eulogy on Rudolf Otto by Theodor Siegfried, one of his Marburg colleagues, someone is quoted as characterizing him: 'After all, he was something of a king ['ein Herrscher']; yet a king who did not lack humility.' 'He was,' someone else averred, 'the prophet of an inexorable God who in his inexorable way visited him and called him home.' Siegfried grasped it well: 'The inexplorability of the love of God remained for Otto the last of revelations and the profoundest of mysteries.'

The most important dates of his life are quickly mentioned. He was born September 25, 1869, in Peine (Hanover), was, from 1904, instructor and professor of systematic theology at Göttingen, taught in Breslau from 1914, and at the University of Marburg from 1917. There, as the most outstanding theologian at that school so rich in theological tradition, he taught until his retirement in 1928. From 1913 to 1918 Rudolf Otto was a member of the Prussian diet. He travelled extensively in the Mohammedan countries, in India and the United States. Oberlin College has the distinction of having invited him as a visiting professor. As his fame grew, professors and students came to Marburg from all parts of the world, to visit him, to study under him, and to learn from him.

His first publication appeared in 1898. From this distance— now nearly half a century has passed—we can reconstruct better than would have been possible a few decades ago the tendencies which prevailed in the intellectual life of Germany at the turn of the century. Three powerful movements had exerted their influence in succession, leaving no single sector of her cultural life untouched: the Enlightenment, Romanticism and Naturalistic Materialism. The history of the after-effects of the Enlightenment, the philosophy of which has been so brilliantly analysed in a well-known treatise by Ernst

Troeltsch, has not yet been written. During the second half of the nineteenth century, motives which reflected its rationalistic temper penetrated with characteristic simplification into the thought-world of the masses, and prepared the way for the philosophy of naturalistic materialism. The counter-movement against the Enlightenment which in the early nineteenth century assembled the most gifted of the intellectual élite of Germany under the Romantic banner, and was to determine the attitudes and the creative work of at least two generations, remained limited to the circles of the intellectuals. Romantic motives had long ceased to exert their lure by the turn of the century, and began to become effective again only with the neo-romantic school and the youth movement of the second decade of the twentieth century. Materialistic naturalism, relentlessly advancing from the eighteen-fifties to the end of the century, became the philosophical creed of the victoriously advancing natural sciences and of the Marxist social teaching with its mass-appeal. Only recently have we begun to understand how great a tribute the Enlightenment exacted from German Protestantism, especially its academic leaders. While at the intellectual centres many of the academic theologians tried to adapt their message to the philosophy of the Enlightenment, the ecclesiastical communities, especially in the north, west, and south of Germany, preserved the religious substance of the Protestant tradition of the Christian faith. The romantic school, primarily a movement of aesthetic character, though not lacking from its start an affinity to religion, endeavoured to develop, from its presuppositions, a new understanding of Christianity or, more exactly, of certain Christian motives. The two great Protestant theologians of the first half of the nineteenth century, Schleiermacher and Kierkegaard, both owe much to Romanticist inspiration. The pietism of the *ecclesiolae* ('Gemeinschaften') and Romanticism, though deeply at variance in their basic attitudes, determined—with the philosophy of Kant—the world-view of the young Schleiermacher and of his famous discourses on religion addressed to the educated among the contemptuous. These discourses were re-edited by the same Rudolf Otto who, as Siegfried reports, called himself in his farewell lecture to his students in 1928 a 'pietistic Lutheran.'

In what sense was Otto a Lutheran? The title of his first treatise gives us a hint: 'The Concept of the Holy Spirit in Luther' (originally: 'Geist und Wort nach Luther'). The young magister here shows how Luther's teaching has to be interpreted with a double front in mind: against Catholic sacramentalism and against the Anabaptists ('Schwärmer'). As against the former, the *intus docere* of the divine Spirit is emphasized; as against the latter the objectivity of the Word of the Scriptures, of preaching as brotherly admonition. Mere historical faith (*fides historica*) has to be excluded, as well as claims to subjective illumination. Otto quotes Luther: 'God first has to preach of his Son through the Spirit, so that it falls into our ears and then sinks into our heart, so that we hear and believe' ('Gott muss anheben und predigen durch seinen Geist vom Sohn, so schlägt dir's in die Ohren und her nach sinkt wieder in unser Herz, dass wir es hören und gläuben'). The author of *The Idea of the Holy* was not one of the conventional traditionalists among the latter-day Lutherans. The numinous experience of Luther, the personality of the mighty prophet-like promulgator of the notion of the hidden and yet mercifully revealing God, fascinated and deeply influenced Otto throughout his life. Yet did he not dwell with more than a purely historical interest on the study of the fathers of Lutheran orthodoxy, such as Hollaz, Quenstedt, and Chemnitz? Not much has been said in this regard by his eulogists. I should like to hazard the guess that, besides the great systematic talent to which their dogmatic works witness, it was the substance of Christian, reformatory faith revealed in their theology which was sensed and admired by Otto. Does that make him a narrow denominationalist? We shall see that this genuinely liberal theologian cannot be designated thus. But he was repelled by the semi-rationalistic theology of his day, by the superficiality with which the nature of religion and the nature of Christianity were frequently defined. As against an ossified intellectualism on the part of many contemporary theologians Otto had to stand by the word of the Apostle that the letter killeth but the spirit giveth life. It was by no accident that the doctrine of the Holy Spirit was a field neglected by the official theologians of the day.

A second great teacher, besides Luther, who deeply influenced the thought of Otto was Kant, who himself had his roots in the Enlightenment; the Königsberg philosopher who excluded metaphysics and religion from the realm of the scientifically ('wissenschaftlich') explorable had yet allowed for a satisfaction of the demand for demonstration of evidence for religious judgements. He had, in his way, safeguarded the domain of religious experience. But the important task of determining the nature of the latter had not been satisfactorily concluded. Four thinkers who were influenced by Kant and tried to find such a solution are important for Otto's theory of religion. Besides Schleiermacher, already mentioned, they are the less-known philosopher Fries, the theologian Albrecht Ritschl, and the theologian and philosopher Ernst Troeltsch. Fries postulated a faculty which he called 'Ahndung' (intuition), by means of which we become aware of the numen. Otto had a high regard for this thinker, whose ideas Leonard Nelson propagated with zeal among his colleagues at Göttingen, as we learn from Otto's treatise on Kant and Fries' philosophy of religion (1904). Albrecht Ritschl, without doubt the most influential Protestant theologian of the second half of the nineteenth century, followed Kant and Schleiermacher in his attempt to demonstrate the existence of a realm of religious experience which he thought was constituted by characteristic value-judgments. In this way Kant's moralistic concept of religion as well as its psychological foundation in feeling which Schleiermacher had proposed could be corrected. In the analysis of Christian consciousness which Ritschl undertakes in his comprehensive studies in the Christian doctrines of justification and reconciliation, the specific character of the Christian experience of redemption is sharply accentuated. However, the exclusiveness with which religion and Christianity are here identified, motivated the protest of Ritschl's most outstanding pupil, Ernst Troeltsch. He did not see much difference between this solution and the old type of apologetics which tried to vindicate the absolute character of Christianity. We may assume that the problem of the religious *a priori* which occupied the mind of Troeltsch especially after 1895, was discussed between him, Rudolf Otto, and his colleague at the

University of Göttingen. What is it that constitutes religious experience? While Troeltsch in far-reaching epistemological and philosophical studies—gathered in the second volume of his *Collected Writings*—continued the attempt to determine the nature of religion without reaching a result wholly satisfactory to himself or to others, Otto preserved silence for a number of years, to issue, in 1917, his book *The Idea of the Holy*, in which a new solution of the problem of the religious *a priori* is suggested. It is not without significance that Troeltsch, who recognized more clearly than any of his theological contemporaries the fundamental import for theology of the study of Non-Christian religions, was not really familiar with any of the non-Christian faiths.

We should be glad to know when and how Rudolf Otto came to study Sanskrit, the sacred language of India, and when and how he acquired his profound and thorough knowledge of the various great religions of the world. As a theologian he was, of course, intimately acquainted with Hebrew and early Christian religion. But it was something of an exception for a liberal Protestant theologian who was not a church historian to indicate his thorough acquaintance with patristic literature by well-chosen quotations from the texts. Of the Non-Christian religions it was Hinduism which attracted Otto most strongly. He devoted to this theme a series of basic, and in part pioneer studies (including valuable translations from the Sanskrit). In 1916 he published his rendering of the *Dīpikā* of Nivāsa with the sub-title: 'A Hindu Doctrine of Salvation.' In 1923 this was followed by *Vishnu-Nārāyana*, texts for the study of Hindu mysticism. In the same year he issued the first German version of the *Siddhānta* (text) of the great medieval theologian Rāmānuja. A work as important for its methodology as for its content was a comparison of the teachings of Meister Eckhardt and of Shankara, who is regarded by the Vedanta School as the greatest thinker of India, under the title *Western and Eastern Mysticism* (1926). A fundamental study followed in 1930 on the similarities and differences in the teachings on *Grace in Christianity and Hinduism*, and in 1930 an inquiry into the Indo-European Pantheon (*Gott und Gottheiten der Arier*). Not much later the author of *The Idea of the Holy* turned to the study of the ancient sacred literature of India. Two publications were devoted to the *Bhagavadgita*, and his German rendering of the *Katha-Upanishad*, one of the shorter philosophical treatises of Brahmanism, is a model translation.

All these studies not only bespeak an intimate acquaintance with the texts and the philological problems involved in their interpretation, not only a comprehensive knowledge of the theological and philosophical systems of India and of the outstanding Hindu thinkers and teachers, but also a deep understanding of Indian devotion. In contrast to many German Indologists Otto was attracted not only to the more ancient forms of it, but especially to its medieval expressions, which had hitherto hardly been studied in his home country. In his last great work on *The Kingdom of God and the Son of Man*, the author of *The Idea of the Holy* displayed also a considerable familiarity with the religions of ancient Iran. His extensive travels, especially in North Africa, had given him the opportunity of studying Islam at first hand. Though the East Asiatic religions were furthest removed from his special field of interest, Otto occupied himself especially with the mystical teachings of China and Japan, and refers to them in various passages in his chef-d'œuvre. He helped us markedly, though not an expert in anthropology, in our understanding of 'primitive' religions by analysing the notions of visions, of power, and of holiness, and thus continued the work of Marett, Söderblom and others.

It would be easy to overlook, amid all these detailed achievements, the results which have accrued from them to the concern for methodological reflection and theological principles. So it will not be amiss to summarize briefly some of the important results for the study of religions. Even in his early essay on naturalistic and religious outlooks (1904) Otto had criticized the naturalistic world-view. In a highly significant review of Wilhelm Wundt's *Social Psychology* (*Volkerpsychologie*) he took exception to that writer's highly schematic construction of development, and demonstrated the impossibility of reducing qualitative changes which occur in the life of nature and of the mind to quantitative differences. Religion does not 'develop' by itself from something that is not yet religion and the profounder insights of the higher religions are not simply the result of gradual evolution. Not only evolutionism but psychologism also came under Otto's attack. Feuerbach and Freud had drawn subjectivistic conclusions from the psychological principle underlying Schleiermacher's theory of religion, declaring religion to be an illusion. The Marxist interpretation had proceeded likewise. As against these 'explanations' Otto was not satisfied to show philosophically their methodological shortcomings, a task which was simultaneously undertaken by Husserl in his *Logische Untersuchungen*, by the Austrian philosophy of values, and, later, by Scheler in his critique of Kant. He attempted, in one of the profoundest analyses of religious experience which have ever been made, to indicate the objective character, the 'meaning' of religion. In the numinous experience man confronts the Wholly Other. This, according to Otto, is not self-deception but rather awareness of ultimate reality. Anthropologists and historians of religion debated around the turn of the century as to how similarities in religious notions and customs occurring in different parts of the world and in different cultural contexts were to be explained. One school favoured the theory of spontaneous origin ('Elementargedanken'), while the other, leaning towards an historical interpretation, postulated *one* centre of diffusion, with different members seeking the original home of the primordial ('Ur-') civilization and religion in different regions (Egypt, Babylonia, Central Asia, China, Europe). Otto submitted his solution of the problem in a treatise on *The Law of Parallels in the History of Religions* which is a methodological paradigm. His theory culminates in the notion of the convergence of types. Examples chosen from various areas show convincingly how similar are the expressions which religious experience has created in divers places, and how parallel forms become in turn qualified by the genius of the individual religion. The task of the historian of religions, requiring much sensitivity, is to weigh carefully both similarities *and* differences.

Before we can discuss Rudolf Otto's solutions of the problem of the religious *a priori*, a problem which had baffled his predecessors, and that of the relation of Christianity to the non-Christian religions, we must look more closely at his two main works, *The Idea of the Holy* and *The Kingdom of God and the Son of Man*.

The former book was published in 1917 and reprinted many times (twenty-five printings in 1936). We have already referred to the profound effect which it created. Translations into various languages—seven of them in 1934: English, Swedish, Spanish, Italian, French, Dutch and Japanese—followed each other rapidly. There can be little doubt that it is not elegance of style or presentation that is responsible for a popularity such as has rarely been accorded to a theological volume. The style not only of this but of all of Otto's books is very concise and crisp, always original. No time is wasted by the author in introductory or embellishing remarks. Several of his books, including *The Idea of the Holy* and its companion volume, are collections of relatively independent essays. In some of them he employed a peculiar orthography—no capitals for German substantives, special type-faces, etc.—which he wished to popularise. Very noteworthy always are Otto's quotations, which testify both to his vast information and his fine taste. It is not without significance that aesthetic considerations are by no means overlooked by this great scholar, whose efforts were so unflinchingly directed towards understanding the specifically religious element in human experience. But then this keen investigator of religious systems and theological opinions was one of those not too numerous students of religion who see its very heart in worship. In all the religions he studied he paid the greatest attention to the cultus, and the reform of worship in contemporary Protestantism was one of his most urgent concerns.

From all this it can be seen that Rudolf Otto was well equipped theologically for the execution of his plan to analyse the nature of religious experience. He stood in a philosophical tradition which was devoted to the solution of the great epistemological problem: What constitutes experience? With his teachers he was convinced of the specific character of religious experience, the categories of which he set out to define. To this task he brought, besides a gift for conceptual analysis, an unusual depth and intensity of religious feeling. It may be said that even if Otto had not been possessed of the talents of a historian and a systematic thinker, he would have contributed greatly to the history of devotion by the very expression of his own personal religious experience. It is, after all, a very mysterious fact that in the history of successive generations one or another individual personality, raised under the same conditions and influences as his contemporaries, reacts to the common tradition not only receptively but creatively, that he is stimulated to new and deepened experiences and a productive interpretation of them. Because our fellowmen are prone to provide anything which deviates from established norms, anything unusual, with a handy label, Rudolf Otto on the publication of his chief work was labelled a mystic. What do we mean by this ambiguous term? Do we want to subsume under this heading the uncommon and bizarre phenomena which the text-books on the psychology of religion have often treated as typical of religous experience, or are there reasons for assuming that all genuine and deep religion possesses a mystical element? Be that as it may, the author of *The Idea of the Holy* has succeeded not only in interpreting meaningfully innumerable religious notions, usages, and institutions by pointing out the religious principles which they illustrate, but also in determining clearly the central experience which is at the bottom of all manifestations of the religious spirit. The third presupposition which enabled Otto to do this was his intimate acquaintance with the variety of forms in which religious life is expressed: his mastery of the history of religions.

Without entering into a detailed discussion of the many fine and searching analyses which are found in Otto's chief work, we shall be satisfied with summing up its main results. Religious experience differs from other kinds, moral, aesthetic, etc., though it appears in interrelation with them. It is a specific category ('Bewertungs-Kategorie'), for which he conceived the term *numinous*, derived from the Latin word *numen*. The religious realm is the realm of the Holy. This statement is not, as one might think, tautological. However, it is not the final word. Some mistakes might have been avoided if the author had started, even more decidedly than he does, with the demonstration of the objective quality of the reality of which we become aware in religious experience. Some of his critics have objected to the fact that Otto prefaces this demonstration with an analysis of a psychological reaction (the feeling of creatureliness, the consciousness of sin ('numinos unwert')). However, I remember the emphasis with which in his lectures on Old Lutheran dogmatics he stressed the fact that they start, without fail, with the *locus de Deo*. The first proposition in *The Idea of the Holy* is that the Holy is mystery (*mysterium*)—an objective quality. The further description of it as that which inspires awe (*tremendum*) and yet attracts (*fascinosum*) seems to lead back to an analysis of subjective states. But it seems so only because the former reaction is explained as a response to an—objective—powerful reality ('energy') and the latter which blends with the former into a characteristic 'harmony of contrast' as an effect of the august nature of ultimate reality. We find the theological formulation of these definitions within and outside of Christianity in the doctrines of the attributes, especially of the 'wrath' and the 'grace' of God. Confronting God man experiences his creatureliness. 'Sin,' according to Otto, is consciousness of one's deficiency in value ('Unwert'). He has treated the question 'What is sin?' in a series of essays which are meant to supplement his main work. The numinous experience of our lack of value points to an 'infinite' value: holiness ('Tu solus es sanctus'). In the last period of his life Rudolf Otto attempted, in the context of his investigation of ethical problems, to outline systematically his theory of values. He developed a phenomenological axiology in his study: *Wert, Würde, Recht* (1931).

How do we have to explain religious experience as characterized by the fundamental categories outlined above? At the time of the publication of *The Idea of the Holy*—as to a great extent even now—the disciplines devoted to the study of the lower and higher religions, anthropology and the history of religions, were dominated by the proponents of the reductionist theory of epigeneticism. The higher was to be 'explained' by the lower. There was little provision made in this unqualified evolutionism for creative spontaneity. In his discussion with Wundt, Rudolf Otto asked humorously if milk, because it may turn into cheese, is to be called the 'same' thing as cheese. From nothing nothing can come. The religious *nisus* which Otto ascribes to man is irreducible. This proclivity and 'predestination' for religion may become a religious quest which will not rest until it rests in God. In a few brilliantly terse chapters the author of *The Idea of the Holy* conducts us through the whole religious history of man and illustrates the articulation of this numinous experience on different cultural and religious levels. His critics have chastised Otto for isolating religious experience from other modes of apprehending values. Though he tries to put in relief the specific nature ('Eigenart') of religion, he does not do so without considering the relationships that obtain between the numinous experience which he defines as irrational and other kinds. It does become united with the rational. Genuine religiosity is characterized by the avoidance of both extremes of rationalism and fanaticism. We shall have to say a word on other ways of blending the religious presently. But there can be no doubt that only 'that which is its core, the idea of the holy itself, and the degree to which a historical religion lives up to it, can be the standard by which the value of a religion can be measured.' What is in common to all as a disposition develops and becomes articulate in prophet and saint. The culmination of this process Otto sees in the figure of Him who has the plenitude of the Spirit, in whose person and work we are able to 'divine' in an incomparable degree the Holy. The last sentence of the book points to Him as 'the Son.'

The last two decades of his life the author of *The Idea of the Holy* devoted to two difficult problems, one of a philosophical, the other of a theological nature. Both resulted from the study of the nature and the manifestation of the 'Holy' in life and in history. The first of these is the question of the relation of religion and morality. We have in this actually a special application of the more general problem of the relation between the experience of the numinous and other kinds of experience. But this special query became a major concern of Otto's in the last years of his life as the fundamental problem of the foundation of ethics. We have seen previously that aesthetic considerations did not play a minor part in his thinking, and therefore it may be asked why the problem of the relationship obtaining between religion and other value-experiences did not lead him to an inquiry into aesthetics rather than ethics. The reason may quite possibly be found in the personality of the thinker to whom the formula of the categorical imperative was so congenial. Nearly all critics agree that the weakest point in Otto's analysis of religious experience is his concept of schematism ('Gefühlsgesellung'). The word he took from Kant, but he changed its meaning. Religious experience becomes schematized in entering into relationships with other modes of experience or of judgement. The central religious notions of sin and of redemption, even that of the Holy, have moral associations. A phenomenological demonstration of the foundation of moral values was the aim of the last endeavours of Rudolf Otto. He planned to include the content of five essays which were dedicated to the topic and had appeared in different journals in a volume to be entitled *Moral Law and the Will of God*. They were to have been the Gifford Lectures which he had been invited to deliver. His death intervened.

The first two treatises: 'Value, Dignity and the Just' ('Wert, Würde, Recht') and 'The Law of Value and Autonomy' ('Wertgesetz und Autonomie') indicate the influence of the Austrian school which had concentrated on the demonstration of the objective validity of values, and that of the phenomenology of Max Scheler and Nicolai Hartmann. The Kantian starting-point is not abandoned but is more strongly qualified than in Otto's main work. The same mastery is displayed in the analysis of subjective reaction to moral values as is found in the investigation of numinous experience. The specific nature and the inexorability of the demands of morality are more clearly stated than the nature of the mysterious value of the Holy. 'The moral law,' Otto says, in the last sentence of the first essay, 'to the extent that it is categorical, is not actually a law but a commandment' ('nicht "Gesetz", sondern "Gebot"'). It is not 'handed down' but discovered ('nicht "gegeben", sondern "ergibt sich"'), as founded in value and justice. To act in accordance with it confers the dignity of good will. The analysis of the basic moral value of freedom offered in the study 'On the Sense of Responsibility,' leads the author back into the realm of religion and metaphysics, to the idea of 'creative making' ('schöpferisches Urheben'). In the sense of responsibility we have, 'per aenigma' (in a mysterious form) 'ein vestigium,' a non-conceptual awareness of the coincidence of necessity and contingence.

We have now to turn to the second, the great theological problem, which had commanded Otto's attention not for the first nor for the last time when he wrote his *The Idea of the Holy*. It is the question: What think you of Christ? In the same year (1902) in which Otto's small popular pamphlet on *The Life and Work of Jesus* was published, Ernst Troeltsch, in his famous essay on the incomparability of Christianity (*Die Absolutheit des Christentums*), had asked the question how, in view of the enormous increase in our knowledge, especially of the non-Christian religions, the old claim to absolute validity could be maintained. His answer was that no religion possesses absolute truth, not even the Christian. Only God, to enter into communion with whom and to be redeemed by whom we mortal men are striving, only God is 'absolute.' Christianity, like the other religions, is a historical phenomenon. This understanding need not imply relativistic consequences. History does not exclude norms, they are rather history's greatest discovery. So the Christian has no reason to despair. Yet the criterion for the evaluation of those religions which compete for the highest prize—their number is not great—cannot be an *a priori* but has to be 'produced in the free struggle of ideas.' Troeltsch himself has spoken in warm, convinced and convincing terms of the imcomparable character of Jesus.

Otto's early essay on *The Life and Work of Jesus* is rather conventional. Yet the way in which he portrays the new devotion of Jesus as against Old Testament piety already betrays the characteristic orientation of his theology. 'Here too,' he says, 'God is the Holy One, the embodiment of the moral law that severely puts us strictly under obligation.' And he adds: 'This new religion of Jesus does not grow out of reflection and thinking, out of speculation and philosophy; it is not artfully construed or demonstrated. It breaks forth from the mysterious depth of the individuality of this religious genius.' It centres—this early tract already stresses the fact—in the preaching of the Kingdom of God. To this cardinal notion the second of Rudolf Otto's major works was to be devoted. We have seen that the earlier one closes with a hint at the highest level of 'divination' where 'the Spirit dwells in its plenitude.' He who dwells there is more than a prophet; He is *The Son.*

The Kingdom of God and the Son of Man is the title of the second work, which does not seem to have become quite as widely known as it deserves. The modest but telling sub-title: *An Essay in the History of Religions*, would hardly make us suppose that this book actually represents one of the major contributions of the last decade to the understanding of New Testament theology and especially to Christological thought. The consequences of the situation which Ernst Troeltsch had characterized so convincingly in his treatise on the absolute nature of Christianity and the history of religions are fully drawn by the author, who had had an opportunity, at Göttingen, to enter into personal contact with leaders of the 'religionsgeschichtliche Schule,' especially with Wilhelm Bousset. Whereas other scholars had elucidated the special contributions to the formation of Christianity of the Jewish, Hellenistic, Egyptian, Mesopotamian and Syrian religions, Otto discussed at much greater length, as had been done before, the influence of Iranian notions upon the concept which played so central a rôle in the *Kerygma* of Jesus, the idea of the Kingdom of God. However, it is improbable from the start that the author of *The Idea of the Holy* would have been satisfied to add just one more proof of the thesis that the Christian message could be explained as an assemblage of foreign influences and nothing more. He could object to such a procedure according to his own methodological principles. Besides the interpretation of the 'religionsgeschichtliche Schule' another exegesis of the *Kerygma* of Jesus had had a considerable influence upon New Testament scholars in the first decade of the twentieth century; Albert Schweitzer's eschatological explanation. Otto also sees in Jesus a 'consistent eschatologist' as John the Baptist had been before him. But he contrasts the new message with that of the Forerunner. 'The Kingdom of Heaven is at hand' is not the same as 'The judgement day is approaching.' The place of the Johannine eschatological sacrament of baptism by water is taken by the announcement, later overshadowed, of the spiritual *dynamis* (power) of the Eschaton in the already-here ('schon-anbruch') of the Kingdom. That we have to comprehend if we wish to understand the 'meaning of Christ,' that he lives, notwithstanding his conviction that the kingdom of God is the future shape of the end of time, in its already apparent glory and power, and that he communicates by word and deed to those who follow him, on the basis of a charisma different from that of the Baptist, the effect of this 'miracle of transcendence' as his gift.

Otto has called his book *The Kingdom of God and the Son of Man*. In the beginning of the second part he discusses the much debated problem of the messianic titles of Jesus, and poses and sets forth a thesis which is characteristic of him as the theologian and historian of religions. The answer to the question: Was Jesus the Christ sent by God? can only be decided by faith, and thus does not fall within the competence of history. We are concerned here with a religious judgement referring to numinous reality, a judgement of a type which is analysed in *The Idea of the Holy*. As far as the messianic consciousness ('das Sendungsbewusstsein') of Jesus is concerned, it is expressed in images, the history of whose meaning might well be illuminated by the work of the historian of religion. Otto has devoted to these concepts, especially to the late Jewish messianic speculations, some analyses which are among the best things he has ever written. Otto shows from Christ's own pronouncements that he knew his own communion with God to be 'unique and incomparable.' His very passion and his glorification are anticipated by Jesus in the interpretation of Jeremiah liii as necessary stages in the coming of the Kingdom. We cannot dwell in this context on Otto's interpretation of the Last Supper as the initiation of the disciples ('Jüngerweihe') into the Kingdom of God which he develops in that part of his book. His discussion on the nature of the Eucharist demonstrates anew his mastery of the exegetical and historical material, and proves the fruitfulness of an eschatological interpretation of the sacrament (which is treated all too frequently without such context), as a symbolic expression of the messianic consciousness of Christ. Otto had discussed previously in two pamphlets the best methods of a dignified celebration of the Eucharist. They are entitled: *The Sacrament as Manifestation of the Holy* ('als Ereignis des Heiligen') and *The Celebration of the Lord's Supper.*

The last section of *The Kingdom* leads back to the question at the beginning of the book: What think you of Christ? Here the interests of the theologian and the sociologist of religion coalesce. According to Otto, we have to see Jesus in the context of notions of charisma and of power as a charismatic: 'If one wants to say what Jesus was, one has to think of the exorcist, the charismatic.' 'Only from his person and its meaning can we derive the meaning of his message concerning the Kingdom.' For the theologian, an understanding of the charisma of Jesus is indispensable; in the words of Rudolf Otto: 'as an anticipated *eschaton* it becomes the foundation of a community which sees itself as the Church of the Nazarene.'

In the foregoing pages we have tried to do justice to the scholar and thinker. We have now to add a few words on Rudolf Otto as a citizen and leader of the academic community in which he lived, as a son of his people and, finally, as a citizen of the world. His inaugural address as Rector of the University of Marburg, on *The Meaning and the Task of a Modern University* (1927) develops the notion of the community of those who teach and those who learn as an ever-changing and ever-growing one, and treats of the work of the mind dedicated to the investigation of truth. Otto points out how it is necessary to integrate into a new idea of the *universitas* elements of truth from three successive movements, idealism, realism and a modern philosophy of life. Rudolf Otto was a good German. As a good German he was also a true cosmopolitan. He documents it in his scholarship and his programmes for a Religious League of Mankind which goes far beyond the ecumenical notion of a union of Protestants. The idea that a devout Christian, a devout Jew, a devout Moslem or Hindu possess something in common which could become the foundation of such a league appeared to many at the time fantastic or even ridiculous. It was overlooked that the author of *The Idea of the Holy* did not advocate an indiscriminate unification in ignorance of the profound differences which separate the great religious communities of the world. It turned out that in spite of his idealism, or very possibly because of it, Rudolf Otto has been the greater realist. To-day, under the violent onslaught of powers hostile to religion everywhere, the recognition begins to spread that in no religious community can there be room for the lukewarm. In all of them men search for a profounder understanding of the essentials in doctrine and in worship. New fronts begin to replace old divisions. Smaller cells begin to be formed, here and there, which draw spiritual nourishment from a common experience of the Holy and hence should be willing and able to understand each other. In such signs Rudolf Otto saw hope for the future of Christianity, of religion and of the world.

CONCLUSION

THE studies collected in this volume deal with various aspects of the history of religion. The attempt has been made to do justice to *individual* phenomena: thoughts and practices, personalities and movements, trends and institutions. Though not a few of these belong to a distant or a more recent past, all of them are believed by the author to be not without significance for the present day and age. Though these phenomena are, in the major portion of the book, treated monographically, a systematic interest has guided the author throughout. Comparisons were made to bring out contrasts as well as similarities. Types of thought, of attitudes, and of grouping emerged out of the investigation of religions as far apart as primitive cults, the national faiths of Asia and the major world religions. Certain beliefs, practices and forms of association in Islam, Buddhism and Christianity were singled out for analysis in the hope that something of the genius and of the possibilities inherent in each of these major faiths might become apparent. It is the author's conviction that we have passed the stage of surveys as they are offered in the current text-books and manuals of the history of religions. A great deal of work still remains to be done in purely historical and philological research. Meanwhile, however, the student of the history of religions is pressed for answers to the quest for the meaning of all these expressions of religious experience, and the meaning and nature of religious experience itself. A circle, though not necessarily a vicious one, seems to exist: if we desire to focus our investigation on phenomena to be called religious, we have to proceed on the basis of some presuppositions as to their nature, and yet, in order to be able to articulate these presuppositions, we have to study the widest possible range of historical phenomena. In one of the essays the problem of the classical and its significance for the study of religion was discussed. In several of them the typological

228

method is employed. Are types then the last word which the historian of religions has to contribute? Very possibly, yes; *qua* historian he cannot go further. He may find in the teachings of a Christian or of a Moslem spiritualist a type of 'religiosity' which, in and through its historical form, reveals one possibility of understanding and interpreting the Christian and the Moslem faiths. He may ascertain if and to what extent the respective religious communities have regarded these teachings as legitimate expressions of their religious experience. The historian *qua* historian will examine the sociological forms under which religiously motivated groups have organized, and he will inquire into the underlying theological assumptions. He will show parallels between different types which belong to different historical contexts. But he cannot *qua* historian go beyond this *descriptive* task to answer the *normative* quest. Again he is within his rights when he traces the ideas of a thinker as to the principles which, according to the latter's philosophy, ought to govern a society, or the teachings of a theologian as to the nature of the Holy, but *qua* historian he is not entitled to judge their normative value. There can be no dispute as to the relative worth of the historian's work. Who would not agree that we have to know what Moslems *qua* Moslems or Buddhists *qua* Buddhists actually believe and do, before we can 'evaluate' Islam or Buddhism? Or that we have to be thoroughly familiar with the notions, attitudes, and practices of Christian teachers and groups before we can ask if their teachings are true? And yet, even if the historian can show the consequences which were drawn from certain premises in speculation, practice and life, and then vindicate them as historical 'possibilities,' we shall feel the need to inquire after their *truth*. We have outgrown historicism and relativism.

It would be too simple to say that the task of the historian of religions is the study of non-Christian faiths, while the theologian, without regard to the work of the former, should tell us what we ought to believe. Actually the historian of religions does not wait for the final quest for help from the theologian. Without pressing his material to conform to a framework and to notions which are alien to it, he will be well advised if he informs himself thoroughly about the work done in the various theological disciplines. But the theologian, the exegete, the church historian and, most of all, the systematic or constructive theologian can ill afford to neglect the material with which the historian of religion is ready to supply him. It will be of a threefold nature: first, individual data covering the whole range of extra-Christian religious experience (and only the most narrow-minded will deny that such data would be of value); second, representative phenomena which, possibly in extreme form, may offer him a clue for the understanding of the range of possibilities within the realm of religious experience and its expression; finally, classical instances which he would compare and evaluate in the light of the norms to which he is committed. Of course, so long as this 'commitment' consists only in lip-service to a historically inherited tradition, it will not make a telling criterion for judgement. Where it is the result of an existential decision, it will involve an orientation on the truth apprehended in this experience. Jesus Christ, his person and his teaching, is the standard by which the Christian theologian will 'evaluate.' He will be ever conscious of the temptation to equate this norm with the derivative norms which have resulted from its interpretation through the ages. In the never-ending process of 'reconception' (Hocking) he will be aided by the understanding of the nature of all 'expression.' There is a place for the history of religions in the study of theology. Not merely for his apologetic task but for the even more central concern of the theologian, namely, to determine the nature and extent of God's revelatory activity in history, he will have to take note of 'prophecies' throughout the ages. An absolute 'No' does not leave room for a reception of the message of Jesus Christ, thorough as the judgment must be which this message entails for *all* human aspiration. It is one thing to understand this, and another to deny that there are degrees and levels of spiritual insight in the religious testimonies of mankind.

If a study of universal features in the expressions of the religious experience of mankind can supply us with a framework within which we find this experience articulated, it must be possible to test the validity of this framework by applying it in the study of primitive cults *and* of the universal religions. It was just that which the outstanding scholar to whom our last essay is dedicated set out to do. Whatever criticism might rightfully be levelled at his epistemology, here is a successful attempt to combine appreciation based on the most thorough acquaintance with different types of religious experience with profound Christian conviction and commitment.

We shall conclude this exposition with a quotation from Max Müller, to whom, notwithstanding certain shortcomings, the study of the history of religions owes so much. 'To my mind the great epochs in the world's history are marked, not by the foundation or the destruction of empires, by the migration of races, or by French Revolutions. All this is outward history, made up of events that seem gigantic and overpowering to those only who cannot see beyond and beneath. The real history of man is the history of religion: the wonderful ways by which the different families of the human race advanced toward a truer knowledge and a deeper love of God. This is the foundation that underlies all profane history: it is the light, the soul, and the life of history, and without it all history would indeed be profane.'

NOTES

INTRODUCTION (Pages xi–xvi)

1. *Das Verstehen. Geschichte der hermeneutischen Theorie im 19. Jahrhundert* I–III (Tübingen: Mohr (Siebeck), 1926–32); 'Verstehen' in *RGG*, V, 1570 ff., and 'Understanding' in *The Albert Schweitzer Jubilee Book*, ed. A. A. Roback (Cambridge, Mass.: Sci-Art Publ., 1945).

2. Reprint from *Journal of Religion*, XXVII, 3 (1947), 157–77. Cf. also: "Teaching History of Religions" in *Pro Regno, Pro Sanctuario* (Nÿkerk, Callenbach, 1950), p. 525 ff.

3. English translation of an essay written in German for *Quantulacunque* in honour of Kirsopp Lake (London: Christophers, 1937), pp. 87–97.

4. *Typen der religiösen Anthropologie* (Tübingen: Mohr (Siebeck), 1926). Considerably shortened and altered.

5. Reprint from *Journal of Religion*, XXVI, 1 (1946), 1 ff.

6. Reprint from *Journal of the History of Ideas*, VII, 1 (1946), 74–90.

7. *Einführung in die Religionssoziologie* (Tübingen: J. C. B. Mohr (Siebeck), 1930); *Sociology of Religion* (London: Kegan Paul, 1947); 'Sociology of Religion' in *Symposium on Twentieth-century Sociology* (New York: Philosophical Library, 1946).

8. Reprint of the M. Dwight Johnson Memorial Inaugural Lecture, published by Seabury-Western Episcopal Seminary, 1946.

9. Translated from the German text of a lecture before the German Literary Society at Chicago, May 1947.

I. THE PLACE OF THE HISTORY OF RELIGIONS IN THE STUDY OF THEOLOGY (Pages 3–29)

1. Henri Pinard de la Boullaye, *L'Étude comparée des religions* (Paris: Beauchesne, 1922), Vol. I.

2. E. Hardy, 'Zur Geschichte der vergleichenden Religionsforschung,' *Arch. für Rel. Wiss.*, IV (1901), 45 ff., 97 ff.; L. H. Jordan, *Comparative Religion: Its Genesis and Growth* (Edinburgh: T. and T. Clark, 1905); J. Wach, *Religionswissenschaft: Prolegomena* (Leipzig: Hinrichs, 1924); E. O. James, *Comparative Religion* (London: Methuen, 1938); Gustav Mensching, *Geschichte der Religionswissenschaft* (Bonn: Universitätsverlag, 1948); G. van der Leeuw, *La réligion* (Paris, Payot, 1948), §112.

3. Ernst Troeltsch, 'Die Aufklärung,' in *Gesammelte Schriften* (Tübingen: Mohr, 1925), IV, 338 ff.; H. Hoffmann, 'Die Frage nach dem Wesen des Christentums in der Aufklärungstheologie,' in *Harnack-Ehrung* (Leipzig: Hinrichs, 1921), pp. 353 ff.

4. Pinard, op. cit., chaps. viii ff.

5. Jordan, op. cit., pp. 7 ff., 26 ff., 62; cf. on the term 'science of religion,' p. 25.

6. E. Troeltsch, 'Die Dogmatik der religionsgeschichtlichen Schule,' in *Ges. Schr.*, II, 500 ff.; 'Religionsgeschichtliche Schule' (art.), in *RGG*, Vol. IV (1898).

7. Cf. Franz Overbeck, *Selbstbekenntnisse* (Basel: B. Schwabe, 1941).

8. E. Troeltsch, *Ges. Schr.*, Vol. IV, chaps. x, xii, xiv, xv, xx.

9. R. Otto, *The Idea of the Holy*, trans. J. W. Harvey (London: Oxford University Press, 1923). Cf. below, Chap. X.

10. 'Was Jesus the Christ of God? This is not a question raised by the history of religion, but a question of faith, and therefore does not arise in our investigation which will proceed along religio-historical lines' (R. Otto, *The Kingdom of God and the Son of Man* (London: Lutterworth Press, 1938), p. 159; cf. pp. 193-4, 333-4, 375-6).

11. Cf. E. Bernheim, *Lehrbuch der historischen Methode* (Leipzig: Duncker & Humblot, 1903); J. G. Droysen, *Grundriss der Historik*, ed. E. Rothacker (Halle: Niemeyer, 1925).

12. J. Wach, *Das Verstehen, Geschichte der hermeneutischen Theorie im 19. Jahrhundert* (Tübingen: Mohr (Siebeck), 1926 ff.), esp. Vol. II.

13. Cf. 'The Symposium on Biblical Theology,' in *Journal of Bible and Religion*, Vol. XIV, Nos. 1 and 3 (1946), and W. A. Irwin, 'The Reviving Theology of the Old Testament,' *Journal of Religion*, XXV (1945), 235 ff.

14. Cf. R. C. Denton, 'The Nature and Function of Old Testament Theology,' *JBR*, XIV, No. 1, 19-20.

15. H. Wheeler Robinson, *The Religious Ideas of the Old Testament* (5th ed.; London: Duckworth, 1934); W. Eichrodt, *Theologie der Alten Testaments* (Leipzig: Hinrichs, 1933); Millar Burrows, *An Outline of Biblical Theology* (New York: Harper, 1946).

16. Schleiermacher's concept of the analysis of the pious self-consciousness ('das fromme Gemüt') had a strong influence upon conservative theologians of the school of Erlangen, to wit, Frank and Ihmels (see below, n. 39).

17. 'Der Ort der Theologie ist die Kirche . . .' (E. Brunner, *Religionsphilosophie evangelischer Theologie* (München: Oldenburg, 1927)), p. 6. See below, n. 104.

18. As the four factors to be considered, Brunner (ibid., p. 23) enumerates scripture, reason, subjective experience, and history, which have to come into their own in the Christian doctrine of revelation. Cf. also H. Cunliffe-Jones, *The Authority of the Biblical Revelation* (London: Clark, 1945).

19. Pinard, op. cit., chaps. ii and iii.

NOTES (Pages 12–14)

20. Cf. Otto Karrer, *The Religions of Mankind* (London: Sheed & Ward, 1936; 1945). Also M. Scheler, *Vom Ewigen im Menschen* (Leipzig: Neue Geist Verlag, 1923), I, 440 ff.

21. But cf. E. Troeltsch, *Vernunft und Offenbarung bei Johann Gerhardt und Melanchthon* (Göttingen: Vanderhoeck, 1912); O. Ritschl, *Dogmengeschichte des Protestantismus* (Leipzig: Hinrichs, 1908). Cf. also n. 104.

22. See the controversy between Karl Barth and Emil Brunner. Cf. also A. Köberle, 'Vernunft und Offenbarung,' in *Zeitschrift für Systematische Theologie*, XV, No. 1 (1938), 28 ff. For the polemic against any natural theology and those who lean towards it see Karl Barth's Gifford Lectures: *Gotteserkenntniss und Gottesdienst nach reformatorischer Lehre* (Zollikon, 1938), First Lecture, esp. p. 43.

23. Troeltsch, *Ges. Schr.*, Vol. IV, chaps. xii, xiv; N. Söderblom, *Natürliche Theologie und allgemeine Religionsgeschichte* (Stockholm: Bonnier, 1913).

24. E. Troeltsch, 'The Ideas of Natural Law and Humanity,' in Otto Gierke, *Natural Law and the Theory of Society*, trans. E. Barker (Cambridge: University Press, 1934), pp. 201 ff.

25. E. Troeltsch, 'Der Historismus und seine Probleme,' in *Ges. Schr.*, Vol. III; E. Rothacker, *Einleitung in die Geisteswissenschaften* (Tübingen: Mohr (Siebeck), 1920), chap. ii.

26. R. B. Brandt, *The Philosophy of Schleiermacher* (New York: Harper, 1941).

27. Rothacker, op. cit., chap. iii; M. Mandelbaum, *The Problem of Historical Knowledge* (New York: Liveright, 1938).

28. Towards the end of the nineteenth century, philosophy of religion rose to unchallenged prominence, a development not unconnected with the decline of Protestant systematic theology. In Germany and in England its norms were those of the idealistic systems of Caird, McTaggart, Pfleiderer, Siebeck, Eucken, Troeltsch, Wundt, Scholz, though with an emphasis upon an empirical method and an epistemology (cf. Troeltsch, 'Das Wesen der Religion und der Religionswissenschaft,' in *Ges. Schr.*, II, 452 ff.; Wach, 'Religionsphilosophie,' *RGG²*, IV, 1914 ff.). In America, realism, pragmatism, and naturalism tended to dissolve philosophy of religion into metaphysics (cf. H. N. Wieman, *American Philosophies of Religion* (Chicago: Willett, Clark, 1936)). Cf. also R. B. Perry, *Philosophy of the Recent Past* (New York: Scribner's, 1926).

29. Troeltsch, 'Der Deismus,' in *Ges. Schr.*, IV, 429 ff., and his article quoted in the previous note.

30. E. S. Brightman, *A Philosophy of Religion* (New York: Prentice-Hall, 1940), p. 22. As the dangers of philosophy of religion are listed: mere dogmatic restatement of tradition, and polemics against tradition without understanding what its contents really are (p. 438).

31. Cf. the problem of the structure of reality, of values, of the moral imperative, of freedom and of evil.

32. H. Kraemer, *The Christian Message in a Non-Christian World*
(Edinburgh: Edinburgh Press, 1938), chap. iv, rightly distinguishes
between the problem of value (of religions) and that of truth (pp.
106–7). Though acknowledging the 'salutary' influence of the work
of 'comparative religion' (fostering openness and honesty towards
non-Christian faiths), Kraemer is inclined to emphasize 'discontinuity.' See also Alan Richardson, *Christian Apologetics* (New York:
Harper, 1947).

33. *Natürliche Theologie*, pp. 53–4.

34. N. Soederblom, *The Nature of Revelation* (New York: Oxford
University Press, 1903; 2nd ed., 1930); *Natürliche Theologie und
Religionsgeschichte* (Leipzig: Hinrichs, 1913).

35. Ibid., p. 8.

36. Ibid., pp. 58, 61; cf. in the same vein: Kraemer, op. cit., pp.
103 ff.

37. *Nature of Revelation*, p. 203; *Natürliche Theologie*, p. 77.

38. Cf. 'Holiness,' *ERE*, VI, 731 ff.

39. *Natürliche Theologie*, p. 63.

40. Ibid., p. 78. Earlier B. Duhm (*Über Ziel und Methode der
theologischen Wissenschaft* (Basel: Schwabe, 1889), pp. 27–8) had stated:
'In der wissenschaftlichen Theologie müssen im Prinzip sämtliche
Religionen mit gleichen Recht auftreten, das allein schon wird der
heillosen Identifizierung von Religion und Theologie entgegen-
wirken.'

41. *Natürliche Theologie*, pp. 63 ff.

42. Ibid., p. 67; *Nature of Revelation*, p. 6.

43. *Nature of Revelation*, p. 8.

44. Ibid., p. 23.

45. Ibid., p. 34.

46. Ibid., p. 40.

47. Ibid., pp. 43–4.

48. Ibid., pp. 45 ff., 78, 99.

49. *Festgabe für Theodor Zahn* (Leipzig: Deichert, 1928).

50. *Nature of Revelation*, pp. 98–9.

51. Ibid., p. 99.

52. Ibid., pp. 200, 204.

53. Ibid., pp. 200 ff.

54. Ibid., p. 130.

55. Ibid., pp. 140 ff.

56. Ibid., pp. 143 ff.

57. *Natürliche Theologie*, pp. 80 ff.

58. Ibid., pp. 82 ff.

59. W. E. Hocking, *Living Religions and a World Faith* (London:
George Allen & Unwin, 1940), and 'Living Religions and a World
Faith,' *Asian Legacy and American Life*, ed. H. E. Christy (New York:
John Day, 1942), pp. 193 ff.

60. Cf. C. W. Morris, *Paths of Life: Preface to a World Religion* (New

York: Harper, 1942); F. S. C. Northrop, *The Meeting of East and West* (New York: Scribner's; London: Macmillan, 1946).

61. *Living Religions*, p. 54.
62. Ibid., p. 57.
63. Ibid., p. 26; *Asian Legacy*, p. 196.
64. *Living Religions*, p. 35.
65. Ibid., pp. 36 ff., 43.
66. R. Otto, *The Idea of the Holy* (cf. above, n. 9).
67. Cf. 'The Concept of the "Classical" in the Study of Religions' below, Chap. III. Also 'Sociology of Religion' in *Symposium on Twentieth-century Sociology*, ed. S. Gurvitch (New York: Philosophical Library, 1946).
68. G. van der Leeuw, *Religion in Essence and Manifestation*, trans. J. E. Turner (London: Allen & Unwin, 1938).
69. F. L. Parrish, *The Classification of Religions* (Scottsdale: Herald Press, 1941), and E. Hirschmann, *Phänomenologie der Religion* (Würzburg: Triltsch, 1940) (discussion of methodologies in the science of religion).
70. *Living Religions*, Sec. II. It is interesting to compare this characterization with that of so ardent an admirer of Eastern thought as R. Guénon (cf. his *Introduction to the Study of the Hindu Doctrines* (London: Luzac, 1945)).
71. *Asian Legacy*, pp. 203–4.
72. *Living Religions*, pp. 63–4.
73. Ibid., pp. 163 ff.
74. Ibid., p. 168.
75. Ibid., p. 167.
76. Ibid., p. 168.
77. Ibid., p. 185.
78. Ibid., p. 191.
79. Ibid., p. 192.
80. Ibid., p. 193. Cf. Brunner's criticism of all quests for 'essences' (op. cit.).
81. *Living Religions*, p. 196.
82. Ibid., p. 197.
83. Ibid., p. 198.
84. Ibid., p. 201.
85. Ibid.
86. Ibid., p. 229.
87. Ibid., pp. 215 ff.
88. Ibid., pp. 163 ff., 228 ff., 275 ff.
89. Ibid., p. 230.
90. Ibid., pp. 232 ff., 249.
91. Ibid., pp. 266, 268.
92. Ibid., pp. 242 ff.
93. Ibid., p. 250.
94. Ibid., pp. 254 ff.

95. E. L. Wenger, 'The Problem of Truth in Religion: Prolego-
menon to an Indian Christian Theology,' in *Studies in History and
Religion Presented to Dr. H. Wheeler Robinson*, ed. E. A. Payne (London:
Lutterworth, 1942), pp. 159 ff.

96. Ibid., p. 160.

97. Ibid., p. 162.

98. Ibid., p. 164.

99. Ibid., p. 166.

100. Ibid., p. 165.

101. Ibid., p. 166; Kraemer, op. cit.

102. Wenger, op. cit., p. 168.

103. Ibid., p. 170.

104. Ibid., p. 171. Cf. now: R. P. Davies, *The Problem of Authority
in the Continental Reformers* (London: Epworth Press, 1946).

105. Wenger, op. cit., p. 178.

106. P. Tillich suggests the term 'encounter' (*Journal of Religion*,
XXVII (1947), 17). Unfortunately, this article came out too late to
be more fully discussed here.

107. Cf. E. E. Aubrey, 'The Holy Spirit in Relation to the
Religious Community,' *Journal of Theological Studies*, XLI (1940),
1 ff. Though a cycle is involved in the 'testimonium spiritus,' it is
not of a vicious nature. Cf. also above, n. 12.

108. Cf. E. von Dobschütz, *Vom Auslegen des Neuen Testamentes*
(Göttingen: Vandenhoeck, 1927), pp. 50 ff., who asks how a dialogue
of Plato could be understood without 'Sinn' for philosophy or
Thucydides without 'Sinn' for history. See also J. Wach, 'Zur
Auslegung heiliger Schriften,' *Theologische Studien und Kritiken* (1930).

109. Kraemer, op. cit., p. 137.

II. UNIVERSALS IN RELIGION (Pages 30–47)

1. William James, *The Varieties of Religious Experience* (New York
and London: Longmans, Green, 1902).

2. Paul Tillich, 'The Problem of Theological Method,' *Journal of
Religion*, XXVII (1947), 23.

3. W. James, op. cit., p. 58.

4. Paul E. Johnson, *Psychology of Religion* (New York: Abingdon-
Cokesbury Press), p. 36.

5. Émile Durkheim agrees with W. James that 'religious beliefs
rest upon a specific experience whose demonstrative value is, in one
sense, not one bit inferior to that of scientific experiments, though
different from them.' (*The Elementary Forms of the Religious Life*,
trans. J. W. Swain (1915), (Glencoe: Free Press, 1947), p. 417.) He
adds, and rightly, that it does not follow from the fact that a
'religious experience exists and has a certain foundation, that the
reality which is its foundation conforms objectively to the idea which
believers have of it.'

6. Johnson, *Psychology*, p. 47, and John M. Moore, *Theories of Religious Experience* (New York: Round Table Press, 1938), who criticizes Rudolf Otto's assumption of the cognitive nature of the numinous feeling (pp. 86 ff., 95 ff.). We distinguish between apprehension and intellectual expression.

7. This point is well brought out by Canon B. H. Streeter, *The Buddha and the Christ* (London: Macmillan, 1932), pp. 157 ff.

8. Bronislaw Malinowski, *Magic, Science, and Religion and other Essays* (Glencoe, Ill.: Free Press, 1948), p. 1.

9. Cf. the methodological prolegomena in J. Wach, *Sociology of Religion* (London: Kegan Paul, 1947); Part I. Cf. there many references and bibliography for statements in the text above.

10. Cf. Aldous Huxley, *The Perennial Philosophy* (London: Chatto and Windus, 1945), chap. xii: 'Time and Eternity.'

11. There is the *analogy* of the senses (sight, hearing, smell, touch; what is experienced is described as 'light,' voices are heard, sweet odours are smelt), then the analogy of physical phenomena (procreating, eating), that of the various activities of man (warfare, peaceful pursuits (agriculture; pastoral life; other professions)), travelling (pilgrimage) and of human relationships (kin, social, marital relations). Professor Bevan has especially studied the symbolic use of time and space notions. Urban again has stressed the analogies of the *sun*—'the Sun with its powerful rays, its warmth and light, its life-giving qualities, becomes a natural symbol for the creating and eliciting power' (Urban, *Language*, p. 589)—and *sex*—'sex love, its heights and its depths, its horrible darkness and its blinding light is never wholly alien to the creative love of which Plato, no less than Christian theologians and philosophers, discourse' (Urban, loc. cit., p. 591). M. A. Ewer (*A Survey of Mystical Symbolism* (London: S.P.C.K., 1933)) analysed the analogies of the senses in mystical symbolic language. E. Underhill has concentrated upon the symbolic notions of pilgrimage (for divine transcendence), of love and of transmutation (*Mysticism* (London: Methuen, 12th ed., 1930), chap. vi).

12. Gerardus van der Leeuw, *Religion in Essence and Manifestation* (London: Allen & Unwin, 1938), pp. 655–7. Mircea Eliade, *Traité d'histoire des religions* (Paris: Payot, 1949), chaps. x, xi.

13. Otto Franke, 'Der Kosmische Gedanke in der Philosophie und dem Staat der Chinesen,' *Vorträge der Bibliothek Warburg* (Leipzig: Teubner, 1928): Wach, *Sociology of Religion*, pp. 49 ff.; T. W. Rhys Davids, 'Cosmic Law in Ancient Thought' (*Proceedings of Brit. Academy* (Oxford: University Press, 1917), pp. 18, 279 ff.). Roger Caillois, 'L'homme et le sacré' (*Mythes et religions* (Paris: Leroux, 1939), pp. 9 ff; Eliade, *Traité*, chaps. x, xi.

14. 'The symbolism of the World Quarters, of the Above, and of the Below, is nowhere more elaborately developed among American Indians than with the Pueblos. Analogies are drawn not merely with

colours, with plants and animals, and with cult objects and religious ideas, but with human society in all the ramifications of its organization, making of mankind not only the theatric centre of the cosmos, but a kind of elaborate image of its form' (Hartley Alexander, 'North American Mythology,' in *The Mythology of All Races* (Archaeological Institute of America, 1936), Vol. X., 185.

15. 'He [the savage] encounters the divine stimulus here, there and anywhere within the contents of an experience in which percepts play a far more important part than concepts' (Marett, *Faith, Hope and Charity in Primitive Religion* (Oxford: Clarendon Press, 1932), p. 144). Cf. also Frankfurt, etc., *Intellectual Adventure of Ancient Man* (Chicago, University Press, 1946), 130 ff.

16. Cf. below, Chap. X.

17. Thus the criticism which J. M. Moore (*Theories*, pp. 91 ff., 103 ff.) levels rightly at Rudolf Otto's concept of 'feeling' does not apply to our theory.

18. Van der Leeuw, op. cit., Part I; Eliade, op. cit.

19. Martin P. Nilsson, 'Letter to Professor A. D. Nock' (*Harvard Theological Review*, XLII (1949), 91).

20. Cf. the excellent chapter 'Curiosity' in Marett, *Faith, Hope and Charity in Primitive Religion* (op. cit., note 15 above), chap. viii. Cf. also: V. Gordon Childe, *Magic, Craftsmanship and Science* (Liverpool: University Press, 1950).

21. Malinowski, 'Myth in Primitive Society' (op. cit., pp. 72 ff., 76, 93 f.). Malinowski's solution—the sociological theory of myth, in his own words—does not satisfy because of his preoccupation with the *pragmatic* aspect of both religious and magical activities. He neglects the problems of meaning, structure and motivation. A more promising approach seems to be Ernesto de Martino's *Il Mondo Magico* (Firenze, Giulio Einaudi, 1948)) who is concerned with the nature of the *reality* to which magic thought and acts refer (p. 11).

22. Cf. for the general framework: Wach, *Sociology of Religion*, Part I, chap. ii.

23. Clyde Kluckholm, 'Myths and Rituals: A General Theory' (*Harvard Theol. Review*, XXXV, 1 (1942), 45 ff.; cf. also C. H. Ratschow, *Magic und Religion* (Gütersloh, Bertelsmann, 1947).

24. Edwyn R. Bevan, *Symbolism and Belief* (London: Allen & Unwin, 1938); Ernst Cassirer, *Philosophie der symbolischen Formen* (Berlin: Cassirer, 1923 ff.); Wilbur M. Urban, *Language and Reality* (London: Allen & Unwin, 1939), esp. chap. xii; Susanne Langer, op. cit., note 27 below (cf. p. 10, n. 2); Mircea Eliade, op. cit., chap. xiii; Wach, *Sociology of Religion*, p. 19; Jean Danielou, "The Problems of Symbolism" (*Thought*, XXV, 1950), 423 ff.

25. 'Images are taken from the narrower and more intelligible relations and used as expressions for more universal and ideal relations which, because of this pervasiveness and ideality, cannot be directly expressed' (Urban, *Language*, pp. 580, 586).

26. Rich inventories of the wealth of expressions of religious experiences are to be found in Gerardus van der Leeuw's *Religion in Essence and Manifestation*, trans. J. E. Turner (London: Allen & Unwin, 1938), of which a revised French translation appeared recently: *La Religion dans son essence et ses manifestations. Phénoménologie de la religion* (Paris: Payot, 1948); and in Mircea Eliade, *Traité d'histoire des religions. Morphologie du Sacré* (Paris: Payot, 1949).

27. Susanne K. Langer, *Philosophy in a New Key. A Study in the Symbolism of Reason, Rite, and Art* (New York: Penguin Books (1942), 1948), p. 169; also Urban, op. cit., pp. 586 ff.

28. Malinowski, op. cit., p. 86.

29. Urban, op. cit., pp. 571 ff., 576 ff.

30. Cf. the penetrating analysis in Maurice Leenhardt, *Do Kamo. La personne et le mythe dans le monde melanésien* (Paris: Gallimard, 5th ed., 1947), esp. chap. XII.

31. Urban, op. cit., pp. 598 ff.

32. Cf., as an example, the development in early Christianity, suggestively traced by Oscar Cullmann, *The Earliest Christian Confessions*, trans. J. K. S. Reid (London: Lutterworth, 1949).

33. Paul Tillich, op. cit., p. 25.

34. Henry N. Wieman, *The Source of Human Good* (Chicago: University of Chicago Press, 1946), p. 217.

35. Evelyn Underhill, *Worship*.

36. Marett, *Sacraments of Simple Folk* (Oxford: Clarendon Press, 1933), p. 18; cf. Ratschow, op. cit., pp. 43 ff., 62, 81 f., 148 f.

37. Marett, op. cit., chaps. ii, iv.

38. For the divine 'archetypes' of the cult: cf. M. Eliade, *Le mythe de l'eternal rétour* (Paris: Gallimard, 1949), pp. 44 ff; cf. also W. Norman Pittenger, *Sacraments, Signs and Symbols* (Chicago, Wilcox and Follet, 1949), I.

39. Langer, op. cit., p. 39; cf. Theodor H. Gaster, *Thespis. Ritual, Myth and Drama in the Ancient Near East* (New York, H. Schumann, 1950).

40. Marett, *Sacraments*, p. 12.

41. 'The attitude which is the worshipper's response to the insight given by the sacred symbol, is an emotional pattern, which governs all individual lives. It cannot be recognized through any clearer medium than that of formalized gesture; yet in this cryptic form it *is* recognized, and yields a strong sense of tribal or congregational unity, of rightness and security. A rite regularly performed is the constant reiteration of sentiments toward "first and last things"; it is not a free expression of emotions, but a disciplined rehearsal of "right attitudes" (S. Langer, op. cit., p. 124).

42. Paul Radin, *Primitive Religion, Its Nature and Origin* (London: Hamish Hamilton, 1938), chap. ii.

43. Cf. *Sociology of Religion*, chap. v, sect. 10: 'Reaction: Protest'; and Paul Tillich, *The Protestant Era* (Chicago: University of Chicago Press, 1948), esp. sect. iv.

44. Underhill, *Worship* (London: Nisbet, 1936), chap. iii.

45. Marett, *Sacraments of Simple Folk;* Ratschow, op. cit.

46. Cf. the chapter on 'The Sacramental Universe' in W. Temple, *Nature, Man, and God,* Lect. XIX.

47. The need of sacraments, according to Dr. Inge, is 'one of the deepest convictions of the religious consciousness. It rests ultimately on the instinctive reluctance to allow any spiritual fact to remain without an external expression.'

'A sacrament is a symbolic act, not arbitrarily chosen, but resting, to the mind of the recipient, on Divine authority, which has no ulterior object except to give expression to, and in so doing effectuate, a relation which is too purely spiritual to find utterance in the customary activities of life' (William R. Inge, *Mysticism in Religion* (London: Hutchinson [1947]; Chicago: University of Chicago Press, 1948), pp. 251 ff.).

48. The sacraments of Baptism and the Lord's Supper are 'symbols of the mystical union between the Christian and his ascended Lord. Baptism symbolizes that union in its inception, the Eucharist in its organic life' (loc. cit.).

49. Cf. below, Chap. VII, on the spiritualist teachings of Caspar Schwenckfeld.

50. William Temple, *Nature, Man, and God,* p. 494.

51. William James, *Varieties,* pp. 30 ff.

52. Durkheim has stressed this point (op. cit., p. 47), that religion is 'something eminently social.' But he has not always taken care to qualify this statement, as when he says (p. 10), 'They [religious representations and rites] are rich in social elements.' The opposite one-sidedness we find in the work of a well-known contemporary of Durkheim, in W. James' classic *The Varieties of Religious Experience*, where the emphasis on the individual dominates. We agree with Durkheim, however, when he states: 'In so far as he belongs to society, the individual transcends himself, both when he thinks and when he acts' (pp. 16 f.). Cf. Wach, *Sociology of Religion,* pp. 27 ff.

53. Lyman Bryson, *The Communication of Ideas (Religion and Civilization Series.* Institute for Rel. and Soc. Studies, New York: Harper, 1948).

54. R. Otto, *The Kingdom of God and the Son of Man,* trans. Floyd V. Filson and B. L. Lee (London: Lutterworth, 1938), p. 164. Cf. below, Chap. X.

55. *Symposium on Twentieth-century Sociology,* art. 'Sociology of Religion' (chap. xiv).

56. Cf. below, Chap. IX, p. 191 for Christian 'notae.'

57. William Temple, *Nature, Man, and God,* Lect. XIII.

58. Max Weber, *The Theory of Social and Economic Organization,* trans. A. M. Henderson and T. Parsons (London: W. Hodge, 1947), pp. 358 ff.; R. Otto, *Kingdom,* Book IV; and J. Wach, *Sociology of Religion,* chap. viii.

59. Op. cit., LXX.

IV. THE IDEA OF MAN IN THE NEAR EASTERN RELIGIONS (Pages 61–79)

1. Since this lecture was given, a useful essay by Frederick Hilliard, *Man in Eastern Religions. Truths from the East about Man in Relation to Christian Belief* (London: Epworth Press, 1946) has appeared. For the section on pre-Socratic Greek anthropology, cf. Werner Jaeger, *The Theology of the Early Greek Philosophers* (The Gifford Lectures, 1936) (Oxford: Clarendon Press, 1947). Cf. Wilhelm Dilthey, *Gesammelte Schriften* (Leipzig: Teubner, 1921), Vols. II and V; Paul Masson-Oursel, *Comparative Philosophy* (London: Kegan Paul, 1926); Filmer S. C. Northrop, *The Meeting of East and West* (London: Macmillan, 1946); Ernst Cassirer, *Philosophie der Symbolischen Formen* (Berlin: Cassirer, 1923 ff.); Friedrich Überweg, *Grundriss der Geschichte der Philosophie* (Mittelalter) (Berlin: Mittler, II, 2nd ed., 1928), Vol. II; Eduard Zeller, *Grundriss der Geschichte der Griechischen Philosophie* (Leipzig: Reisland, 11th ed., 1914); Carl M. Becker, *Vom Werden und Wesen der islamischen Welt* (Leipzig: Quelle und Meyer, 1924 ff.); Tjitze J. Le Boer, *Geschichte der Philosophie im Islam* (Stuttgart: Fromann, 1901); Isaac Husik, *A History of Mediaeval Jewish Philosophy* (Philadelphia: Jewish Publication Society of America, 1940); Harry A. Wolfson: *Philo: Foundations of Religious Philosophy* . . . (Cambridge, Mass.: Harvard U.P., 1947; George Vajda, *Introduction à la pensée juive du moyen âge* (Paris, Vrin, 1947). Also: H. Frankfort, etc., *The Intellectual Adventure of Ancient Man* (Chicago, Univ. Press, 1946); Simone Petrement, *Le Dualisme chez Platon, les gnostiques et les manichéens* (Paris: Presses Universitaires, 1947). Gershom G. Scholem, *Major Trends in Jewish Mysticism* (New York: Schocken, 1941); H. R. Willoughby, *Pagan Regeneration* (Chicago: University of Chicago Press, 1929); H. Wheeler Robinson, 'The Concept of Corporate Personality,' in *Das Werden des Alten Testamentes* (Leipzig: Teubner, 1936); Reinhold Niebuhr, *The Nature and Destiny of Man. A Christian Interpretation* (London: Nisbet, 1941 ff.).

V. SPIRITUAL TEACHINGS IN ISLAM WITH SPECIAL REFERENCE TO AL-HUJWIRI (Pages 80–103)

1. A. J. Toynbee, *A Study of History* (abridged version) (London: Oxford Press, 1947); F. S. C. Northrop, *The Meeting of East and West* (London: Macmillan, 1946).

2. There is no dearth of handbooks outlining Islam. Cf. G. F. Moore, *History of Religions* (New York: Charles Scribner's Sons, 1928), II, 386 ff.; E. J. Jurji, *The Great World Religions* (Princeton: Princeton University Press, 1946), pp. 178 ff.

3. Cf. D. B. MacDonald, *Aspects of Islam* (New York: Macmillan Co., 1911); I. Goldziher, *Vorlesungen über den Islam* (2nd ed.; Heidelberg: Winter, 1926), chap. iv.; H. A. R. Gibb, *Mohammedanism* (Home Univ. Library, Oxford, 1949).

4. I. Goldziher, *Die Richtungen der islamischen koranexegese* (Leyden: Brill, 1920), esp. pp. 180 ff.

5. H. A. R. Gibb, *Modern Trends in Islam* (Chicago: University of Chicago Press, 1947), pp. 20, 31 ff.

6. A thorough comparison of the teachings of a Christian and a Moslem theologian as to similarities and differences comparable to the work done by R. Otto in his *Mysticism, East and West*, trans. B. L. Bracey (New York: Macmillan Co., 1932), wherein he compares Meister Eckhardt and Shankara, has as yet not been undertaken. But cf. M. Smith, *Studies in Early Mysticism in the Near and Middle East* (London: Sheldon Press, 1931) and J. W. Sweetman, *Islam and Christian Theology* (London: Lutterworth, 1945), Vol. I. The aim of the present paper is not a comparison but simply an exposition of the teachings of one representative theologian.

7. R. A. Nicholson, 'Mysticism in Persia,' *Proceedings of the Iranian Society*, I, No. 6 (1938), 60 ff. It was the merit of L. Massignon in his monumental studies in the development of early Islamic mysticism to point out the central role of meditation upon the Koran as a source of its piety (cf. op. cit. on Hasan al-Basri, father of the 'knowledge of the heart'; cf. also below, n. 13). The oldest type of mysticism in Islam was ascetic and devotional rather than speculative, and the word 'Sufi' first appears in literature as applied to a certain class of ascetics (R. A. Nicholson, *The Idea of Personality in Sufism* (Cambridge: University Press, 1923) and his *The Mystics of Islam* (London: Bell, 1914); I. Goldziher, *Vorlesungen*, pp. 133 ff.).

8. Smith, op. cit., chap. viii.

9. One of the younger English orientalists, A. J. Arberry, has recently surveyed the fascinating history of the rediscovery of Sufism by Western scholars in his *Introduction to the Study of Sufism* (London: Luzac, 1942). English, French, and German philologists and poets share the merit of having edited and interpreted Arabic, Persian, Turkish, and Hindustani sources for the study of the lives of the Sufi and their teachings. '*Suf*' (wool) was the material of the garment worn by the early ascetics. Different explanations of the term 'Sufi' have been suggested by the Sufi themselves (cf. below).

10. Cf. the brief but excellent survey by M. Smith, *Al-Ghazali, the Mystic* (London: Luzac, 1944); cf. also G. von Grunebaum, *Medieval Islam* (Chicago: University of Chicago Press, 1946), pp. 124 ff.

11. Ali b. Uthman al-Jullabi al-Hujwiri, *The Kashf al-Mahjub: The Oldest Persian Treatise on Sufism* (originally published as Vol. XVII of the 'Gibb Memorial Series'), now edited and translated by R. A. Nicholson (London: Luzac, 1936). On the author, who died between A.D. 1087 and 1091, and the text cf. the Preface. The title of the book is *The Unveiling of the Veiled*. In the following pages numbers in parenthesis refer to the pagination of Nicholson's translation.

12. L. Massignon, *La Passion d'al Husayn . . . al Hallaj: Martyr mystique de l'Islam* (Paris: Geuthner, 1922).

13. Cf. the excellent exposition of al-Muhasibi's theology by M. Smith, *An Early Mystic of Baghdad* (London: Sheldon Press, 1935).

14. A. E. Affifi, *The Mystical Philosophy of Muhyid Din Ibn ul 'Arabi* (Cambridge: University Press, 1939).

15. Smith, *Al-Ghazali, the Mystic;* cf. also S. Zwemer, *A Moslem Seeker after God* (New York: F. H. Revell Co., 1920).

16. Other texts in translation are: R. Hartmann, *Al Kuschairis Darstellung des Sufitums* ('Türkische Bibliothek,' Band 18 (Berlin: Mayer & Müller, 1914)); A. J. Arberry, *The Doctrine of the Sufis (Kitab al Ta'arruf* of al-Kalabadhi) (Cambridge: University Press, 1935). The former Sufi died in 1074, the latter in 990 (995). Both of these earlier treatises seem to us inferior to the *Kashf al-Mahjub.*

17. For the Sufi terminology cf. L. Massignon, *Essai sur les origines du lexique technique de la mystique musulmane* (Paris: Geuthner, 1922); and the articles on 'dervish,' 'tasawwuf,' and 'tariqa' in *Encyclopaedia of Islam,* I, 949 ff.; IV, 687 ff.; 667 ff.; and 'Sufis' in *ERE,* XII, 10.

18. Cf. esp. *Kashf al-Mahjub,* chap. xiv.

19. Cf. the discussion on the saintliness of the *imams* (first caliphs) and their successors (chaps. vii ff.). On Ali as the *shaikh* ('leader') of the theory and practice of Sufism see ibid., p. 74.

20. The notion of 'veiling' is developed further by al-Ghazzali (cf. Smith, *Al-Ghazali, the Mystic,* pp. 147 ff.; W. H. T. Gairdner, *Al Ghazzali's Mishkat al anwar* (London: Royal Asiatic Society, 1924), pp. 5 ff.).

21. Al-Muhasibi (d. 857) first systematically classified 'states.' Cf., for his teachings, Massignon, *Essai,* pp. 211 ff.; Smith, *An Early Mystic,* esp. chap. x; Arberry, *Introduction,* pp. 62–3; Smith, *Al-Ghazali,* pp. 123–4.

22. For other important references in al-Hujwiri's refutation of the erroneous teachings of his predecessors, see especially the numerous 'excursuses' of his book.

23. Cf. Hartmann, op. cit., pp. 56 ff.; Arberry, *Doctrine,* chaps. xxi, xxii; Smith, *An Early Mystic,* chap. vi.

24. For al-Muhasibi's doctrine of grace cf. Smith, *An Early Mystic,* pp. 178 ff.

25. Cf. Arberry, *Doctrine,* chap. lix; cf. Nicholson, *Idea of Personality,* pp. 13 ff.

26. On the notion of union of al-Junaid and al-Qushairi see Massignon, *La Passion;* Hartmann, op. cit., pp. 48 ff.; for that of al-Muhasibi see Smith, *An Early Mystic,* chaps. ix, xii; of al-Kalabadhi see Arberry, *Doctrine,* chaps. xxxii, l, lv, lxi.

27. On *dhikr,* the practice of the cultivation of Divine Presence, cf. also Hartmann, op. cit., pp. 34 ff.; for al-Ghazzali's teaching and its resemblance to that of Brother Lawrence cf. Zwemer, op. cit., p. 248, and Smith, *Al-Ghazali,* pp. 96 ff.

28. For al-Muhasibi, who first outlined methodologically a

psychology in Sufism, and his notion of the 'lower soul' (*nafs*), cf. Smith, *An Early Mystic*, p. 90.

29. Cf. Hartmann, op. cit., pp. 107 ff.; Smith, *An Early Mystic*, pp. 150 ff.; Arberry, *Doctrine*, chap. xxxv; Zwemer, op. cit., pp. 243 ff.

30. Dhu'l Nun was the first to distinguish the mystical knowledge of God (*ma'rifat*) from the intellectual (*'ilm*) by connecting the former with the love of God (*mahabbat*) (R. A. Nicholson, *The Idea of Personality in Sufism*, p. 9). For Rabia cf. Smith, *Rabia the Mystic* (Cambridge: University Press, 1928); for al-Muhasibi see Smith, *An Early Mystic*, pp. 233 ff.; for Kalabadhi see Arberry, *Doctrine*, chap. li; for al-Qushairi see Hartmann, op. cit., pp. 62 ff., 75; for al-Ghazzali see Smith, *Al-Ghazali, the Mystic*, chap. xii.

31. Love for the prophet, surpassing belief and reverence, is an important feature of Sufism. 'Um ihre Gefühle für den Propheten auszudrücken, greifen die Mystiker immer auf das Wort Liebe, ja der Prophet wird gleichsam in die mystische Gottesliebe mithineingezogen' (Tor Andrae, *Die person Muhammeds* (Stockholm: Norstedt, 1918), p. 384; cf. pp. 367 ff.).

32. Al-Hujwiri is preceded in his *via media* by al-Muhasibi (cf. Smith, *An Early Mystic*, p. 254). See, for al-Kalabadhi, Arberry, *Doctrine*, chaps. xxv ff.; for al-Ghazzali, whose spiritual interpretation of the ordinances is especially impressive, Zwemer, op. cit., pp. 239 ff.

33. But cf. al-Kalabadhi's definition (Arberry, *Doctrine*, pp. 78–9).

34. Cf., for al-Muhasibi's devotional teachings, Smith, *An Early Mystic*, chap. xi.

35. Concerning the novices as 'masters of their hearts' and the adepts as 'under the dominion of their hearts,' see *Kashf al-Mahjub*, p. 85.

36. Cf. von Grunebaum, op. cit., pp. 250 ff.

37. 'Futuwwa' (art.), *EI*, II, 123 ff.; R. Hartmann, 'Futuwwa and Malama,' *ZDMG*, LXXII (1918), 193 ff.; and J. Wach, *Sociology of Religion* (London: Kegan Paul, 1947).

38. Hartmann, *Al-Kushairi*, pp. 113 ff.

39. Cf. Zwemer's discussion of al-Ghazzali's *Al adab fi din* ('Ethics in Religion'), op. cit., pp. 175 ff., 201 ff. The division of the respective chapters of Ghazzali's main work clearly reflects al-Hujwiri's work (op. cit., p. 180).

40. *The Ante-Nicene Fathers* (Buffalo: Christian Literature Pub. Co., 1885), II, 231 ff.

41. For Mohammed as the prototype of the spiritual guide (*shaikh*) in Sufism see Andrae, op. cit., pp. 367 ff.

42. Cf. Hartmann, *Al-Kuschairi*, pp. 101 ff., 176 ff.; for Suhrawardi see J. Wach, *Meister und Jünger* (Leipzig: Ed. Pfeiffer, 1925), pp. 72 ff.; for Ghazzali see Smith, *Al-Ghazali, the Mystic*, p. 152. Cf. also generally M. Buber, 'Der Ort des Chassidismus in der Religionsgeschichte,' *Theol. Zeitschrift*, II (1946), 438 ff.

43. Cf. Hartmann, *Al-Kuschairi*, pp. 148 ff.; Andrae, op. cit., pp.

NOTES (Pages 99–105)

371 ff.; R. Otto, *The Kingdom of God and the Son of Man* (London: Lutterworth, 1938), pp. 333 ff.

44. The development of orders (dervish communities) in Sufism does not begin before the twelfth century; here the notion of *Shuyukhiyat* (spirit guidance) was to play a decisive rôle.

45. Hartmann, *Al-Kuschairi*, chap. iv; Arberry, *Doctrine*, chap. lxxv; Smith, *An Early Mystic*, p. 71, and *Al-Ghazali, the Mystic*, chap. vi.

46. Cf. al-Muhasibi's views on temptation (Smith, *An Early Mystic*, esp. chap. vii).

VI. THE STUDY OF MAHĀYĀNA BUDDHISM
(Pages 104–131)

1. Notes 9, 10 and 11 list important general works. Since their publication a great deal of valuable research has been done to which reference is made in the notes of the following treatise (cf. the previous study of J. Wach, *Mahāyāna, besonders im Hinblick auf der Saddharmapundarika-Sūtra* (München: O. Schloss, 1926).

2. Betty Heimann, *Indian and Western Philosophy. A Study in Contrasts* (London: Allen and Unwin, 1937).

3. F. Otto Schrader, 'Zur Bedeutung der Namen, "Mahāyāna" and "Hīnayāna"' (*Zeitschrift der Deutschen Morgenländischen Gesellschaft*, XLIV (1910), 341 ff.).

4. Ananda K. Coomaraswamy, *Hinduism and Buddhism* (New York: Philosophical Library, Inc.), s.a.

5. Cf. the as yet unpublished thesis by Robert H. L. Slater, *'Nirvana' in Burmese Buddhism*, and esp. Th. Stcherbatsky, *The Conception of Buddhist Nirvana* (Leningrad: Academy of Sciences, 1927, reprint Shanghai, 1940).

6. Th. Stcherbatsky, *The Central Conception of Buddhism and the Meaning of the Word 'Dharma'* (London: Royal Asiatic Society, 1923); O. Rosenberg, *Buddhistische Philosophie*.

7. A. Berriedale Keith, *Buddhist Philosophy in India and Ceylon* (Oxford: Clarendon Press, 1923).

8. J. G. Jennings, *The Vedāntic Buddhism of the Buddha. A Collection of Historical Texts translated from the Original Pāli* (London: G. Cumberlege, Oxford University Press, 1948).

9. Louis de la Vallée-Poussin, *Bouddhisme. Opinions sur l'histoire de la dogmatique* (Paris: Beauchesne, 1925); Keith, *Buddhist Philosophy*; E. J. Thomas, *History of Buddhist Thought*.

10. James B. Pratt, *The Pilgrimage of Buddhism* (New York: The Macmillan Co., 1928).

11. Sir Charles Eliot, *Hinduism and Buddhism* (London: E. Arnold, 1921).

12. On Tocharian notions cf. Walter Couvreur, 'Le charactère Sarvāstivādin-Vaibāshika des fragments Tochariens' (*Le Muséon*,

LIX (1946), 577 ff.). For South-east Asia: Kenneth P. Landon, *South-east Asia, Crossroads of Religions* (Chicago: University of Chicago Press, 1949); Bernard H. M. Vlekke, *Nusantara* (Cambridge, Mass.: Harvard University Press, 1944). For Tibet: Charles Bell, *The Religion of Tibet* (Oxford: Clarendon Press, 1931).

13. Since a knowledge of these languages cannot be expected from the reader of this article, no data on editions of the texts are given, but in the case of each translation the exact place where it can be found has been indicated. Diacritical signs are omitted.

14. L. Renou, 'Sylvain Lévi' (*JA*, CCXXVI (1936), 1 ff.); P. Masson-Oursel, 'Louis de la Vallée-Poussin' (*JA*, CCXXX (1938), 287 ff.).

15. A recent survey: E. Lamotte, 'Chronique Bouddhique' (*Le Muséon*, LIV (1941), 199 ff.). Cf. also now the great translation of Nāgārjuna's Mahāprajñāpāramitā-śāstra by the same author (*La Traité de la grande vertu de sagesse*, Louvain, 1944–9).

16. Cf. Burnett H. Streeter, *The Buddha and the Christ* (Bampton Lectures, 1932) (London: Macmillan, 1932); Hendrik Kraemer, *The Christian Message in a Non-Christian World* (New York: Harper & Bros., 1947); Arnold J. Toynbee, *A Study of History* (Abridged by D. S. Somerville) (London: Oxford Press, 1947), pp. 21 ff., 390 ff.; F. S. C. Northrop, *The Meeting of East and West* (New York: Macmillan, 1946), IX, cf. pp. 346 ff.

17. Art. 'Mahāyāna,' *ERE*, VIII, 330 ff.; Chantepie de la Saussaye, *Lehrbuch der Religionsgeschichte*, 4 Aufl. (Tübingen: 1924); G. F. Moore, *History of Religions* (New York: Charles Scribners, rev. ed. 1937), I, 304 ff.; August K. Reischauer, 'Buddhism' in Edward J. Jurji, *The Great Religions of the Modern World* (Princeton: University Press, 1946), pp. 121 ff.; William M. McGovern, *An Introduction to Mahāyāna Buddhism* (London: Kegan Paul, 1922); B. L. Suzuki, *Mahāyāna Buddhism* (London: Marlowe, 1948). The best presentation of Mahāyāna Buddhism is still: L. de la Vallée-Poussin, *Bouddhisme, Opinions sur l'histoire de la dogmatique* (4th ed. Paris: Beauchesne: 1925). E. Lamotte, *La Somme du Grand Véhicule* (Louvain: 1938–9), was not available to me.

18. Cf. Junjiro Takakusu, *The Essentials of Buddhist Philosophy* (ed. by W. T. Chan and Charles A. Moore) (Honolulu: University of Hawaii, 1947); Masaharu Anesaki, *History of Japanese Religion* (London: K. Paul, Trench, Trubner, 1930); D. T. Suzuki (cf. below); O. Rosenberg, *Buddhist Philosophy* is the only Western work which incorporates the studies of the Japanese commentaries and modern writings. Cf. the extensive bibliography, pp. 270 ff. and 278 ff. Cf. also R. Tajima, *Étude sur le Maha-vairocana-Sūtra* (Paris; Maisonneuve, 1936).

19. Benoytosh Battacharyya, *The Indian Buddhist Iconography* (London: Oxford University Press, 1924); Alice Getty, *The Gods of Northern Buddhism, their History, Iconography and Progressive Evolu-*

tion (Oxford: Clarendon Press, 1914), with a list of earlier publications, pp. 183 ff.; Ludwig Bachhofer, *Early Indian Sculpture* (New York: Harcourt, Brace, 1929); Ananda K. Coomaraswamy, 'La Sculpture de Bodhgayā' in *Ars Asiatica*, XVIII (Paris: Éditions d'art, 1935); Ananda K. Coomaraswamy, *Elements of Buddhist Iconography* (Cambridge, Mass.: Harvard University Press, 1935); Alfred C. A. Foucher, *La Vie du Bouddha d'après les textes et monuments* (Paris: Payot, 1949). Cf. also below, Note 50.

20. Stcherbatsky, *The Central Conception*, p. 3. This understanding is also stressed by Rosenberg (op. cit.) who states that the basic problems of Buddhist systematic literature are the quest for the nature of the 'real' and for salvation (p. 229).

21. For the notion of celestial archetypes, cf. Mircea Eliade, *Le Mythe de l'éternel rétour* (Paris: Gallimard, 1949).

22. Cf. L. de la Vallée-Poussin's criticism of the theses of H. Oldenberg, *Opinions*, pp. 219 ff.

23. A good survey of the historical development of Mahāyāna doctrine in its main stages gives Stcherbatsky, *Nirvāna*, pp. 60 ff.

24. R. Otto, *The Idea of the Holy* (tr. John Harvey), rev. 1929. (London: Oxford University Press, 1928). Cf. below, Chap. X.

25. W. E. Soothill, *The Lotus of the Wonderful Law* (Oxford: Clarendon Press, 1930), preface.

26. R. Otto, op. cit., chap. v.

27. On *Chinese Buddhism*, cf. Samuel Beal, *A Catena of Buddhist Scriptures* (London: Trubner, 1871); Jan J. M. de Groot, *Le Code du Mahāyāna en Chine* (Amsterdam: J. Müller, 1893); Reginald F. Johnston, *Buddhist China* (London: J. Murray, 1913); Lewis Hodous, *Buddhism and Buddhists in China* (New York: Macmillan, 1924); Karl L. Reichelt, *Truth and Tradition in Chinese Buddhism* (Shanghai: The Commercial Press, 1934); cf. also his 'Buddhism in China' (*International Review of Missions*, XXVI (1937), 153 ff.); John Blofeld, *The Jewel in the Lotus* (London, Sidgwick, 1948).

28. For *Japanese Buddhism*, cf. Sir Charles N. E. Eliot, *Japanese Buddhism* (London: E. Arnold, 1935); Rosenberg, op. cit.; August K. Reischauer, *Studies in Japanese Buddhism* (New York: Macmillan, 1917); E. Steinilber-Oberlin, *The Buddhist Sects of Japan* (tr. from French by Marc Logi) (London: Allen and Unwin, 1938); Masaharu Anesaki, *Nichiren, the Buddhist Prophet* (Cambridge, Mass.: Harvard University Press, 1916); A. Lloyd, *Shinran and His Work* (Tokyo: Kyobunkwan, 1910; Harper H. Cooks and Ryugaku Ishizuka, *Honan the Buddhist Saint* (Kyoto: Chiomin, 1925); Gessho Sazaki, *A Study of Shin Buddhism* (Kyoto: The Eastern Buddhist Society, 1925); Daisetz T. Suzuki, *Essays in Zen Buddhism* (London: Luzac, 1927); *Manual of Zen Buddhism* (Kyoto: The Eastern Buddhist Society, 1935), *Zen Buddhism and its Influence on Japanese Culture* (Kyoto: The Eastern Buddhist Society, 1938). For Shingon esp. Tajima, op. cit., Introd.

29. The denominational differentiation of Mahāyāna Buddhism cannot be discussed in detail in this paper. For the philosophical aspects of Chinese-Japanese denominationalism cf. Junjiro Takakusu, *The Essentials of Buddhist Philosophy* (ed. by W. T. Chan and Charles A. Moore) (Honolulu: University of Hawaii, 1947).

30. A good survey of the Japanese Buddhist denominations can be found in Pratt, *The Pilgrimage of Buddhism*, chaps. xxiii ff., Steinilber-Oberlin, op. cit., and Reischauer, op. cit.

31. For the differentiation between denomination and sect, cf. J. Wach, *Church, Denomination and Sect* (below, Chap. IX). Cf. also Rosenberg, *Buddhist Philosophy*, chap. xix, who also rejects the term 'sect' for the 'schools' ('Konfessionen') of the Great Vehicle (p. 246).

32. Cf. the critical classification of the other groups by Kegon: Takakusu, op. cit., pp. 114 ff.; by Tendai: pp. 131 ff.; by Shingon: pp. 147 ff.

33. The best survey of the lives and teachings of the outstanding theologians and thinkers of the Great Vehicle in *ERE* (Aśvagosha, II, 159 f., Nāgārjuna, Āryadeva, Asanga, II, 62, Vasubhandu, XII, 595b f., Chandrakīrti, Śāntideva, VIII, 89a, etc.) and in Winternitz, *Geschichte der indischen Literatur* (Leipzig: Amelang, 1920), pp. 201 ff., 250 ff. Cf. also Keith, *Buddhist Philosophy*, pp. 227 ff., Stcherbatsky, *Nirvāna*, pp. 65 ff., and articles in *ERE*, II, 159 f., 62; VIII, 330 ff., 89a; XII, 595b f., etc.

34. Rosenberg, *Buddhist Philosophy*, pp. 107 ff., 229, 245.

35. Cf. the important study of Stcherbatsky, *The Central Conception* with the analysis of the classes of dharmas.

36. Rosenberg, op. cit., p. 108.

37. 'In Hīnayana . . . we have a radical Pluralism, converted in Mahāyāna into as radical a Monism' (Stcherbatsky, *Nirvāna*, p. 41).

38. For the texts cf. below. *Nāgārjuna* is the foremost thinker of the first, *Asanga* and *Vasubandhu* of the latter school. For the major treatises of the Mādhyamika cf. below note 131; Rosenberg, op. cit., pp. 37 ff., 92 ff. for the Yogācāra; Th. de Stcherbatsky, 'La littérature Yogācāra d'après Bouston' (*Le Muséon*, VI (1905)); L. de la Vallée-Poussin,'Vasubandhu's Traité des Vingt Ślokas' (*Le Muséon*, XIII (1912), 53 ff.); Sylvain Lévi, *Asanga's Mahāyāna-Sūtrālamkāra. Exposé de la doctrine du Grand Véhicule selon le système Yogācāra* (Paris: H. Champion, 1911), II, 1 ff.; on Asanga, pp. 16 ff.; Hermann Jacobi, *Trimśikāvijñāpti des Vasubandhu mit Bhāsya des Sthiramati* (Stuttgart: Kohlhammer, 1932). Though belonging to Vasubandhu's Hināyāna period, his *Abhidharma-kośa* is of fundamental importance for all Buddhist epistemology, as Rosenberg (op. cit., pp. 41, 90 ff.) rightly insists. (French translation by L. de la Vallée-Poussin, Société Belge d'Études Orientales (Paris: P. Geuthner, 1922–31). For the connection between the ancient discipline of Yoga and the Yogācāra thought cf. Lévi, op. cit., pp. 18 ff. and Mircea Eliade, *Techniques du Yoga* (Paris: Gallimard,1948).

39. L. de la Vallée-Poussin, *Opinions*, pp. 186 ff., 195 ff., 200 ff. Cf. also Mādhyamika; article 'Philosophy: Buddhist,' *ERE*, IX, 848b. Keith, op. cit., chap. xiii; Lamotte, *Traité*, I, Pref. X.

40. The method of the 'four branches' (things neither exist by themselves, nor by others, nor by both, nor by neither) is known as *prasanga*. (Keith, op. cit., p. 230; Stcherbatsky, *Nirvāna*, p. 67). Cf. there, p. 81, n. 1, an excellent exposition of the meaning of madhyamā pratipāda ('middle path').

41. Stcherbatsky, *Nirvāna*, p. 69.

42. L. de la Vallée-Poussin, *Opinions*, pp. 204, 290 ff., esp. pp. 188 f. The teachers of the Great Vehicle are familiar with Hinayāna texts and quote from them (*ERE*, VIII, 336a). The following threefold teaching can be distinguished: the doctrine of the Ego is erroneous; the doctrines of the elements of the Ego and of causation experience; the true doctrine which contradicts experience is the doctrine of the void, revealed in the writings and treatises of the Great Vehicle (p. 189). As long as belief in the reality of suffering prevails, the 'heresy' that the suffering is *my* suffering is easily succumbed to (pp. 194, 292). Cf. also *ERE*, IX, 851.

43. 'This amalgamation [*soudure*] of charity and devotion on the one hand, and the most extreme [*outrancière*] metaphysics on the other, is the masterwork of Hindu dialectics and an object of astonishment or admiration for the historian.' (L. de la Vallée-Poussin, *Opinions*, p. 290.) Cf. Lamotte, op. cit.

44. On the divisions within the Mādhyamika School, cf. L. de la Vallée-Poussin, *Opinions*, p. 198, n. 1; Keith, op. cit., pp. 240 ff.; Stcherbatsky, *Nirvāna*, pp. 65 ff., 87 ff.

45. Cf. below, Sect. IV. This text approaches a pantheistic position. (Cf. the teaching of the Elements of Buddhahood according to the U.: Obermiller, 'The Sublime Science' (*Acta Orientalia*, IX (1931), 104 ff.)

46. Cf. Keith, op. cit., chap. xv.

47. Loc. cit., pp. 255, 253.

48. L. de la Vallée-Poussin, 'Note sur les Corps de Buddha' (*Le Muséon*, n.s., XIV (1913), 257 ff.); *ERE*, IX, article 'Philosophy: Buddhist,' p. 852; *Opinions*, pp. 260 ff.; T. Suzuki, *Studies in the Lankāvatāra Sūtra* (London: Routledge, 1930), pp. 308 ff.; Rosenberg, op. cit., p. 236; Keith, op. cit., chap. xvi.

49. Cf. the enumeration of the acts of devotion (pūja); L. de la Vallée-Poussin, 'Introduction à la pratique des futurs Bouddhas' (*Bodhicaryāvatāra*) (*Revue d'histoire et de littérature religieuse*, XI (1906), 445 ff., 454 ff.)

50. L. de la Vallée-Poussin, *Opinions*, chap. iii. A. Getty, *The Gods of Northern Buddhism*, pp. 26 ff.; M. T. de Mallmann, *Introduction à l'étude d'Avalokiteçvara* (Paris: Civilisations du Sud, 1948), IV, V.

51. *ERE*, II, 740a; Keith, op. cit., pp. 298 ff.

52. Cf. p. 11, n. 3.

53. Suzuki, *Studies*, p. 229.

54. L. de la Vallée-Poussin, *Introduction*, p. 434.

55. Cf. below. S. Lévi (in his Introduction to the *Sutrālamkara*, p. 18), refers to *prajñā* as the twin-sister of *Sophia* and the Gnosis of Greek Asia. Cf. Lamotte, op. cit., and notes 15, 109, 131 here.

56. L. de la Vallée-Poussin, *Opinions*, p. 282.

57. Cf. the 'Vows of the Bodhisattva' (Samantabhadra) cf. Suzuki, *Studies*, pp. 220, 230 ff., 356 f.; Mallmann, op. cit.

58. On Avalokiteśvara's vows cf. Suzuki, op. cit., p. 356, who renders in English some passages of the main text in praise of this Bodhisattva, the *Avatamsaka*, of which the *Karandavyūha* forms a part. It has never been translated fully in any European language. The edition of the *Gandavyūha* was not available to me. (Kyoto: Buddhist Text Society, 1934.)

59. L. de la Vallée-Poussin, *Opinions*, pp. 280 ff., 296 f.; cf. Keith, op. cit., pp. 283 ff. on devotion and transfer of merit.

60. L. de la Vallée-Poussin, *Introduction*, p. 435.

61. For the distinction between the 'beginning' bodhisattvas (*ādikarmika*) who may still lack morality or knowledge, and may sin though they have at least the desire of charity, and the Bodhisattvas who, sinless, possess the body of bliss (cf. above) and become incarnate for the salvation of creatures, cf. L. de la Vallée-Poussin, *Introduction*, p. 433.

62. L. de la Vallée-Poussin, *Opinions*, pp. 283 f., 287 f.

63. *ERE*, II, 740b; cf. Keith, op. cit., pp. 275 ff.

64. For the word: *Le Muséon*, VIII, 190 f., 277 ff., and *ERE*, II, 740b. For the texts cf. below. Cf. Suzuki, *Studies*, pp. 365 ff.; L. de la Vallée-Poussin, *Opinions*, pp. 311 ff.; also *ERE*, II, 750 ff. and the analysis of the content of the *Bodhicaryāvatāra* below, Sect. VI, p. 119 and Lamotte, *Traité*, Vol. I, 255 ff., and II.

65. For the distinction between Buddhas and Bodhisattvas, cf. the excellent definition of L. de la Vallée-Poussin: 'In this reality [middle path] the Buddha's knowledge is wholly purified, whereas the Bodhisattva's knowledge is simply directed toward it, "ripened toward it by the path of study." Its name is wisdom (*prajñā*). It is the "Great Resource" to supreme Enlightenment' (*Le Muséon*, VII (1906), p. 222); Lamotte, op. cit., I, VIII.

66. 'The beginner relying on the favour of the Buddha' (*ERE*, II, 749).

67. The major texts—besides the Great Sūtra—are the *Mahāyāna-Sūtrālamkāra* (tr. by Sylvain Lévi in *Bibliothèque des Hautes Études* (Paris: H. Champion, 1907), p. 159. A summary of the teachings: II, 16 ff.), and the *Bodhisattvabhūmi* (Cecil Bendall and L. de la Vallée-Poussin, *Le Muséon*, VI (1905), 38 ff., VII (1906), on

pp. 213 ff. a summary of the contents). Cf. Har Dayal, *The Bodhi-sattva Doctrine in Buddhist Sanskrit Literature* (London: Kegan Paul, 1932). Cf. above, note 15.

68. *Le Muséon*, VI, 40 ff.

69. Ibid., VI, 40 ff.

70. Cecil Bendall, *Cikshāsamuccaya* (St. Petersburg: Academy of Sciences, 1902, Vol. XXXI).

71. 'One is lost if one lets go saving a single creature; what should one say of the injustice done to all the living inhabitants of infinite space?' (L. de la Vallée-Poussin, *Introduction*, IV, 10).

72. Art. 'Bodhisattva,' *ERE*, II, 749. (Cf. there on the ritual of supreme worship (*anuttarapūjā*)). Dayal, op. cit., chap. iii.

73. Loc. cit., p. 740a.

74. Dayal, op. cit., chap. vi. A comparison of the Buddhist *bhūmis* with the Yoga and the Sufi 'stations' is suggested by Rahder, op. cit., p. 152. Cf. J. Wach, 'Spiritual Teachings in Islam' (*JR*, XXVIII (1948), 263 ff.), and above, Chap. V.

75. No translation exists, as yet, of the *Daśabhūmaka-Sūtra*. Cf. J. Rahder, *Le Muséon*, XXXIX (1926), 125 ff. Winternitz, *Geschichte*, p. 244. Suzuki, *Studies*, pp. 221 f. with extracts from the text. According to the *Compendium* the vow can be taken even by one who has not entered on the *bhūmis*. (*Śiksāsamuccaya*, XXXII).

76. *ERE*, II, p. 744b, n. 6. Cf. Lévi, *Introduction to the Sūtralamkāra*, pp. 21 ff.

77. Art. 'Bodhisattva' (*ERE*, II, 745b).

78. Loc. cit., p. 747a. Long periods have to elapse before the Yogacāra attains to Bodhisattvahood, and again from this state to Buddhahood (Lévi, op. cit., p. 21).

79. Loc. cit., pp. 745b ff. The principal texts, according to L. de la Vallée-Poussin, are the *Astasāhasrika-Prajñāpāramitā* (cf. below, p. 131), the *Daśabhūmaka*, the *Bodhicaryāvatāra*, the *Bodhisattvabhūmi*, the *Mādhyamikāvatāra* and the *Sūtrālamkāra*. For the ten stages of the *Mahāvastu*, cf. loc. cit., p. 744b.

80. Cf. for the seven stages of the *Bodhisattvabhūmi: Le Muséon*, VI, 38 ff., VII, 213 ff.

81. *Mādhyamikāvatāra* (*Le Muséon*, XIII, 249 ff.; XI, 271 ff.); *ERE*, II, 748.

82. For the Buddha's prediction that Ānanda, the favourite disciple, would be reborn in the 'joyful stage' as Nāgārjuna, cf. loc. cit., p. 746a.

83. *ERE*, p. 746b, cf. *Le Muséon*, VIII, 300, 305 ff.

84. Soothill, *Lotus*, chap. ii.

85. *ERE*, II, 747–8.

86. Ibid., II, 748a.

87. Lévi, *Introduction*, p. 23.

88. *ERE*, II, 748a. Cf. there Candrakīrti's theory of stages (in the *Mādhyamikāvatāra*).

89. *Bodhisattvabhūmi* (*Le Muséon*, VI, VII). Cf. Lamotte, op. cit., I, chap. X.

90. For *siddhi*: Mircea Eliade, *Techniques de Yoga* (Paris: Gallimard, 1948), pp. 156, 189.

91. *Le Muséon*, VI, 43.

92. Ibid., VI, 44. On the conduct of the Bodhisattva very detailed rules are given: *Bodhicaryāvatāra*, chap. v.

93. Ibid., VII, 214.

94. Ibid., VII, 216 ff.

95. *ERE*, II, 748. Dayal, op. cit., chaps. v, vi. Cf. above and also *Le Muséon*, VI, 48, VII, 218.

96. Selections from the following texts were the subjects of reports in the above-mentioned course. Cf. above, p. 232, n. 2.

97. Unfortunately no full English translation of Śantideva's *Sikshāsamuccaya* (the fragmentary one of Bendall and Rouse was not available to me) exists. Cf., however, the summarizing of the teachings of this compendium of Mahāyāna Buddhism which its author adorns with many quotations, by C. Bendall in his edition of the text (*Bibliotheca Buddhica* (1897), XXXI ff.). The *Kārikās* (memorial verses) are translated by L. D. Barnett, *The Path of Light* (London: John Murray, 2nd ed. (1947), pp. 103 ff.).

98. A very good short selection in German is M. Winternitz, 'Der Mahāyāna-Buddhismus' (*Religionsgeschichtliches Lesebuch*, ed. Alfred Bertholet, 2. Aufl. (Tübingen: Mohr (Siebeck), 1930), Nr. 15.

99. Cf. E. J. Thomas, *The Life of the Buddha in Legend and History* (London: Kegan Paul, Trench, Trubner, 1927).

100. Cf. M. Winternitz, *Geschichte der indischen Literatur* (Leipzig: Amelang, 1920), II, 187 ff. on the *Mahāvastu;* pp. 194 ff. on the *Lalitavistara*. A French translation of the latter from the Tibetan, Ph. E. Foucaux; a translation of the *Nidānakathā*, an extracanonical biographical Pali work, in T. W. Rhys Davids, *Buddhist Birth Stories* (London, Trubner, 1877); cf. also Lamotte, *Traité*, I.

101. *The Lotus of the Wonderful Law* or *The Lotus Gospel*, tr. by W. E. Soothill (Oxford: Clarendon Press, 1936). See also J. Wach, *Mahāyāna, besonders im Himblick auf das Saddharmapundarīka* (München: O. Schloss, 1925).

102. Cf. esp. the parables of the Prodigal Son (chap. iv), of Trees and Herbs and of the Magic City (v) and of the Good Physician (xvi).

103. Avalokitésvara in chap. xxiv. Cf. Mallmann, op. cit.

104. *Lotus*, chap. ii.

105. Ibid., chap. x.

106. Ibid., chaps. xviii, xix.

107. *Sacred Books*, XLIX.

108. Ibid., XLIX, cf. for the theory of meditation in the Lesser and the Great Vehicle: Mircea Eliade, *Techniques du Yoga* (Paris: Gallimard, 1948), chap. iv.

109. L. de la Vallée-Poussin, 'Introduction à la pratique des futurs Bouddhas par Çantideva' (*Revue d'histoire et de la littérature réligeuse*, XI (1906), 430 ff., XII (1907), 97 ff. Cf. also by the same, 'Une version chinoise du Bodhicaryāvatāra' (*Le Muséon*, n.s., IV (1908), 313 ff.). Cf. also now in Lamotte, *Traité* (below, n. 131), vol. II.

110. Op. cit., p. 435.

111. Op. cit., p. 389.

112. Op. cit., chap. ii.; Lamotte, op. cit., II, Chaps. xvii ff.

113. Op. cit., chap. v., cf. Dayal, op. cit., chap. v.

114. Op. cit., chap. vi.

115. Op. cit., chap. vii.

116. Op. cit., p. 389; Lamotte, op. cit., II, chaps. xxiv, xxv.

117. Op. cit., chap. viii, cf. Eliade, op. cit., pp. 164 ff., 175 ff.

118. Op. cit., p. 404.

119. Op. cit., chap. ix; cf. Lamotte, op. cit., II, chaps. xxix, xxx.

120. Op. cit., p. 429, s, 1.

121. *Açvagosha's Discourse on the Awakening of Faith in the Mahāyāna*, tr. from the Chinese by Teitaro Suzuki (Chicago: Open Court, 1900). This text is an early Yogācāra treatise.

122. Loc. cit., pp. 53 ff., 67.

123. Loc. cit., p. 78.

124. Loc. cit., p. 82. S. Lévi in his introduction to the *Sūtrā-lamkāra* (p. 18) suggests Manichean influences on the Yogācāra theory of 'defilement.' (Cf. below on the *Lankavātara*.) On the (*ālaya*) *vijnāna:* p. 20.

125. Loc. cit., p. 95.

126. Loc. cit., p. 89.

127. Loc. cit., p. 92.

128. Loc. cit., p. 93.

129. Loc. cit., p. 116.

130. Loc. cit., pp. 132 ff.

131. Cf. Winternitz, *Geschichte*, pp. 247 ff.; Max Walleser, *Prajñāpāramitā. Die Vollkommenheit der Erkenntnis* (Göttingen: Vandenhoek, 1914), sect. 5, I, II; Stcherbatsky, *Nirvāna*, with extracts from the *Mādhyamika-śāstra* and the *Prasannapadā;* T. Matsumoto, *Die Prajñāpāramitā-Literatur* (Stuttgart: Kohlhammer, 1932). E. Lamotte, *Le Traité de la Grande Vertu de Sagesse* (1944–9) became available to me, unfortunately, only after the completion of this essay.

132. E. Obermiller, 'The Doctrine of Prajñā-pāramitā' (*Acta Orientalia*, XI, 7) (cf. below).

133. *Sacred Books of the East*, XLIX, 145 ff.

134. Ibid., XLIX, 111 ff. German translation in Walleser, op. cit., pp. 140 ff.

135. A translation of the *Astasāhasrikā Prajñāpāramitā* into German in Walleser, op. cit., pp. 32 ff.

136. The *Kārikās* of Nāgārjuna and his own commentary, the

Akutobhayā, have been translated into German by Max Walleser, *Die Mittlere Lehre des Nāgārjuna* (Heidelberg: Winter, 1911) from the Tibetan. Extracts from his *Shastras* and Candrakīrti's commentary in English: Stcherbatsky, *Nirvāna*, pp. 65 ff., 81 ff.

137. L. de la Vallée-Poussin, 'Mādhyamakāvatāra, Introduction au traité du milieu de l'ācārya Candrakīrti avec le commentaire de l'auteur.'

138. E. Obermiller, 'The Sublime Science of the Great Vehicle' (*Acta Orientalia*, IX).

139. E. Obermiller, 'The Doctrine of Prajñā-pāramitā as exposed in the Abhisamayālamkāra of Maitreya' (*Acta Orientalia*, XI (1933), 1 ff.).

140. E. Obermiller, 'Doctrine,' p. 9.

141. Op. cit., p. 16, cp. pp. 21 ff., 30 ff.

142. Op. cit., pp. 90 ff., cf. L. de la Vallée-Poussin, *Opinions*, p. 196; Keith, *Buddhist Philosophy*, pp. 240 f. on Bhāvaviveka and the Svātantrikas, also Stcherbatsky, *Nirvāna*, pp. 79 ff.

143. On these cf. E. Obermiller, 'The Sublime Science of the Great Vehicle to Salvation, being a Manual of Buddhist Monism. The work of Arya Maitreya with a Commentary by Aryasanga,' translated from the Tibetan (*Acta Orientalia*, IX (1931), 81 ff.). The first of these five treatises to be translated into any European language was the *Mahāyāna-Sūtrālamkāra* which Sylvain Lévi translated into French (Paris: H. Champion, 1907) and which is another of the most interesting treatises on theology and ethics of the Great Vehicle. E. Obermiller (op. cit., pp. 89 ff.) gives a survey of its main contents. It is one of the major Yogācāra texts.

144. E. Obermiller, 'Sublime Science,' p. 82.

145. Op. cit., p. 89, cf. *Mahāyāna Sūtrālamkāra*, chaps. iii, vi.

146. Op. cit., p. 106.

147. Op. cit., pp. 156 ff., 104.

148. Op. cit., pp. 203 ff., 240 ff.

149. Op. cit., p. 105.

150. Op. cit., p. 107.

151. Op. cit., p. 110, cf. pp. 122, 147 ff.

152. Op. cit., pp. 123 ff., 131 ff., 137 ff. Cf. *Sūtrālamkāra*, chap. ii.

153. Op. cit., p. 83. Cf. L. de la Vallée-Poussin, *Opinions*, p. 196, and Keith, op. cit., pp. 240 f. on the Prāsangikas (Buddhapālita and Chandrakīrti).

154. Daisetz T. Suzuki, *The Lankāvatārasūtra. A Mahāyāna Text.* (London: Routledge, 1932).

155. Suzuki, *Studies in the Lankāvatārasūtra* (London: Routledge, 1930).

156. On logical and psychological doctrines: *Studies*, pp. 153 ff., 169 ff.

157. L.S., XVII.

158. L.V., XXI ff., 182 ff.

159. *Studies*, p. 177.
160. L.V., XXV, 105 ff.
161. Loc. cit., XXVI.
162. *Studies*, pp. 96 ff., 101 ff., 110 ff., 132 ff.
163. Op. cit., p. 116.
164. Op. cit., pp. 128 ff.
165. Op. cit., p. 102.
166. Op. cit., pp. 105, 202 ff.
167. Op. cit., pp. 44 ff., 89 ff., 102 f., 171.
168. Op. cit., pp. 101, 177, 202 ff. Cf. above on the *Lotus*.
169. Op. cit., p. 216.
170. Op. cit., pp. 222 ff.
171. Cf. the text and quotations in Albert J. Edmunds–M. Anesaki, *Buddhist and Christian Gospels. Being Gospel Parallels from Pali Texts* (Chicago: Open Court, 1905), pp. 23 ff. (history of conversions).
172. Cf. Giuseppe Messina, S.J., *Cristianesimo, Buddhismo, Manicheismo nell'Asia Antica* (Roma: N. Ruffolo, 1947).
173. Cf. on this much discussed subject: J. Estlin Carpenter, *Buddhism and Christianity, a Contrast and a Parallel* (London: Hodder and Stoughton, 1923); Streeter, *The Buddha and the Christ*, chaps. iv and viii, Hendrick Kraemer, *The Christian Message to the Non-Christian World* (London: Edinburgh House, 1938), esp. chaps. v and vi; Frederick Hilliard, *Man in Eastern Religions* (London: Epworth Press, 1946); Robert E. Hume, *The World's Living Religions* (New York: Scribners), 2nd ed. (1946), chap. xiii.

VII. CASPAR SCHWENCKFELD. A PUPIL AND TEACHER IN THE SCHOOL OF CHRIST (Pages 135–170)

1. Since the writing of this essay a factual biography of Schwenckfeld has been published: Selina Gerhard Schultz, *Caspar Schwenckfeld von Ossig (1489–1561)* (Norristown, Penn.: Board of Publication of the Schwenckfelder Church, 1946). Cf. also A. Koyré, 'Caspar Schwenckfeld' in *Annuaire 1932–3 École Pratique des Hautes Études* (Melun: Impr. Administr., 1932), and Franklin H. Littell, 'The Anabaptists and Christian Tradition' (*Journal of Religious Thought*, IV, No. 2 (1947), 167 ff.).
2. 'The Historiography of the German Reformation during the Last Twenty Years,' *Church History*, IX (1940), 314 ff. For the methodological problem of bias in the understanding of religion and its documentary evidence, cf. J. Wach, *Das Verstehen*, Vols. I–III (Tübingen: J. C. B. Mohr (Siebeck), 1926–33).
3. Charles D. Hartranft, E. E. Schultz Johnson, and A. A. Seipt (eds.), *Corpus Schwenckfeldianorum* (Leipzig: Breitkopf & Härtel, 1911——). Published under the auspices of the Schwenckfelder church (Pa.) and the Hartford Theological Seminary (Conn.).

Seventeen volumes are planned; fourteen have appeared thus far. All quotations are from this edition, and will be cited by volume and document or volume and page. The spelling in the quotations follows Schwenckfeld's somewhat arbitrary use.

4. Pauck, op. cit., p. 336.

5. Three examples: E. Hirsch, 'Zum Verständnis Schwenckfelds,' *Festgabe für Karl Müller* (Tübingen: J. C. B. Mohr, 1923), pp. 154 ff.; H. Bornkamm, 'Mystik, Spiritualismus und die Anfänge des Pietismus im Luthertum' (in *Vorträge der Theol. Konferenz*) (Giessen: Töpelmann, 1926); Erich Seeberg, 'Der Gegensatz zwischen Zwingli, Schwenckfeld und Luther,' *R. Seeberg Festschrift* (Leipzig: A. Deichert, 1929), I, 43 ff.

6. Cf. Robert Friedmann, *Mennonite Piety through the Centuries* (Goshen, 1949).

7. Cf. R. M. Jones, *Spiritual Reformers in the Sixteenth and Seventeenth Centuries* (London: Macmillan & Co. Ltd., 1914); E. Troeltsch, *The Social Teachings of the Christian Churches* (London: Allen and Unwin, 1931); J. Kühn, *Toleranz und Offenbarung* (Leipzig: F. Meiner, 1923); J. Horsch, *Mennonite History* (Scottsdale, Pa.: Mennonite Pub. House, 1942), Vol. I; R. Friedman, 'Conception of the Anabaptists,' *Church History*, IX, No. 4 (1940), pp. 341 ff.; F. Heyer, 'Der Kirchenbegriff der Schwärmer' (in *Schriften des Vereins für Reformationsgeschichte*, No. 166 (Leipzig: M. Heinsius, 1939)); *Mennonite Quarterly Review*, XXIV, 1950.

8. K. Ecke, *Schwenckfeld, Luther und der Gedanke einer apostolischen Reformation* (Berlin: M. Warnecke, 1911).

9. Cf. above, n. 6.

10. Between 1523 and 1562 no less than 112 tracts by Schwenckfeld were published; 1547 was the most fertile year (*Corpus*, I, Introd., x).

11. A sketch of the development of Schwenckfeld studies and bibliography are given in the *Corpus*, I, lxv ff.

12. Vol. III, Doc. LXXIX: 'Ain klarer bericht von Christo'; Vol. VII, Doc. CCCIV, and VIII, 91 ff. Cf. also: 'Mir ists je an nichts mehr gelegen auf dem ganzen Erdboden . . . weder dass Christus Jesus der ware Son Gottes in vielen hertzen recht bekannt unnd dass viel frommer rechtschaffner Christen würden . . .' (V, 351); 'Christus qui vera et unica salus est' (II, 342); 'Unus est omnium magister Christus' (III, 343); 'lapis ipse angularis super quod aedificium domus spiritalis [*sic!*] struitur' (II, 593); cf. also XIV, 251, 832.

13. Typical are the quotations in 'The Confession' of 1541, Vol. VII, Doc. CCCLIV, esp. Part II; cf. also Hirsch, op. cit., p. 148.

14. For the most illuminating study of the influence of Luther on Schwenckfeld see E. Hirsch, op. cit., pp. 145 ff.

15. Much confusion exists, e.g., in Bornkamm's typology and terminology (cf. above, n. 4). We agree with Seeberg (op. cit.,

p. 157) that it is the 'Geistgedanke' which separates Schwenckfeld from all types of mysticism.

16. Cf.'Kein haufen noch anhang'(Vol. XIII, Docs. DCCCXXII, DCCCXXXIII). For the relation to the Anabaptists cf. J. Loserth, *Quellen und Forschungen der oberdeutscher Taufgesinnten* (Wien, 1929).

17. For Schwenckfeld's concept of the church cf. Vol. XIII, Doc. CCCXXXIV; and Heyer, op. cit., pp. 50 ff.

18. Cf. V, 590 ff., 640.

19. The study of Schwenckfeld as a forerunner of pietism will be dealt with in a separate monograph. It is sufficient here to list some passages which anticipate pietism: I, XXVI; III, 385 ff.; IV, 106, 528; V, 7, 212, 616, 650; VI, 3; IX, 206, 401, 409, 448 ff., 632; X, 876, 963, 970 ff.; XI, 555, 825; XII, 543 ff., 645; XIII, 317, 597; XIV, 65, 418. Cf. now Friedmann, *Mennonite Piety*.

20. Cf. above n. and the biographical data in I, xi ff.; for his birth-year see XI, 663, 667. His mother was Barbara von Kreckwitz (IX, 252 n.). Of his house, of his brother and sister whom he left behind, and the places he turned to, Schwenckfeld speaks in 'Rechenschafft der gnedigen Versehunge Gottes' (Vol. VIII, Doc. CCCCXII; cf. also IX, 249).

21. Cf. XIV, 876.

22. Cf. the later (1533) reference, IV, 781.

23. Vol. II, Doc. XVIII.

24. IV, 775; V, 100.

25. Vol. II, Doc. XLI.

26. His relation to Zwingli is discussed by Schwenckfeld in Vol. XIV, Doc. DCCCCXII.

27. Cf. IV, 822, and V, 309, where Bucer's and Zwingli's rôles are discussed; cf. also Hirsch, op. cit., p. 164.

28. For a testimony of the impression that Schwenckfeld's manners and behaviour made upon his adversaries cf. V, 97.

29. Blaurer is called (V, 303) Schwenckfeld's first enemy on earth after Bucer. Cf. Th. Pressel, *Abraham Blaurer* (Elberfeld, Friderichs, 1861).

30. Cf. esp. XIII, 217 ff., 301 ff., 361 ff., 508 ff., 525 ff., 548 ff., 732 ff., 907 ff. Cf. now Werner Näf, *Vadian Studien und Analekten* (St. Gallen: Fehr, 1945).

31. Cf. IX, 821 f., 1020; X, 923; XI, 509, 522, 772 f., 878 ff.; XIII, 267. Yet the years 1546–7 were the most productive period of Schwenckfeld's religious activity (X, xi). On his pseudonyms ('Grisswarter,' 'Eliander') cf. XI, 546, 551.

32. In his letter (to J. S. Werner), 'The School of Christ' (January 1, 1545): 'Das heisst die Schule Christi, die Christen sein die Schüler, Christus ist der Meister, sine lehre ist die einschreibung des Gesetzes . . . in die taffeln des hertzens' (Vol. IX, Doc. CCCCLXI).

33. XI, 840 f.; XII, 358.

34. I, 440; cf. also X, 26.
35. On the Suderman Codex ('Epistolar') cf. IX, 116 ff. Schwenckfeld wrote as many as twenty letters a week (XII, 24).
36. Cf. the 'Ratio vocationis meae' (XI, 968 f.) and the beautiful admonition on patience (Vol. V, Doc. CCXXXIX).
37. I, 35.
38. Cf. the statement of J. S. Zabern: An arch-heretic (*Ertzketzer*) if one asks his enemies, a saint if one reads him (that is Schwenckfeld) (I, xv).
39. I, 16.
40. I, v and xlvi.
41. Cf. the magnificent letter of comfort to a dying friend, Vol. XII, Doc. DCCLXXXV.
42. Schwenckfeld speaks of his writing method in Vol. IX, Doc. DXXVI.
43. Reply to the accusation of being a 'Weiber Prediger' (XI, 930 f.).
44. I, xv, lix; typical is V, 549. Cf. the letter to a clockmaker, M. Rhöt, Vol. VIII, Doc. CCCLXXIX; to a married couple, Doc. CCCLXXXII; to a wine merchant, H. Weiss, on Christian administration of his business, Doc. CCCXCIX; to a pastor, on remuneration, Doc. CCCC; to a knight, Vol. IX, Doc. DXXVII; to a prince-abbot, Vol. X, Doc. DXLVIII. On property, Vol. III, Doc. LXIII.
45. VII, 60 ff.
46. Among his most important doctrinal statements are: VI, 510 ff.; VII, 451 ff.; VIII, 251 ff.; IX, 157 ff.; XI, 78 ff., 390 ff.; XII, 192 ff., 664; XIII, 574; XIV, 255 ff., 381, 419 ff., 898, 950.
47. An interesting document is his discussion of the planets (Vol. VI, Doc. CCLIX), which is more technical than most of his letters.
48. Hirsch, op. cit., p. 150. Melanchthon had already criticized Schwenckfeld for the lack of a 'summa' of Christian doctrine (XIII, 1001).
49. Cf. the unusually sharp but brilliant reply to an attack by V. Vannius, Vol. VII, Doc. CCCIX; cf. also Vol. VIII, Doc. CCCCXXI.
50. For Luther's unfriendly communications see VIII, 686 and 719 f.; for Schwenckfeld's answer see Vol. IX, Doc. CCCCXXXIX; IX, 86 ff.; Vol. XII, Doc. DCCLXIX; cf. also XIII, 58 ff.; for refutation of Melanchthon see Vol. XIV, Doc. DCCCCLX.
51. On humility and warning of hasty judgment see III, 844. Schwenckfeld is no 'Zänker' (IV, 253 f., 820 f., 828). He knows (p. 831) 'quod Christianus neminem persequitur.' Cf. Vol. V, Doc. CXCII, also p. 316 and XIV, 826.
52. A special study of the influence of Thomas à Kempis' *Imitation of Christ* (cf. Schwenckfeld's edition, Vol. IV, Doc. CXXIII) and of Tauler (I, 252 ff., 389 f.; V, 427; VIII, 404; IX, 242, 361;

XII, 139 ff., 500, 554; esp. Vol. XIV, Doc. DCCCCXXVIII) on Schwenckfeld seems highly desirable. For the 'Teutsche Theologia' see IX, 315, 319, 359 ff.

53. I, 79. Cf. 'Denn ess ist . . . unser zunehmen inn der gnade des Herren nicht so vil am lesen alss am tieffen bedencken und nachtrachten . . . gelegen' (IX, 411). In XII, 714, he gives suggestions for meditation for each day of the week. 'Lesen, betrachten, beethen, studieren . . .' (XIV, 841).

54. Vol. IV, Doc. CXLIX.

55. Cf. his exegesis of Ps. 25 (V, 35 ff.); see also IV, 873, and VII, 45: 'Wer on liebe bettet, der wird nicht erhört, wer recht liebet, der bettet recht, wer nicht liebet, der bettet nicht, ob er auch viel Psalter spreche. Das ware anbetten Gottes ist in dem lieben Gottes, das der hl. Geist im hertz geusst welches kein Mensch das andere kan leeren so wenig als essen oder trinken, sondern allein Gott lehret lieben.'

56. X, 965 ff.

57. X, 964, 1011.

58. Cf. 'Prayer for the Church of Christ,' Vol. XI, Doc. DLII; 'In Time of War,' Doc. DLIII.

59. X, 968, 1042.

60. X, 1012; cf. the exposition of the *Miserere*, V, 640 f.

61. X, 970.

62. Vol. X, Doc. DCX.

63. X, 1018 ff. Cf. now on the *Passional* Friedmann, *Mennonite Piety*, 5, 29, 193 ff.

64. IV, 560; cf. also his annotation of Luther's book (VI, 290); his work on his 'Confession' (VII, 462 ff.); his 'amanuensis' (IX, 178, 366); his method of annotations (XI, 499, 517).

65. II, 597; cf. also E. Hirsch, op. cit., pp. 155 ff., 158.

66. Vol. II, Docs. XLI and LII (Appendix).

67. II, 596.

68. II, 595.

69. II, 343, 454, 494 ff.; V, 524.

70. II, 345.

71. On the word 'faith' see IV, 31; cf. also below, Sec. VII.

72. II, 592, 675.

73. II, 594; cf. esp. Vol. XI, Doc. DCXL, and Gregory the Great (*Mor.* v. 28): 'Cum igitur divina aspiratio sine strepitu mentem sublevat, verbum absconditum auditur, quia sermo Spiritus in *aure cordis* silenter sonat' (Migne, *Patr. Lat.*, LXXV, 710).

74. II, 494 ff., 593; cf. also pp. 696 ff.

75. III, 36; cf. also Doc. LXVIII and Sec. IX below (on grace). Gott würket in der seel on ainig eusserlich mittel oder bild allein durch ein gleiches mittel seines lebendigen wortes und athems' (III, 86). 'So viel erkenne ich aber Christum wieviel er mich erkennt. . . . So viel ergreiffe ich ihn, soviel ich von ihm ergriffen

werde' (IV, 84). It is Schwenckfeld's conviction 'dass auch kein eusserlich ding in Gottes Sachen weder erkannt, recht verstanden und verbracht mag werden wa nicht das innerliche liecht göttlicher gnaden und des glaubens zuvor im hertzen ist' (II, 676). 'Es mag niemand Gottes Wort noch Gott recht verstehen er hab es denn one mittel von dem heiligen Geiste. Niemand kans aber von dem heiligen Geiste haben, es erfahr es, versuchs, und empfinds denn (ibid.).

76. II, 456; cf. also I, xxvii ff.

77. Cf. W. J. Sparrow Simpson, *St. Augustine on the Spirit and the Letter* (London: Society for Promoting Christian Knowledge, 1925).

78. IV, 777.

79. II, 456.

80. II, 557 ff.

81. II, 459, 521.

82. IV, 820, 861.

83. III, 383 ff.; IV, 639, 819 f., 861; V, 99 ff., 107; VII, 38.

84. For main statement on his ideas on worship see Vol. XI, Doc. DCLXXIX; for his criticism of the Mass, Vol. XI, Docs. DCCXXXVIII f.

85. III, 96; cf. the classic exegesis of John vi: Vol. V, Doc. CCXXXVI and Vol. VI, Doc. CCLXII.

86. On the relative value of images see Vol. XIII, Doc. DCCCXXXIX.

87. III, 86. But cf. Vol. VII, Doc. CCCVIII, in which he states that, though eternal happiness is not bound to any external thing, he is far from rejecting the sacraments which Christ has instituted (though not considering them necessary for salvation). He holds that the unregenerated ('fleischliche Wiegenkinder') should not be admitted (VIII, 97 ff.).

88. Vol. IV, Doc. CXI; also IV, 85. On the ministry cf. esp. Vol. X, Docs. DXLVIII and DLI, and Vol. XIV, Doc. DCCCCXL.

89. Cf. the treatise 'The Holy Scriptures,' Vol. XII, Doc. DCCLXXX. Part II deals with the misuse of the Scriptures. Flacius Illyricus wrote against this book. Cf. also Vol. XII, Doc. DCCCXIII.

90. Cf. IV, 656.

91. 'Es ist aber die Schrifft im grund nit wider sich selbs, der hl. gaist ir schreiber ist allweg ainhellig, weiset immer fur und fur auf den einigen Christum sonder so der mensch der die Schrifft handelt des rechten maisters und aines gaistlichen Urtails mangelt, so er Christum nit recht kennet von welchem die Schrifft zeuget und durch sein naturliche Schicklichkeit oder durch menschliche weisshait die Schrifft sich understeet auszulegen die spruch aber nit vergleichen kan, so fällt er dann auf etwas das ihm am anmutigsten ist da braucht er seiner subtilen vernunfft an stat des hailigen gaists und das ander muss alles falsch sein' (IV, 108).

92. IV, 561. Hirsch says rightly (op. cit., p. 160) that Schwenck-

feld was the first to describe rebirth as a process in the soul, developing with organic necessity through various stages.

93. III, 163; IV, 562, 696. Cf. Schwenckfeld's edition of Georg Schmaltzing's Psalter (Vol. V, Doc. CCLIV).

94. III, 163. Cf. 'On the Word of God' (against Flacius), Vol. XIII, Docs. DCCCLXXXIX, DCCCXC, and DCCCXCI.

95. III, 488. Cf. Ecke, op. cit., chap. ii. Schwenckfeld's exegetical method can best be studied in his Postils, Vol. X, Docs. DLVI–DXCV; cf. also Vol. XI, Doc. DCLXIII.

96. IV, 766, 810; VIII, 94. Cf. Wach, op. cit., Vols. I, Introd., and II.

97. IV, 810.

98. Ibid.

99. IV, 815 f., 861.

100. V, 52 ff.

101. V, 94.

102. XIII, 217 ff., 301 ff., 361 ff., 508 ff., 525 ff., 545 ff., 732 ff.; XIV, 152 ff., 514 ff., 981 ff.; cf. also Vol. XIV, Doc. DCCCXCV.

103. Vol. I, Doc. V; cf. also the late summary of his views on the monastic life and vows, Vol. XIV, Doc. DCCCCXI.

104. I, 118, 124.

105. I, 118; II, 675.

106. II, 593; Vol. III, Doc. LXXIX, esp. 388.

107. II, 593.

108. II, 594, 596.

109. II, 690 f., 596: 'Sintemal ein natürlicher Mensch des dinges nicht vernimpt, die da Gottes Geist angehören. Mus aber der mensch zuvor geistlich und übernatürlich sein ehe er die wort der eusserlichen promission und die schrift als ein werck des heiligen Geists verstehen kann.'

110. V, 218; cf. also the treatise on 'The Good and Evil Conscience,' Vol. III, Doc. LXXXII.

111. V, 221 ff.

112. James L. Connally, *John Gerson, Reformer and Mystic* (Louvain: Librarie Universitaire, 1928), p. 87.

113. V, 227. On the 'Milchlehre' cf. IX, 125, 145 ff., 448 ff.

114. V, 224.

115. V, 226.

116. V, pp. 226 f.: 'Will einer die jugent zur kirchen bringen und er täglich im brettspiel oder zechhaus sein, so wird er nicht mehr schüler finden, welche jme im Brettspiel oder wirtshauss denn in der kirche nachgehen.'

117. V, 231.

118. V, 228.

119. V, 230; cf. VI, 651; I, 79; and XIII, 225 f.

120. Cf. the editors' Introd. to Schwenckfeld's edition of Schmaltzing's Psalter, V, 830 ff.; also Vol. VIII, Docs. CCCXCVIII and CX; and DLV.

121. V, 232 f.

122. V, 243.

123. V, 245.

124. Vol. IX, Doc. DXXI.

125. For martial analogies in description of Christian perfection cf. 'Christian Warfare and the Knighthood of God,' Vol. IV, Doc. CXXXIV; cf. also A. von Harnack, *Militia Christi* (Tübingen: J. C. B. Mohr, 1905).

126. IX, 708; cf. also the 'New Song on the Regeneration, Nurture, and Growth of the Children of God,' Vol. X, Doc. DLV (1546).

127. X, 754; cf. also XI, 154.

128. XI, 665 f.

129. XI, 794, 879: 'Es sind da vil staffeln das mans nicht bald einsmals alles kan ersteigen, verstehen noch vernehmen. . . . Es müssen am leibe Christi auch Kleine zehen sein und mancher helt des Leyen statt, der kaum noch kann Amen Auffs gebet singen.'

130. Vol. IX, Doc. D.; cf. also XIII, iii.

131. Cf. V, 695, on the rose and cross; cf. also Vol. VI, Docs. CCLXXVII and CCLXXXIII.

132. Søren Kierkegaard, *Tagebücher*, I, 122.

133. K. Holl, 'Luther,' in *Gesammelte Schriften*, II, 577a.

134. Cf. 'The Consolation for a Bearer of the Cross of Christ,' Vol. V, Doc. CCLIII; and the letter to M. Engelmann, Vol. XI, Doc. DCXXI, esp. pp. 44 ff. Cf. also 'Von der Gelassenheit,' Vol. VI, Doc. CCLV; and 'Ermanung zum Creutz Christi,' Vol. IX, Doc. DXVII. Caspar's motto: 'Nil Christo triste recepto' (XIII, 89).

135. Cf. XII, 712.

136. IX, 416; cf. also V, 479, 505, 617.

137. IX, 416.

138. Vol. VII, Doc. CCCXXXIII.

139. VII, 268 f. The reference is to Ps. 101: 7, 8: 'Similis factus sum pellicano solitudinis: factus sum sicut nycticorax in domicilio.' Cf. also St. Francis of Sales, *Introduction to the Devout Life*, trans. Thomas Barnes (London: Methuen & Co., 1906), p. 116.

140. Vol. X, Doc. DXLII; cf. also Vol. V, Doc. CCLIII, and VI, Doc. CCLXVII; also Vol. XIII, Doc. XXIX, esp. pp. 589 f.; and IX, Doc. CCCCXCIX.

141. Cf. XII, 549: 'Es muss gestritten, gelitten und gemieden sein.' His 'proba,' 'persecution, exilio und tribulation' . . . (IX, 166 f., 312 ff.; 402).

142. X, 46 f.; cf. also XI, 522 ff.; V, 336: 'Es muss das faule widerspenstige fleisch im worte des creutzes durch trübsall, angst und leidenn also eingesalzen, vertzeret und ausgeetzt werden.' Cf. reference to the 'prächtigen mulieres die nicht gern opprobria Christi tragen' (IX, 204).

143. X, 49.

144. Cf. VI, 330; IX, 179, Doc. D.

145. X, 62, 64.

146. Cf. I, 62; VIII, 79; and V, 813; for the meaning of death see X, 38.

147. V, 814; cf. also his edtion of Crautwald's 'Novus homo,' Vol. VIII, Doc. CCCLVIII.

148. X, 50.

149. Vol. IX, Doc. DXIV; cf. also Vol. III, Doc. LXXXIII, and V, 481.

150. IX, 534 ff. Søren Kierkegaard, *The Sickness unto Death* (London: Oxford University Press, 1941). Cf. also Hugo of St. Victor, *Sermones centum* (Migne, *Patr. Lat.*, Vol. CLXXVII), Sermo XI, 'De spirituali sanitate'; and Richard of St. Victor, 'De statu interioris hominis' (Migne, *Patr. Lat.*, Vol. CXCVI, cols. 1115 ff.).

151. IX, 513 ff. On his influence on pietism cf. Hirsch, op. cit., pp. 168 ff.; on Hoburg see *RGG* (2nd ed.), II, 1942; and above, n. 18.

152. IX, 545 ff.

153. IX, 560 ff., on diagnosis; cf. also VI, 431.

154. IX, 573 ff.

155. IX, 526, 557, 592 ff.

156. IX, 529, 605 ff. Hugo of St. Victor also considers *Aegrotus, vulnera, medicina, vasa, antidota, diaeta, dispensatores, locus, tempus, sanitates, gaudia de ipsis sanitatibus recuperatis* (op. cit., cols. 922 ff.).

157. IX, 530.

158. IX, 564 ff.; cf. also Kierkegaard's *Concept of Dread* (London: Oxford University Press, 1944).

159. IX, 578, 620.

160. IX, 598.

161. IX, 603, 611, 619.

162. Vol. IX, Doc. DXXXIV.

163. IX, 832 ff.

164. IX, 834.

165. IX, 841 ff.

166. Vol. VI, Doc. CCLVI; cf. also V, 5423.

167. VI, 22 ff., 27; cf. also XIII, 535 ff., and Vol. XIV, Doc. DCCCCVI.

168. XII, 728; cf. also Vol. X, Doc. DXCVI.

169. VI, 16. Cf. against Flacius on spiritual birth, XIII, 811, 916; against Anabaptists, Vol. XII, Doc. DCCXCIX, esp. pp. 672 f.

170. XIII, 580.

171. Vol. VII, Doc. CCCXLVIII.

172. VII, 395 ff.; cf. also Vol. X, Doc. DCI, and Vol. XI Doc. DCLXIII.

173. Vol. VIII, Doc. CCCLVIII.

174. IX, 170 ff. On his teachings on regeneration cf. Hirsch,

op. cit., pp. 159 ff. 'Der lebendige Glaube als Träger der Wiedergeburt' (p. 170). Cf. also Bornkamm, op. cit., p. 16, who wrongly states that 'der' (wiedergeborene) 'Fromme des strengen Bussgebets nicht mehr bedarf.'

175. IX, 171; for love as key to his system see I, 476; cf. also V, 291, 309. Cf. Vol. IX, Doc. CCCCXLIV on 'Spiritual Brotherhood.'

176. Vol. X, Doc. DXCVI.

177. Cf. A. Hyma, *Christian Renaissance* (New York, 1924), on the conversion of G. Grote, chap. i.

178. X, 744; cf. X, 754, on the three stages of love.

179. Vol. XI, Doc. DCXXI; cf. also the homiletic letter on 'The Pure in Heart' (Matt. v, 8), Vol. XII, Doc. DCCLXXIII.

180. XI, 38.

181. XI, 41; cf. also Ecke, op. cit., pp. 106 ff.

182. XI, 41, 43: 'Die liebe des irdischen reichthumb ist unersetlich und peiniget das gemüt vil mehr denn sie das erfreut mit seinem gebrauch' and 'Wer aus morgen den gewinn sucht, der findet am abent seiner seelen hindernus.' On the right use of property see Vol. III, Doc. LXIII. Sooner than become a captive of his riches, man will sell all he has (III, 68).

183. XII, 704 f.

184. IX, 859 ff.; cf. also IV, 737 ff., on Christian virtue.

185. IX, 860 ff.; cf. pp. 938 ff.

186. 'Denn wer da wil selig werden, der muss sich kurtz umb von dem unordigen gemenge dieser welt und von dem weltwesen absondern. Er muss nit mehr mit den weltkindern in der eitelkeit lauffen, uund jrem pracht nachfolgen, auch so fern nicht dass er sich von allem bösen schein soll hüten' (V, 108 f.).

187. III, 164; cf. also St. Augustine's 'De disciplina Christiana' (Migne, *Patr. Lat.*, XL, 669).

188. XII, 261; III, 147 f.

189. III. 106.

190. V, 287.

191. II, 649; cf. also Ecke, op. cit., chap. iv.

192. For the Anabaptists see VII, 152; IX, 313; and XII, 103 ff., 121, and Doc. DCCCXI; and Hirsch, op. cit., p. 164.

193. III, 384; IV, 681 f.

194. IV, 765 ff.

195. IV, 768, 769; cf. also V, 530. Cf. also the very interesting letter to Nic. Rosul, who, a monk, left his monastery, Vol. VII, Doc. CCCXLI. Schwenckfeld exhorts him to leave it for a 'stricter order,' that of the mortification of the self.

196. Cf. Vol. II, Doc. VIII.

197. II, 46.

198. II, 54; cf. 'A Treatise on the Forgiveness of Sins,' Vol. X, Doc. DCIX.

199. II, 54. Cf. the reference to Wycliffe, Huss, and Wessel (Gansfort), who have written 'vil gewisser und besserlicher vom ewigen bestendigen glauben den Luther' (IV, 821). For Wessel cf. Edward W. Miller, *Wessel Gansfort: Life and Writings* (New York: G. P. Putnam's Sons, 1917), esp. Vol. II.

200. XI, 589 f.; cf. Vol. XI, Doc. DCCXX.

201. XII, 375 f. Cf. the beautiful characterization of faith as a spark of the eternal sun which is God, in a letter to a blind friend of his youth (Vol. VI, Doc. CCCXXIV, 156).

202. XII, 376 f.; cf. also pp. 884 ff.

203. XII, 375; cf. also pp. 370 ff.; cf. the exposition of Gal. v, 5, in CXIII, 43 ff.

204. XIII, 766, 873; XIV, 411 ff.

205. XIII, 866.

206. XIII, 864.

207. XIII, 873.

208. XIII, 874 ff.

209. XIII, 878; cf. also XIV, 415.

210. XIII, 882.

211. XIII, 883.

212. XIV, 412.

213. Vol. XIV, Doc. DCCCLXXXVI.

214. XIV, 418.

215. XIV, 790 ff.

216. Vol. XII, Doc. DCCXXV.

217. XII, 370 f.

218. II, 25, 57 ff.; XII, 880 ff.

219. II, 58; in VIII, 435, he speaks of the 'wilden Gebirge dieser schalkhafftigen Welt, die inn unns selbs ist.'

220. XII, 894.

221. II, 60; cf. also XII, 892 ff.

222. II, 64.

223. XII, 895.

224. XII, 897.

225. XII, 910.

226. XII, 914 f., 916.

227. XII, 912.

228. XII, 917; cf. also XIII, 114, esp. pp. 119 ff.

229. XII, 918; cf. also IV, 723.

230. XII, 925 f.

231. XII, 654 ff.; cf. esp. Vol. XIII, Docs. DCCCXXVII and DCCCXXIX.

232. XII, 927 ff., 951 ff.

233. XII, 945 ff.

234. XII, 932 ff., 942 ff.

235. On Lucifer see XIII, 142.

236. On war and the sword cf. X, 926; XI, 177 ff.; XII, 792.

237. Cf. correspondence with Bernhard Egetius, Vol. IX, Docs. DXXIV ff., esp. pp. 682, 699 ff.; and with Katharina Zell, Vol. VIII, Doc. CCCXCII. See also XI, 951.
238. IX, 682, 699, 709.
239. XIII, 859 f.; cf. also VI, 44 f.

VIII. THE RÔLE OF RELIGION IN THE SOCIAL PHILOSOPHY IN ALEXIS DE TOCQUEVILLE (Page 171–186)

1. Since the publication of this essay *A Symposium on Alexis de Tocqueville's Democracy in America*, ed. by William J. Schlaerth (New York: Fordham Univ. Press, 1945), and *The Recollections of A. de T.*, tr. by A. T. Mattos and ed. by J. P. Mayer (London: The Harvill Press, 1948), have been published.
2. Alexis de Tocqueville's main works are *De la démocratie en Amérique* (1835–40; tr. by Henry Reeve, ed. by Francis Bowen, 1862; re-edited by Phillips Bradley (New York, 1945), and *L'Ancien régime et la révolution* (1st ed., 1856). His *Œuvres complètes* were published 1851–65.
3. The most important recent publication on de Tocqueville is G. W. Pierson, *Tocqueville and Beaumont in America* (New York, 1938), which makes use of much unpublished material. Cf. also W. Ohaus, "Volk und Völker im Urteil von Alexis von Tocqueville": in *Romanische Studien*, XXIII (1938); J. P. Mayer, *Alexis de Tocqueville: A Biographical Essay in Political Science*, tr. M. M. Bogman and C. Hahn (1940); J. S. Schapiro, 'Alexis de Tocqueville, Pioneer of Democratic Liberalism in France' (*Political Science Quarterly*, LVII (1942), 545 ff.).
4. Cf. *Memoir, Letters and Remains of Alexis de Tocqueville*, 2 vols. (1861); *Correspondance entre Alexis de Tocqueville et Arthur de Gobineau 1843–1859*, ed. L. Schemann (2nd ed., 1909). *The Correspondence and Conversations of Alexis de Tocqueville with Nassau W. Senior (1834–1859)*, ed. M. C. M. Simpson (1872) are less important for our purpose. For a bibliography of de Tocqueville's Correspondence cf. Pierson, loc. cit., pp. 782 ff. On Senior cf. S. Leon Levy, *Nassau W. Senior* (Boston, 1943).
5. *Democracy* (ed. Reeve), p. 14. Cf. A. Salomon, 'T., Moralist and Sociologist,' *Social Research*, II (1935), 405 ff.
6. *Memoir*, I, 400.
7. J. P. Mayer, op. cit., pp. 7, 31, 121; cf. pp. 165 ff.
8. *Memoir*, II, 238.
9. Ibid., I, 400; *Democracy*, pp. 15, 55.
10. *Democracy*, p. 13.
11. *Memoir*, I, 360.
12. Ibid.
13. *Memoir*, I, 397.
14. Ibid., II, 71.

15. Ibid., II, 254.
16. J. S. Schapiro, op. cit., p. 558.
17. *Correspondance entre de Tocqueville et de Gobineau*, op. cit., p. 195.
18. *Democracy*, p. 6.
19. *Correspondence with Gobineau*, pp. 192 f.
20. Ibid., pp. 183 f.
21. Ibid., p. 184.
22. Ibid., p. 306.
23. Ibid., p. 307.
24. Ibid., p. 309.
25. Ibid., p. 311.
26. Ibid., p. 311.
27. Ibid., pp. 311–12.
28. Ibid., p. 312.
29. Ibid., p. 333.
30. Ibid., pp. 312, 334.
31. Ibid., p. 313.
32. Ibid., p. 313.
33. Ibid., p. 288.
34. G. W. Pierson, op. cit., pp. 153, 106 ff.
35. Ibid., p. 153.
36. Ibid., p. 156.
37. *Democracy*, p. 384.
38. Ibid., p. 385.
39. Ibid., p. 397.
40. Ibid., p. 385.
41. Ibid., p. 385.
42. Ibid., p. 386.
43. Ibid., p. 156.
44. See also ibid, pp. 385, 155.
45. Ibid., pp. 153 f., 106.
46. Ibid., p. 154.
47. Ibid., p. 154.
48. Ibid., p. 157.
49. Ibid., pp. 157, 421 ff.
50. Ibid., p. 158.
51. Ibid., p. 387.
52. Ibid., p. 154.
53. Ibid., pp. 154, 106.
54. Ibid., p. 106.
55. Ibid., cf. pp. 275, 283, 292.
56. Ibid., p. 500.
57. Ibid., pp. 138, 200, 222, 284, 298, 300, 500, 620, 722, 753.
58. Ibid., p. 383.
59. Pierson, op. cit., p. 424.
60. *Democracy*, p. 54.
61. Ibid., pp. 54, 393.

62. Ibid., p. 384.
63. Ibid., I, 383 ff.; II, 22 ff.
64. Ibid., p. 390.
65. Ibid., p. 39.
66. Ibid., p. 391.
67. Ibid., p. 393.
68. Ibid., p. 393.

IX. CHURCH, DENOMINATION AND SECT (Pages 189–194)

1. Since this lecture was given (1946), the following important publications have appeared: 'Organized Religion in the United States' (*Annals of the American Academy of Political and Social Sciences* (Philadelphia, 1948)); H. R. Niebuhr, 'The Norm of the Church' (*Journal of Religious Thought*, IV (1946–7)); Roland Bainton, "The Sectarian Theory of the Church" (*Christendom XI*, 1946), 382 ff.; Charles S. Braden, *These Also Believe. A Study of Modern American Cults* (New York: Macmillan, 1949).

2. Cf. the Papers prepared by members of the American Theological Committee on the conception of the Church in *Christendom*, IX, 3, 4 (1944), 409 ff., 548 ff.

3. *Sociology of Religion* (London: Kegan Paul, 1947). *Symposium on Twentieth-century Sociology* (New York: Philos. Library, 1945).

4. *ERE*, art. 'Heresy,' VI, 614 ff., and 'Schism,' XI, 232.

5. Ernst Benz, *Ecclesia Spiritualis. Kirchenidee und Geschichts-Philosophie der Franziscanischen Reform* (Stuttgart: Kohlhammer, 1934).

6. A. Hyma, *Christian Renaissance, A History of the Devotio Moderna* (New York: Century Co., 1925).

7. O. Karrer, *Religions of Mankind* (London: Sheed and Ward, 1945), chap. xii.

8. W. Köhler, *Dogmengeschichte als Geschichte des Christlichen Selbstbewusstseins* (Zürich, 1938), p. 525.

9. H. Mulert, 'Congregatio Sanctorum' (*Augustana*, Vol. VII) in Harnack-Ehrung; M. Schian, 'Sichtbare und Unsichtbare Kirche' in *Z. f. Syst. Theol.*, IX (1931–2), 535 ff.

10. E. Seeberg, *Gottfried Arnold, die Wissenschaft und die Mystik seiner Zeit.* (Meerane: Herzog, 1923).

11. J. Calvin, *Institutes of the Christian Religion*, ed. Allen (Philadelphia: Presbyterian Board, 1930).

12. These Notae are formulated in contemporaneous statements: G. W. Richards, 'The Conception of the Church as Held by the Evangelical and Reformed Churches' (*Christendom*, IX, 3 (1944), 409 ff.). The presbyteral order is for him not a part of the *esse* but of the *bene esse* of the church. For the Presbyterian view: F. W. Loetscher (op. cit., pp. 573 ff.), 'It is expedient and agreeable to Scripture and the practice of the primitive Christians that the

Church be governed by congregational, presbyterial, and synodal assemblies.'

13. 'Never,' says L. C. Lewis in his report on the *Anglican Concept of the Church* (loc. cit., p. 568), 'does the Anglican Church think of itself as a creation of the Reformation but always as a reformed part of the much older Universal Church.'

14. R. Hooker, 'Books of the Laws of the Ecclesiastical Polity' (*Works*, ed. Keble, Oxford, 1841).

15. *Doctrines of the Church of England, the Report of the Commission on Christian Doctrine* (London: S.P.C.K., 1938), pp. 99 ff., 112.

16. Cf. also: L. S. Thornton, *The Common Life in the Body of Christ*, 2nd ed. (Westminster: Dacre Press, 1944).

17. Article 13 of the *New Hampshire Baptist Confession*: 'We believe that a visible church of Christ is a congregation of baptized believers, associated by covenant in the faith and fellowship of the gospel' (cf. J. L. Neve, *Churches and Sects of Christendom* (Burlington: The Lutheran Literature Board, 1940), p. 520). 'The Congregational Churches,' says W. Horton in his report to the American Theological Council (op. cit., IX, 3 (1944), 427 ff.), 'find their distinction in not being distinctive.' The Church for him too is the 'continuation of the Incarnation' and 'a fellowship of those ruled by the spirit of Christ, but it is also a voluntary society since in it the will of God and that of man can co-operate.' The Disciples consider themselves, according to Garrison (op. cit., p. 434), as 'neither *the* Church nor a church but a movement.'

18. H. W. Clark, *History of English Non-Conformity* (London: Chapman, 1911–13), pp. 197, 202. F. Heyer, 'Der Kirchenbegriff der Schwärmer', (*Schriften des Ver. Ref. Gesch.*, No. 166 (Leipzig:Heinsius, 1939)); Wach, *Caspar Schwenckfeld*, cf. above, Chap. VII.

19. Morrison, *Builders of Back Bay Colony* (Boston: Houghton Mifflin, 1938); Perry Miller, *Orthodoxy in Massachusetts* (Cambridge: Harvard Univ. Press, 1933).

20. De Jong, 'The Denomination as the American Church-form' in *Neue Theol. Tijdschrift* (1938), pp. 347 ff.

21. R. B. Perry, *Puritanism and Democracy* (New York: Vanguard Press, 1944).

22. It is represented, to-day, by the Congregationalists, Baptists and Disciples. 'Our denomination,' says Carver in his statement (op. cit., pp. 552 f.), 'stresses the concept of the Church as a voluntary society for carrying on the work of Christ, but we would insist that it is more than a "merely voluntary" society, for it is a creation of the Holy Spirit and locally the body of Christ. It is limited to those who have experienced the grace of salvation and who seek the fellowship under the constraint of the spirit of Jesus. Its roots and life have been and remain in principle individualism and voluntarism in religious experience, relation and responsibility.' The Quakers are the only denomination which 'admittedly does,' in E. Cadbury's words,

'regard its organization as in exact correspondence with the New Testament teaching and practice respecting the Church, knowing that its own organization originated in the seventeenth century to meet the needs of the Quaker movement.' He cites R. Barclay's statement: 'It is the life of Christianity, taking place in the heart, that makes a Christian, and so it is a number of such being alive, joined together in the life of Christianity, that make a Church of Christ, and it is all those that are thus alive and quickened, considered together, that make the Catholic Church of Christ' (loc. cit.).

23. E. T. Clark, *The Small Sects in America* (Nashville: Cokesbury Press, s.a., 2nd ed. 1949). Wach, *Sociology of Religion*, chap. v, 12b.

24. Cf. E. M. Wilbur, *A History of Unitarianism* (Cambridge, Mass.: Harvard Univ. Press, 1945).

25. As Reinhold Niebuhr ('Sects and Churches' in the *Christian Century*, LII, July 31, 1935, 885 ff.) phrased it: 'It is difficult to perpetuate undefined religious beliefs.'

26. R. Friedman, 'The Concept of the Anabaptists' (*Church History*, IX (1940), 341 ff.).

27. Cf. J. Wach, *Das Verstehen, Geschichte der Hermeneutischen Theorie im 19. Jahrhundert* (Tübingen: Mohr (Siebeck) 1926), Vol. II.

28. Cf. Hauck, 'Der Gestaltwandel der Kirchlichen Bekenntnisse mit Nachtrag über das Wesen der Sekte' (*Z. f. Syst. Theol.*, XIV (1937), 393 ff.).

29. Friedman, loc. cit.

30. *Report of the Archbishop's Commission*, p. 110.

31. Cf. Wach, op. cit., pp. 283 f.; St. Clair Drake, *Black Metropolis* (New York: Harcourt, Brace and Co., 1945).

32. *Sociology of Religion*, chap. i, p. 1.

33. L. Pope, *Millhands and Teachers, A Study of Gastonia* (New Haven: Yale Univ. Press, 1942). Walter G. Mueder, 'From Sect to Church' in *Christendom*, X, 4 (1945), 450 ff.

34. H. P. Douglas, 'Cultural Differences and Recent Religious Divisions' in *Christendom*, X, 1 (1945), 89 ff.

35. Mueder, loc. cit., p. 456.

36. Max Weber, 'Wirtschaft und Gesellschaft' (*Grundriss der Sozialökonomik*, III (Tübingen: Mohr, 1921)), No. 7, esp. p. 296, cf. E. Fischhoff, 'Protestant Ethics' (*Soc. Research*, XI (1944), 53 ff.).

37. E. Faris, *Nature of Human Nature*, chap. 'The Sect and the Sectarian.'

38. Cf. *Sociology of Religion*, pp. 196 ff.

39. J. S. Whale, *Christian Doctrine* (Cambridge: Univ. Press, 1941).

X. RUDOLF OTTO AND THE IDEA OF THE HOLY
(Pages 209–227)

1. Robert F. Davidson, *Rudolf Otto's Interpretation of Religion* (Princeton: Princeton University Press, 1949). (Cf. the bibliography,

pp. 207 ff.) This study is a very careful and balanced presentation of Otto's thought and discusses also some of the criticism levelled at his position or certain aspects of it. Cf. also the special issue dedicated to Otto of the *Zeitschrift für Theologie und Kirche*, N.F. (1938), op. 1–162, esp. pp. 46 ff. and, finally, John M. Moore, *Theories of Religious Experience with Special Reference to James, Otto, and Bergson* (New York: Round Table, 1938).

Of the two publications which Werner Schilling, "Das Phänomen des Heiligen" (*Zeitschrift für Religion- und Geistesgeschichte*, 1949–50, 206 ff.) rightly criticises for not doing justice to R. Otto's thought (Friedrich K. Feigel, *Das Heilige* (Tübingen: Mohr, 1947, 2 Aufl., 1948) und W. Bätke, *Das Heilige im Germanischen* (Tübingen, 1942) only the former was (belatedly) available to me.

INDEX

Abraham ibn David, 79
Affifi, 83
Agricola, Johann, 166
Albertus Magnus, 79
Amsdorff, Nik., 165
Ananda, 55
Anaxagoras, 66, 68
Anesaki, M., 106
Anselm, 79
Aristotle, 67, 69, 76, 78, 171
Arnold, Gottfried, 192
Asanga, 123
al-Ashari, 79
Asin y Palacios, M., 83
Asvaghosha, 117, 125
Augustine, St., 44, 55, 75, 93, 150, 167, 169, 189, 190, 208
Averroes, see Ibn Rushd

Bahya ibn Pakudah, 79
Bancroft, Richard, 193
Barth, Karl, 24, 47, 209–10
Beaumont, 184
Becker, C. H., 77, 206
Benz, Ernst, 189
Berengar, 79
Bernard, St., 79, 81, 169
Bevan, Edwyn, 37
al-Bistami, 86, 90, 93
Blaurer, Ambrosius, 142
Bodhidharma, 124
Boethius, 78
Bonaventura, 79, 169
Bousset, W., 224
Brunner, 47, 79
Bucer, Martin, 142, 147
Buddha, the, 50, 111, 118, 129, 146
Bugenhagen, 141
Burckhardt, Jacob, 172, 175
Burnouf, 106

Callois, R., 65
Calvin, 167, 190, 192
Candrakirti, 122
Carlstadt, 191
Casey, R. P., 206
Cassirer, E., 37, 63
Channing, 183
Chemnitz, 213

Clark, E. T., 197, 203, 206
Clement XI, 190
Clement of Alexandria, 98
Comte, 39
Confucius, 67
Crautwald, V., 148, 153, 160
Cusanus, Nicolaus, 190
Cyprian, 189

Damianus, Petrus, 79
de Jong, 195, 196, 201
de la Vallée-Poussin, L., 106, 111, 113, 114
Democritus, 66
Descartes, 61
Dilthey, W., 61, 62, 171
Donatus, 189
Douglas, H. P., 203
Drake, St. Clair, 202
Dryden, 183

Eckhart, 34, 51, 79, 215
Eichrodt, 9
Eliade, M., xiv, 49
Eliot, Sir C., 106
Emeranus, 155
Empedocles, 66
Engelmann, Margaret, 161
Epicurus, 167
Erasmus, 190

al-Farabi, 79
Faris, R., 206
Faucet, 202
Ferdinand of Bohemia, King, 142
Feuerbach, 61, 217
Fichte, 55
Flacius, Mathias, 138, 142, 147, 152, 164, 165, 169
Flourens, 177
Francis de Sales, 169
Frank, 16
Franke, O., 65
Frecht, Martin, 142, 147
Freud, 217
Frick, 206
Friedman, R., 199, 200
Fries, 214

INDEX

INDEX

Nilsson, M., 36
Nivasa, 215
Northrop, F. S. C., 20, 63, 81
Novatian, 189
Nuri, 99
Nyberg, 83

Obermiller, E., 106, 123
Occam, 79
Oecolampadius, 141
Oldenberg, H., 130
Origen, 16
Osiander, Andreas, 164
Otloh, 79
Otto, Rudolf, 6, 15, 18, 35, 36, 45, 49, 72, 108, 128, 209 ff.

Parmenides, 68
Parsons, 42
Pauck, Wilhelm, 135
Paul, St., 166
Perry, R. B., 195
Philo, 76
Pius IX, 190
Plato, 67–9, 78, 149
Plotinus, 78
Pope, Liston, 203
Porphyry, 78
Pribilla, 190
Proclus, 78
Protagoras, 67
Pythagoras, 15

Qosta ibn Luqa, 76
Quenstedt, 213
Quesnel, 190

Rabia, 93
Radin, P., 42
Ramanuja, 215
Ranke, Leopold von, 172
ar-Razi, 78
Ritschl, 138, 214
Robinson, 9, 25, 71
Robson, William, 65
Rosenberg, O., 106

Saadya Gaon, 78, 79
Sahl al-Tustari, 91
Sakyamuni, see Buddha
Santideva, 107, 119, 120
al-Sayrafi, 84
Schaeder, 83
Schapiro, J. S., 175–6
Scheler, M., 217, 222
Schelling, 49, 110
Scherbatsky, T., 106, 110, 122
Schleiermacher, 13, 15, 55, 61, 138, 212, 214, 217

Schomerus, 128
Schweitzer, A., 224
Schwenckfeld, C., 135 ff.
Scotus, Duns, 79
Seeberg, Erich, 192
Shankara, 51, 110, 215
al-Shibli, 92, 100
Siegfried, Theodor, 211, 212
Smith, Margaret, 83
Smith, Robertson, 71
Socrates, 67–8
Söderblom, N., 14–18, 19, 20, 23, 24, 26, 216
Sombart, Werner, 202, 204
Soothill, 108
Staupitz, Johannes, 160
Suzuki, D. T., 106, 124
Sweet, W. W., 195, 202

Takakusu, J., 106, 118
Tawney, R. H., 202
Taylor, Jeremy, 169
Temple, W., 45, 46, 47
Tertullian, 11
Thomas Aquinas, 79, 189
Tiele, C. P., 18
Tillich, P., 32, 40, 206
Tocqueville, Alexis de, 171 ff.
Toynbee, A., 81
Troeltsch, E., xi, 6, 13, 185, 199, 202, 206, 212, 214, 215, 223, 224
Tsong-kha-pa, 123
at-Tusi, 79

Underhill, E., 40, 44
Urban, 37

Vadianus, see Watt
van der Leeuw, G., xiv, 18, 49
van Gennep, 42
Vasiliev, V., 106
Vermigli, Peter Martyr, 168

Walleser, M., 106
Watanabe, K., 106
Watt, Joachim von, 142, 147
Weber, Max, 47, 56, 185, 202, 204
Wenger, 23–7
Wiemann, 40
Williams, Roger, 195
Willoughby, H. R., 71
Winternitz, 106
Wogihara, W., 106
Wundt, W., 18, 49, 216, 221

Zeno, 69
Zoroaster, 50
Zwingli, 141, 167, 190, 200